Gatsby E-Commerce

A Practical Introduction to Creating E-Commerce Sites with the Gatsby Framework

Alex Libby

Apress®

Gatsby E-Commerce: A Practical Introduction to Creating E-Commerce Sites with the Gatsby Framework

Alex Libby
RUGBY, UK

ISBN-13 (pbk): 978-1-4842-6691-5   ISBN-13 (electronic): 978-1-4842-6692-2
https://doi.org/10.1007/978-1-4842-6692-2

Managing Director, Apress Media LLC: Welmoed Spahr
Acquisitions Editor: Louise Corrigan
Development Editor: James Markham
Coordinating Editor: Nancy Chen

Cover designed by eStudioCalamar

Cover image designed by Freepik (www.freepik.com)

Distributed to the book trade worldwide by Springer Science+Business Media New York, 1 New York Plaza, New York, NY 10004. Phone 1-800-SPRINGER, fax (201) 348-4505, e-mail orders-ny@springer-sbm.com, or visit www.springeronline.com. Apress Media, LLC is a California LLC and the sole member (owner) is Springer Science + Business Media Finance Inc (SSBM Finance Inc). SSBM Finance Inc is a **Delaware** corporation.

For information on translations, please e-mail booktranslations@springernature.com; for reprint, paperback, or audio rights, please e-mail bookpermissions@springernature.com.

Apress titles may be purchased in bulk for academic, corporate, or promotional use. eBook versions and licenses are also available for most titles. For more information, reference our Print and eBook Bulk Sales web page at http://www.apress.com/bulk-sales.

Any source code or other supplementary material referenced by the author in this book is available to readers on GitHub via the book's product page, located at www.apress.com/9781484266915. For more detailed information, please visit http://www.apress.com/source-code.

Printed on acid-free paper

This is dedicated to my family, with thanks for their love and support while writing this book.

Table of Contents

About the Author xiii

About the Technical Reviewer xv

Acknowledgments xvii

Introduction xix

Part I 1

Chapter 1: Getting Started 3

What Is PWA E-Commerce? 4

Exploring the Benefits of Using Gatsby 5

Setting the Scene 7

Exploring the Planned Architecture 7

Setting Up a Development Environment 9

Getting Accounts Set Up 10

Creating the Placeholder Site 13

Understanding the Changes Made 15

Summary 16

Chapter 2: Laying the Foundations 19

Some Housekeeping 19

Displaying the Site Architecture 20

Updating the Main Index Page 22

Understanding What Happened 25

Altering the Site Layout 26

Exploring the Code Changes 28

Adding a Navigation Menu 28

Understanding the Changes Made 30

Updating the Header 31

    Understanding What Happened 33

Creating Site Components and Pages 33

Adding in the Gallery and Blog Pages 35

Implementing New Components for Pages 37

    Exploring the Code in Detail 39

Summary 40

Part II **43**

Chapter 3: Styling the Shop **45**

Deciding on the Approach 45

Choosing a Color Theme 46

Adding Custom Fonts 48

    Understanding What Happened 49

Refactoring the SVG Images 50

    Breaking Apart the Changes 53

Taking Things Further 54

    Converting Styling to Use CSS Preprocessors 54

    Breaking Apart the Code Changes 58

    Implementing More Changes Using Sass 59

    Breaking Apart the Changes 61

Taking Things Further 63

Summary 65

Chapter 4: Sourcing Data **67**

Getting Started with DatoCMS 67

    Setting Up the Database and Adding Media 70

    Creating the Database Fields 73

    Adding Data to Our Shop 76

    Integrating DatoCMS 77

Implications of Using DatoCMS 79

Constructing Data Queries for Our Shop 80

Setting Up the Site Pages 82

Updating the Main Index Page 82

Adding Entries to the Navigation Menu 85

Reviewing Data for Page Layout 87

Hooking in Data for Pages and Components 88

Exploring the Code in Detail 90

Testing the Shop 90

Uploading to Netlify 91

Reviewing the Demo 93

Summary 94

Chapter 5: Building the Catalog 95

Exploring the Structure 95

Assessing the Implications of This Approach 97

Sourcing Data for the Product Catalog 97

Understanding What Happened 99

Adding Products to Shopify 100

Testing the Shopify GraphQL 100

Understanding the Query Used 103

Reviewing the ProductGrid GraphQL 103

Exploring the gatsby-node Component and GraphQL 105

Breaking Apart the ProductPage GraphQL 106

Adding the Cart and Remaining Pages 107

Reviewing the Code in Detail 108

Adjusting the Cart 110

Breaking Apart the Code Changes 113

Implementing Some Fixes 113

Updating the Test Version on Netlify 115

Summary 117

Chapter 6: Checkout and Order Processing **119**

Dealing with Security 119

Breaking Apart the Process 121

Some Points to Consider 122

Constructing the Cart 123

Exploring the Options 129

Integrating Our Payment Processor 131

Performing a Run-Through of the Cart 132

Adding Shipping Options 134

Understanding the Impact of Our Changes 137

Adding Taxes 138

Using the Payment Request API 140

Customizing the Cart Offer 142

Applying Discounts 142

Tweaking the Cart's Appearance 145

Limiting Delivery 147

Displaying Inventory Levels 150

Summary 154

Part III **155**

Chapter 7: Adding a Blog **157**

Setting the Scene 157

Installing the Required Plugins 159

Understanding the Changes 161

Creating the Main Blog Page 161

Breaking Apart the Code 165

Creating the Blog Template 166

Understanding the Changes Made 167

Tying It All Together 168

Exploring the Changes 170

Styling the Blog Pages 171

Adding Content to the Blog 174

Adding Images to the Blog 175

Refining Our Blog: Taking Things Further 178

Summary 180

Chapter 8: Finessing the Site 181

Implementing SEO 181

    Exploring the Code in More Detail 185

    Adding in Metadata 186

Adding Comments 187

    Understanding the Changes Made 190

Setting Up a Sitemap 191

Adding a Contact Form 192

    Reviewing the Code in Detail 195

    Updating the Link 196

Taking It to the Next Level 198

Summary 199

Chapter 9: Testing and Optimization 201

Some Housekeeping 201

    Breaking Apart the Issue 202

Testing the Site 205

    Exploring the Demo in More Detail 210

    Taking It Further 211

Performing a Lighthouse Audit 212

    Exploring the Results in Detail 215

Responding to Issues 215

    Exploring the Background 216

Fixing the Performance Issues 217

    Understanding the Changes 222

Fixing the Accessibility Issues 223

    Breaking Apart the Changes 225

Viewing the Results 226

Where Next from Here? 227

Summary 229

Chapter 10: Deployment into Production 231

Working Through the Final Steps 231

Considering the Steps in Detail 238

Preparing the Host 239

Uploading Content 242

Breaking Apart the Changes 245

Deploying Content Automatically 246

Exploring the Steps in More Detail 248

Adding a Custom Domain Name 249

Summary 253

Part IV 255

Chapter 11: Migrating from WooCommerce 257

Why Migrate to Gatsby? 257

Some Basic Housekeeping 259

Creating the New Site 260

Understanding What Is Happening 262

Outlining the Proposed Solution 263

Understanding the Scope 264

Sourcing Data 264

Breaking Apart the Changes 276

Exploring Alternative Options 277

Taking It Further 278

Summary 280

Chapter 12: Adapting for Mobile 283

Why Is Mobile So Important? 283

Testing the Existing Layout 284

Assessing the Layout 285

Simplifying the Original Design 286

    Breaking Apart the Code 294

Making the Menu Responsive 295

    Breaking Apart the Code Changes 300

Making the Basket Responsive 300

Auditing the Site with Lighthouse 303

    Analyzing the Performance Report 304

Fixing the Issues 307

    What We Didn't Cover 310

    Breaking Apart the Code 312

    Adding PWA Support: A Postscript 313

Summary 314

Chapter 13: Updating the Payment Process **317**

Introducing the API 317

Before Getting Started 319

Setting Up the Project 321

    Exploring the Changes in Detail 322

Setting Up the Payment Request API 323

    Reviewing the Code Changes: How Does the API Operate? 327

    Understanding the Wider Picture 327

Extending Functionality 329

    Understanding the Changes Made 333

Adding the Finishing Touches 334

    Breaking Apart the Code 341

Taking the Next Steps 342

Summary 344

Index **347**

About the Author

Alex Libby is a front-end engineer and seasoned computer book author, who hails from England. His passion for all things open source dates back to the days of his degree studies, where he first came across web development, and he has been hooked ever since. His daily work involves extensive use of React, Node.js, JavaScript, HTML, and CSS. Alex enjoys tinkering with different open source libraries to see how they work. He has spent a stint maintaining the jQuery Tools library and enjoys writing about open source technologies, principally for front-end UI development.

About the Technical Reviewer

Alexander Chinedu Nnakwue has a background in
mechanical engineering from the University of Ibadan,
Nigeria, and has been a front-end developer for over 3 years
working on both web and mobile technologies. He also has
experience as a technical author, writer, and reviewer. He
enjoys programming for the Web, and occasionally, you can
also find him playing soccer. He was born in Benin City and
is currently based in Lagos, Nigeria.

Acknowledgments

Writing a book can be a long but rewarding process; it is not possible to complete it without the help of other people. I would like to offer a huge vote of thanks to my editors – in particular Nancy Chen and Louise Corrigan. My thanks also to Alexander Nnakwue as my technical reviewer, James Markham for his help during the process, and others at Apress for getting this book into print. All have made writing this book a painless and enjoyable process, even with the edits!

My thanks also to my family for being understanding and supporting me while writing. I frequently spend lots of late nights writing alone or pass up times when I should be with them, so their words of encouragement and support have been a real help in getting past those bumps in the road and producing the finished book that you now hold in your hands.

Lastly, it is particularly poignant that the book was written at a time when the world faced global events of an unprecedented nature; it was too easy to think about those who lost the greatest thing we as humans could ever have. Having a project to work on – no matter how simple or complex it might be – helped me get through those tough times, and with the hope that we face a better future.

Introduction

Gatsby E-Commerce is for people who want to quickly create e-commerce sites that are efficient and fast, using the Gatsby framework and associated tools.

This project-oriented book simplifies the setting up of a Gatsby site as a starting point before beginning to explore the benefits of using Gatsby in an e-commerce environment and developing it into an e-commerce offer that we can customize according to your needs. It will equip you with a starting toolset that you can use to create future projects, incorporate into your existing workflow, and allow you to take your websites to the next level.

Throughout this book, I'll take you on a journey through constructing our example site. We will touch on subjects such as adding data sources, creating the catalog, and implementing a payment function and more – showing you how easy it is to develop simple e-commerce sites that we can augment later quickly. With the minimum of fuss, we'll focus on topics such as sourcing data using GraphQL, turning it into useful content, and more – right through to producing the final result viewable from any browser!

Gatsby is based on JavaScript, React, and Node.js, three of the most powerful tools available for developers: you can enhance, extend, and configure your site as requirements dictate. With Gatsby, the art of possible is only limited by the extent of your imagination and the power of JavaScript, React, and Node.js.

Gatsby E-Commerce gets you quickly acquainted with creating and manipulating e-commerce sites using a static site generator (SSG) approach. It's perfect for website developers who are already familiar with JavaScript and React and are keen to learn how to leverage the Gatsby framework. You may also be a developer for whom time is of the essence and simplicity is key; you need to produce efficient and properly optimized content in modern browsers using tools already in your possession.

PART I

CHAPTER 1

Getting Started

E-commerce is big business. It's huge.

Let me hit you with a couple of facts:

- Experts forecast that retail e-commerce sales will hit $4.8 trillion by 2021.

- Over 69% of shoppers abandon their shopping carts, with only 5.2% converting if prompted by an email within 20 minutes of leaving the cart.

Ouch. Those are some significant figures! Customers are spending more and more online, with (strangely) purchasing by men outstripping women when it comes to the battle of the sexes. At the same time, we are becoming more and more time-poor, with increasing demands placed on us; as customers, we expect sites to be fast, reliable, and easy to use. Gone are the days of waiting for websites to load, with less-than-perfect images, or being told to switch sites or install an app if you happen to prefer using a mobile device!

Sounds like a tall order, right? Wrong. Welcome to the world of progressive web app (or PWA) e-commerce! Throughout the next few pages, I will take you through what PWA e-commerce is and why it's beneficial to both customers and companies. We'll see what makes Gatsby such an excellent fit for this paradigm and begin to set the scene for what we will start to develop as our demo shop in this book. We've got a lot to cover, so without further ado, let's begin with a look at what PWA e-commerce is and why Gatsby is a great tool to use to construct PWA e-commerce sites.

© Alex Libby 2021
A. Libby, *Gatsby E-Commerce*, https://doi.org/10.1007/978-1-4842-6692-2_1

What Is PWA E-Commerce?

I suspect many of you may already be familiar with progressive web apps, or PWAs. After all, one cannot help but notice the meteoric rise of frameworks such as React or Gatsby, which developers frequently use to create PWAs!

For the uninitiated, though, this term was coined by Google engineers not to describe a prescriptive framework, but a set of development principles. These principles include the likes of service workers, push notifications, HTTP-based access, and access across any device; there are three critical principles though that sum up this whole approach:

- Reliability – Owing to the use of service workers, a PWA is always responsive to user requests, irrespective of the device used or state of the network connection (online or offline).

- Performance – PWAs use techniques such as compression, pre-caching, and code splitting to help keep the time-to-interactive to a minimum. These techniques help to reduce the number of "pogo-sticking" users, who abandon websites that are slow to use.

- Engagement – Owing to the use of web app manifests, we can easily install a PWA onto a mobile device, which helps maintain one codebase for multiple platforms. We can also use targeted push notifications to help better engage customers.

These are great principles, but how does this translate into the world of e-commerce? Implementing a PWA translates into several direct benefits for businesses and ultimately customers:

- We can make our application available to a broader market, across multiple devices, using a single codebase. At the same time, we can allow for varying network connection speeds, as well as provide an offline capability – customers can use this to browse and place orders when they are back online.

- PWAs make use of pre-caching to help provide a fast, smooth shopping experience for customers. This pre-caching helps improve conversion rate, decrease bounce rates, and boost user engagement – all critical to SEO (Search Engine Optimization) ranking for any website.

- It reduces the need for a significant development budget, as we avoid the need to develop separate apps for both desktop and mobile use. We can use push notification and "add to home screen" functions to make our e-commerce PWA look and feel like a native mobile application.

Hopefully, by now, you can begin to see how developing an e-commerce PWA will be of benefit to both customers and your business! They are perfect for addressing some of the comments I outlined at the start of this chapter. If your site is not performant and unreliable and you force customers to have to go to a separate website for mobile devices, then your site will struggle to survive! Okay, perhaps this might sound a little too extreme, but in this dog-eat-dog world of e-commerce, only the strongest will survive.

Enough of that. Let's move on: we've seen how implementing an e-commerce PWA can help a business; it's time to understand what makes Gatsby such a perfect fit for this approach.

Exploring the Benefits of Using Gatsby

Why *is* Gatsby a good choice as the basis for an e-commerce PWA?

Frequently seen as a static site generator (or SSG) for React, Gatsby offers much more – it's a full-sized framework that has become a firm favorite among JAMstack developers. It does away with the age-old principles of using a database such as MySQL or Oracle by default and instead relies on JavaScript, markup, and APIs to access data (hence the term JAMstack!).

However, what makes it perfect for e-commerce can be summed up perfectly by this statement from Kyle Matthews, the original creator of Gatsby:

> *Google does a lot of research about how to make fast websites, and PWA is sort of an umbrella term for these patterns. So, with Gatsby, we just asked ourselves, why not bake these patterns, all these things that make a website fast, into a website framework?*

In a blog post on the Gatsby website, he explains how Gatsby acts as a meta-compiler – it doesn't make performance considerations optional, but instead bakes them in by default. Gatsby offers CSS inlining, prefetching, data splitting, and more, all of which make it highly performant and perfect as a basis for fast e-commerce sites!

You can read the original blog post at `www.gatsbyjs.org/blog/2017-09-13-why-is-gatsby-so-fast/`.

To take things further, here are a few more features offered as default by Gatsby:

- Automatic routing is built-in by default – this is based on your directory structure, so no need to add additional code to manage routing.

- HTML code is generated server-side, which makes it superfast.

- Gatsby comes with a preconfigured webpack-based build system that takes care of creating an optimized version of your site for production use.

- We can easily extend Gatsby with plugins, either from other plugin authors or by ones you create.

- Gatsby loads only the critical parts of your site, keeping site speed as optimal as possible. Gatsby also prefetches resources for other pages, which helps to reduce loading time between pages.

- Although we are not using databases in our project (at least in the traditional sense), Gatsby can connect to a host of data sources, such as CMSs, SaaS services, APIs, the file system, and, yes, even databases too!

Judging by this list, Gatsby has a lot going for it! This statement might seem as being overly confident, but in reality, customers are demanding performant sites and will vote with their feet if a website is anything but fast. The design of Gatsby is based on research by Google engineers around what makes sites fast, so it makes sense to make use of this research by default when it comes to creating our website.

Just in case you need some extra ammunition, Gatsby has an excellent section on how to win over stakeholders. You can see the article in full on the main Gatsby website at `www.gatsbyjs.org/docs/winning-over-stakeholders/`.

Setting the Scene

Okay, enough selling methinks. Let's get on with the technical detail!

As a project, Gatsby is already well served by excellent documentation. For this book, we will take a different spin and put some of this into practice in the form of developing a simple e-commerce PWA. I'll bet you're wondering what exactly we're going to create, right? Well, wonder no more, my friends – let me reveal all.

As I am sure someone once said, the way to a man's heart is frequently food – and to put a (typical?) developer's spin on it, cake. I've lost count of the number of times someone manages to find an excuse to come into the office with a tray of doughnuts or cake of some kind. It can be a double-edged sword, though, as while it is nice to partake, too much will inevitably lead to an expanding waistline!

Dieting aside, we're going to create a simple e-commerce PWA to sell one of my favorite foods, which is cupcakes. We'll go through the steps required to set up our starting website and turn it into an e-commerce PWA using Gatsby; we'll use principles you can apply across any e-commerce PWA in your future projects. As with any project, we need to start somewhere, so let's first take a more detailed look at how we will architect this project and the tools we will need to get our project off the ground.

Exploring the Planned Architecture

When designing the architecture of a site, we can crack that proverbial nut many different ways; each has its benefits and drawbacks that might not suit all. For this book, we'll be using the following tools, in addition to Gatsby:

- DatoCMS (`www.datocms.com`) – We need somewhere to store our content; for this, we will use DatoCMS, as it offers a free tier option that we can query using GraphQL to get our data. There is a twist though as to how we will use it; this is something we will cover later in this book.

- Shopify (`www.shopify.com`) – Although we will use a pre-built Gatsby starter template to construct the product pages and cart, we clearly need something to allow our customer to check out and pay for the goods they've ordered! Shopify is a perfect fit for us; it is hosted remotely, which reduces the amount of work required to link into our site. It offers payment processing internally, so removing the need for a dedicated solution while testing; we can always include new providers later, when we move our project to production.

- The layout – To create the basic layout, we will use the gatsby-shopify-starter theme by Alexander Hörl (available from `https://github.com/AlexanderProd/gatsby-shopify-starter`). This is based on the default starter theme offered by Gatsby, but which has been adapted to do a lot of the heavy lifting around Shopify. There will still be some code changes we need to make, but without this theme, it would require a lot more work!

- Netlify (`www.netlify.com`) and GitHub Pages (`https://pages.github.com`) – We will use these for hosting. We could use any hosting provider, such as Heroku and others; they would work perfectly fine here. However, GitHub Pages is free, which is one less cost to worry about, and it even allows us to hook in a custom domain to boot. This said, we won't be deploying code until much later in the book; I don't know about you, but that is far too long to wait! To get around this, we will use the free tier service from Netlify to test our site at regular intervals – it provides a quick and easy upload and preview process.

We should be aware, though, that there are other ways to crack this nut – we could choose to use a different hosting provider such as Netlify or Heroku, for example. Or we might decide to build that checkout from scratch. These options will work perfectly fine. Ultimately though, getting the right mix of components is critical to the success of any site; the ones I've chosen to use represent a good selection of tools that will work together well and allow us to create something of an appropriate size for this book.

Okay, let's move on: now that we know how this site will be architected, it's time to dig into the details. We'll begin creating our website toward the end of this chapter, but before we do so, we need to get our development environment set up and ready for use. There are a few tasks we need to complete for this, so let's dive in and take a look at what we need to do in more detail.

Setting Up a Development Environment

So, for our project, what do we need? We've covered the important ones at a high level, but this isn't the full list. There are a few more that we need, so let's take a look at the complete list in detail:

- We, of course, need a text editor – any good text editor is perfect for this project. I use Sublime Text 3, but there are plenty of options available if you don't already have a suitable editor.

- As dependencies of Gatsby, we need to install both Node.js and NPM, using a version suitable for your platform.

- We've talked about using DatoCMS as our back end, so we will need an account to access their services.

- We will host the site on GitHub Pages, so we will need at least a new repo and preferably a separate account.

- We will also use Netlify to test our project, so we will need to set up a free account for this service.

- As part of hosting, I will attach a custom domain name to the site to give it a little extra realism – this isn't obligatory, but will provide you with an idea of how it will work as an end-to-end solution.

- We will use Shopify to process the checkout and payments. The normal account only provides a 14-day trial period, so instead, we will sign up as a Shopify Partner which will give us much longer. Don't worry – it's a free service. You can decide if you want to continue with Shopify later!

- To get at the data from DatoCMS, we will use the Apollo GraphQL tool – this comes bundled in with Gatsby by default.

- Last but by no means least, we will need some photos of cakes for our store – these we will source from `https://unsplash.com/s/photos/cupcakes`.

All of the demos in this book were written for Windows, as this is the author's development platform. Please adapt if you are using macOS or Linux on your PC.

Excellent! The next task is to get accounts set up for our site; this will cover DatoCMS, GitHub Pages, Shopify, and Netlify. At the same time, we'll also get the prerequisite software installed and ready for use. Let's give in and run through the steps required in more detail.

Getting Accounts Set Up

For this project, we're not going to go old school and develop the solution from the ground up. While this would be a valid option, it is overkill for our needs!

Instead, we're going to follow the route of using existing third-party services to help support our site. The use of these services has the benefit of allowing them to worry about security, while we focus on integrating each into our solution. The first stage in this process is to sign up for accounts, so let's dive in and take a look at what we need to do in more detail.

GETTING ACCOUNTS SET UP

We have four accounts to set up, so let's work through each one in turn:

1. The first account we need to set up is for DatoCMS – go ahead and browse to `www.datocms.com/`, and then click Try it now for free on the main page. You don't need any credit card details – it will just ask for your name and email address and a password. You can provide a company name if you wish, but this is not compulsory.

2. Next up is GitHub Pages – for this, we need first to visit `https://github.com/join?source=login` to create an account, before adding a new repo to this account. Go ahead and add in suitable details as requested on this login screen, before clicking Create Account. As part of signing up, you will also need to validate your email address – go ahead and follow the instructions on the screen.

Note   If you already have an account you can use, feel free to skip step 2 and move straight onto the next step in this exercise.

---

3. With a suitable GitHub account in place, we now need to add a repo – click the + symbol at the top right of the page and then New repository.

4. On the next page, fill in the name of the repository, using the format XXXXX. github.io, where XXXXX is the name you choose to use for your repo. I've called mine havecakeeatcake.github.io, but feel free to use something different if you prefer.

The choice is essential, as we will use this to access the site when we've finished construction.

---

5. A little further down, tick the box marked Initialize this repository with a README, and then select Node for the Add .gitignore option.

6. In the license drop-down, select MIT.

The choice of license here isn't critical – I use MIT for convenience, but you can select another if you prefer. Make sure you change any setting later to this license if you decide to use something different.

---

7. At this point, click Create repository – if all is well, you should see something similar to the screenshot shown in Figure 1-1.

Figure 1-1. *Our repository set up, ready for use*

8. The next account to set up is a Shopify Partner account. Don't worry – you don't have to become a Partner if you don't want to! This account gives us longer than the 14-day standard trial period for normal accounts. To get registered, head over to www.shopify.com/partners, enter your email address when prompted, and click Join Now. You will be prompted for some basic information; please follow instructions on-screen as directed.

9. We have one more account to create, which is for Netlify – browse to www.netlify.com, and click Sign up in the top-right corner. You will be prompted to choose a sign-up method; I would recommend using GitHub. Make sure you've logged into your GitHub account first though. If you have several (as I do), Netlify doesn't give you the option to choose: it will often log you into the wrong one! Logging into the GitHub site first will mean that Netlify will automatically log into the right account.

You may be prompted to authorize access to Netlify from your GitHub account – this is necessary. Please follow instructions when prompted.

Although we've covered some routine steps in this first exercise, they do highlight one crucial trend that is becoming increasingly popular with developers across the world.

More and more developers are turning to the use of JAMStack principles when it comes to creating websites – this means making use of third-party services and APIs to surface data through to the customer.

In this exercise, we've set up several accounts with different providers; as well as the expected hosting, we've also set up one for storing our content and another for handling payments during the checkout process. We will add more services and features later in the book, but these are enough for us to get something created as a starting point for our site.

Okay, let's move on: with our accounts now set up and ready for use, it's time for us to get the site set up. For this, we're going to use Gatsby to create a website based on a starter template which will install the main elements for our PWA, ready for us to use.

Creating the Placeholder Site

This next task is a simple one, but probably the most important – we need something that we can use to build our site! Fortunately, Gatsby makes this very easy to complete; the first step is to get the framework installed before using a template to create our starter site.

DEMO: CREATING OUR BASE SITE

To get our base site set up, go ahead with these steps:

1. First, we need to install Node.js – go ahead and browse to `https://nodejs.org/`, and click the left-hand green button (marked "Recommended for Most Users").

2. Go ahead and double-click the installer to start the wizard; when prompted, accept all default settings, which will be sufficient for this demo.

3. Once done, fire up a Node.js terminal session, and then enter this command at the prompt to install Gatsby:

    ```
    npm install gatsby -g
    ```

4. Once done, enter this command at the prompt (all on one line) to set up our base site – this may take a while, so be patient:

    ```
    gatsby new havecakeeatcake https://github.com/AlexanderProd/gatsby-shopify-starter
    ```

5. It will show a message to say that it has been installed – at the prompt, enter this command and press Enter: `gatsby develop`.

6. Gatsby will eventually display a message similar to the screenshot shown in Figure 1-2, shown overleaf.

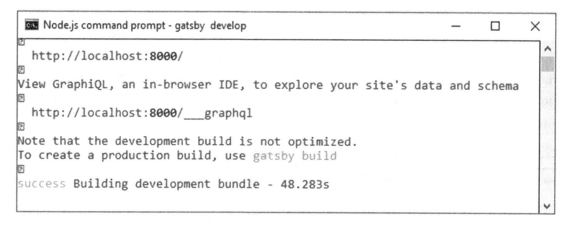

Figure 1-2. *Confirmation that the Gatsby server is running*

7. At this point, fire up your browser, and browse to `http://localhost:8000`; if all is well, you should see the screenshot shown in Figure 1-3.

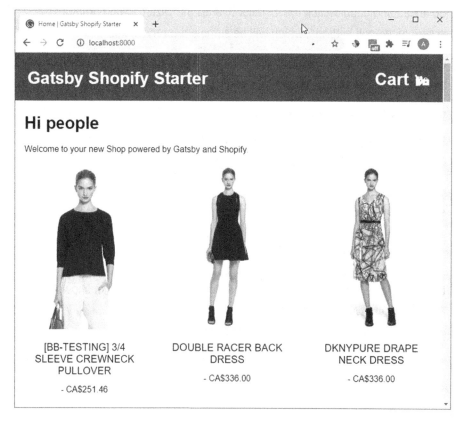

Figure 1-3. *Verifying that our base site is operational*

For those of you already familiar with Gatsby, this last exercise will be something you've likely done before; it's the standard method to install Gatsby and provision a starter site. I've deliberately chosen this theme to keep the basic design as clean as possible so that we're not introducing dependencies or plugins that we are not going to use in our project. With that in mind, let's take a quick look over the steps we took in the last exercise and the base site this has given us in preparation for turning into a simple e-commerce site.

Understanding the Changes Made

If we open up the havecakeeatcake folder stored on our PC, it might at first glance look like we have a lot of content – particularly compared to what was displayed when we previewed the results at the end of the last exercise!

Don't worry – all of it is needed. There are some key areas we will use (and which will likely be familiar to those who may have already used Gatsby before). To get to this point though, we first set up Node.js as a dependency, before swiftly moving on to install Gatsby via the command line, as a global package.

A quick peek at the contents of the havecakeeatcake folder will display a list of files similar to that shown in Figure 1-4.

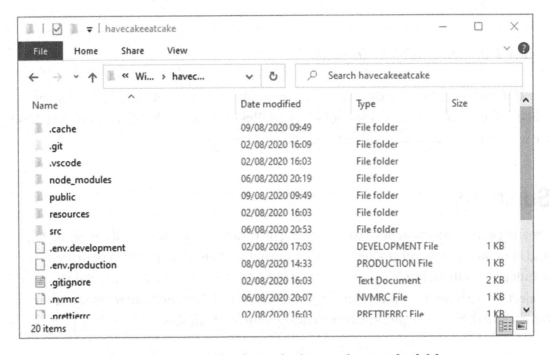

Figure 1-4. *A partial listing of files from the havecakeeatcake folder*

Go ahead and browse to the src folder – inside it, we will see the following folders (Figure 1-5).

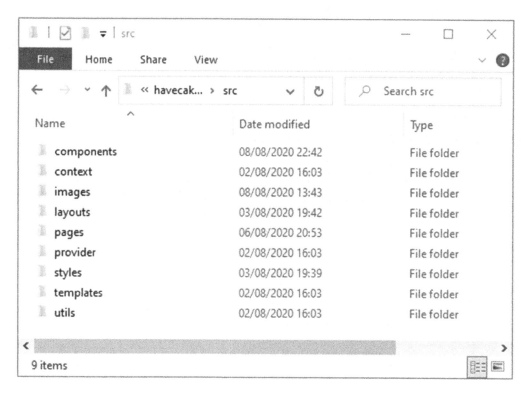

Figure 1-5. *Contents of the src folder*

This folder is where we will spend 90% of our time – there will be some changes we will need to make to some of the configuration files such as gatsby-config.js, but these we will cover as and when requirements dictate in our project.

Summary

Creating a website can be seen as something of an adventure – there will always be highs and lows, successes, and challenges, as we begin to develop what will become our final solution. Over these last few pages, we've detailed some of the background theory to our project, so we have the critical elements in place – let's take a moment to review what we have learned, before beginning the real development of our site.

We kicked off with a quick recap of what PWAs are and saw how principles initially created by Google engineers form the basis for all PWA sites. We then explored some of the critical tenets of PWAs and how they are particularly useful in an e-commerce environment. At the same time, we also covered how Gatsby bakes in these principles by default, helping to make it performant, reliable, and an excellent tool for creating sites available across multiple devices from one codebase.

We then moved on to detailing our proposed architecture for the site we would be creating for this book. We examined some of the reasons for choosing the applications that we will feature in this book, but at the same time understood that there is no hard-and-fast rule as to what we have to use and we could use other choices if preferred.

We then rounded out the chapter by setting up our development environment – this included getting accounts set up and installing our base site using Gatsby.

A nice short chapter, I hope you agree – enough for us to get things ready so that we can get stuck into developing our site. The next part of this adventure is where the fun starts: it's time to get pages set up, add in navigation, apply some styling... In a nutshell, there's plenty to do, so let's move on and get started with fleshing out our cake shop website in the next chapter.

CHAPTER 2

Laying the Foundations

We've got our tools in place, and we've worked out what we're going to build – so it's time to get into creating our shop!

As I am sure, anyone will say that laying solid foundations is essential; throughout this chapter, we will set up our site and start to add in the key elements such as page structure, header, footer, and theme for the site.

I do, however, have a confession to make – you may well find that the code won't appear to work fully, at least until we get to Chapter 4. Don't worry – this is deliberate. The focus of this chapter is about getting the foundations in place so that we can then supplement the code with calls to our chosen CMS (which will happen in Chapter 3). I know this might seem like a bit of a leap of faith, but bear with me – it will all come right, I promise!

On that note, let's get started with writing code – before we put pen to digital paper (so to speak), there are a few points we need to cover off first that will affect how we work in this chapter.

Some Housekeeping

Yes, I know – housekeeping isn't everyone's favorite job, but hey, it's something we have to do sometimes!

The points we need to cover off are purely informational rather than ones that require action; they are as follows:

- I've shortened some of the placeholder text for brevity. Where I've done this, full versions are available in the code download that accompanies this book. You can, by all means, add in the remaining text; not adding it will not impact how the component operates.

© Alex Libby 2021
A. Libby, *Gatsby E-Commerce*, https://doi.org/10.1007/978-1-4842-6692-2_2

- The section headings in this chapter and the next will appear similar – this is by design. We'll work on adding the core pages and features in this chapter, before inserting the code required to hook in the data in the next chapter. Where this happens, I will add a comment to represent the location for any GraphQL calls we make in Chapter 3.

- Any references to "project folder" are to the one we created back in Chapter 1 – I will assume yours is called `havecakeeatcake` and is at the root of your C: drive. If it is in a different location, please amend the instructions where appropriate.

- Make sure you have a copy of the code download available locally – although we will create most files from scratch, some we will need to get from the code download. Extracting from the code download is something we're doing for convenience, but also space constraints mean we can't display all of the components in full in this chapter!

- We also need to set up a template folder inside of our project area – using your File Explorer, browse to the root of the project folder and then into the `src` folder, and create a new folder called `templates`. We will make use of this later in the book.

Okay, we're almost at the point where we will start to write code. We have a lot of code to write, so to help with this, I've drawn up a mini schematic of how each component will link into each other.

The schematic will help give you a visual representation of how we will construct our site – hopefully, it will all begin to make sense when we get to the end of the chapter! With this in mind, let's take a look at that schematic in more detail before making a start on updating our website.

Displaying the Site Architecture

Although it may seem like we'll be working on a lot of code over this chapter, in reality, our site isn't that big. We can see a schematic of how the site will look in Figure 2-1.

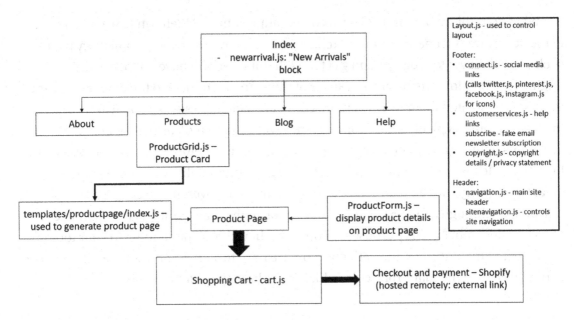

Figure 2-1. *Schematic of the site's page structure*

You may find it easier to view the PDF of the site architecture that is in the code download that accompanies this book.

In total, we will have six physical pages – this covers the main homepage, as well as the about, products, blog, and help pages. Yes, the sharp-eyed among you will notice that I've only listed five pages; there is a good reason for this, so let me explain.

Creating product pages for all six products is technically feasible, but not a sensible idea; we can get away with it on sites that will only ever sell a handful of products, but what if we needed to make a change to the layout? Have you got time to edit all X pages? I don't think so!

Instead, we will use a template file (represented here by the index.js file from within the templates folder); React allows us to create the page dynamically, using information sourced from DatoCMS. It avoids the need to develop hard-coded pages for each product and means that if we need to implement a change, it will apply to all products at the same time.

What does this mean for us in terms of updating content? Well, while we won't have to create any product pages from scratch, we will still have to create the ancillary pages, such as delivery.js, blog.js, and gifts.js. In total, we will have ten pages which might seem a lot for a small site, but some of these are not critical to the core purchasing process. I've created them to give a more complete feel to the site. As you will soon see, most are created as placeholders for now; they will be updated later in the book.

At this point, there is one thing we need to be aware of before we continue: you will find that code may not run until we've set up pages, added styling, and hooked in the data. Don't worry – it's all planned. There is too much to cover in one chapter! We will, however, go through a full test as soon as we hook in the data; it means we can make use of an excellent tool for this purpose and one you should consider adding to your toolbox!

Okay...without further ado, let's crack on: we have to start somewhere, so there's no better place than the main index.js, which is the homepage for our site.

Updating the Main Index Page

Right, now that we know how our site will look, let's crack on and make it happen!

Our starting point is index.js, which is what customers will see when they enter the site. This page will include three sections in total, in addition to the standard header and footer – we will have a header image, a (mocked-up) part for new cake arrivals, and a (placeholder) section about us as a company.

We have a lot to cover over the next few pages, so to give you an idea of what our site will look like when we finish developing it, Figure 2-2 shows a screenshot of the finished article.

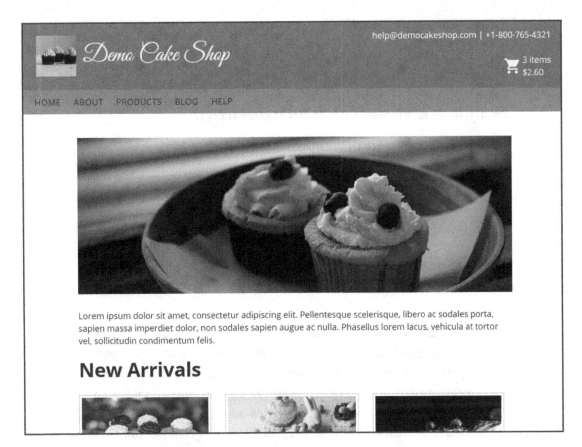

Figure 2-2. *A screenshot of the finished demo*

Okay, let's crack on and make a start with updating the index.js file in our demo.

UPDATING THE MAIN INDEX PAGE

For our first exercise, we're going to set up our welcome page – this is the index.js file, which you can find in the /src/pages folder. Let's work through the steps required to get it ready for our project:

1. The first step is to crack open a copy of the index.js file from the code download that accompanies this book – we will need to copy some parts of it from there into our new file. Keep this file open, but you can minimize it for now.

2. Next, we need to adjust the number of imported components used by index.js – go ahead and crack open index.js in the \src\pages folder of our new site, and modify the code as highlighted:

23

```
import React from "react"

import SEO from "../components/seo"
import PropTypes from "prop-types"
import { graphql } from "gatsby"
import NewArrival from "../components/newarrival"

import headerImage from "../images/header.png"
```

3. Next, we need to update the content rendered in the `IndexPage` constant – for this, first add in the data object into the initial declaration:

```
const IndexPage = ({ data }) => (
```

4. Next, go ahead and remove everything from the opening React fragment () to the end of the file, and add in the following code:

```
<Layout>
  <SEO title="Home" keywords={[`gatsby`, `application`, `react`]} />
  <p><img src={headerImage} alt="header" height="326" width="920" /></p>
  <p>Lorem ipsum dolor sit amet, consectetur adipiscing elit.
  Pellentesque scelerisque, libero ac sodales porta, sapien massa
  imperdiet dolor, non sodales sapien augue ac nulla. Phasellus lorem
  lacus, vehicula at tortor vel, sollicitudin condimentum felis. </p>
    <h1>New Arrivals</h1>
  {/*[...INSERT DATA MAP HERE...]*/}
```

Note   The insert data map here comment will be replaced by data when we cover this in Chapter 4.

---

5. The next section to add in is "Who We Are" – for this, go ahead and insert the following code before the closing):

```
<h1>Who We Are</h1>
<p>Lorem ipsum dolor sit amet, consectetur adipiscing elit.
Pellentesque scelerisque, libero ac sodales porta, sapien massa
imperdiet dolor, non sodales sapien augue ac nulla.
```

[rest omitted for brevity]

```
</p>
```

```
    )

IndexPage.propTypes = {
  data: PropTypes.object,
}
```

I've shortened the placeholder text for reasons of space – you can find the full version of the placeholder text in the index.js file that accompanies this book.

---

6. Last, but by no means least, go ahead and add in this comment below the export default IndexPage line – we'll replace it with proper data in Chapter 3:

   ```
   {/*[...INSERT DATA CALLS HERE...]*/}
   ```

7. Go ahead and save the file – Gatsby will automatically update the page. It will likely throw an error, but this is to be expected. At this stage, we need to focus on getting pages together before making sure it all works!

If you've gotten this far, thank you for believing in that leap of faith! As you will see, building even a simple e-commerce site still requires creating quite a few pages, so we won't necessarily understand how our site will look until most (if not all) of the pages are in place.

We've started with the most important one – let's take a moment to review the code changes we've made, so we can begin to see how it fits into the bigger picture of our site.

Understanding What Happened

For our first exercise, we've had to make a few changes to the index.js file that came with our starter template; we started by adjusting some of the import statements to add in at least one component and image that we will use on this page.

We then moved on to altering the parameters passed as part of initiating IndexPage as an object; we added in the data object, in preparation for hooking in the data in Chapter 4. We then replaced the existing <h1> and <p> tags with a new image and content – the latter will form what will become the New Arrivals section on our homepage. We left a blank space for what will be the call to a new NewArrivals component; this will display the information on the page, once we've called it from the DatoCMS system.

Moving on, we then added in the Who We Are block; for now, we've set it up with hard-coded text from the Lorem Ipsum generator, but we would need to move it into DatoCMS before going into production. We then rounded out the first exercise by updating the export statement at the end of the demo; we then added in a comment as a placeholder for the GraphQL call we will add in the next chapter.

Okay, first page down, another dozen or so to go! What makes Gatsby so great is the wealth of starter templates on offer – rather than having to create a site entirely from scratch, we can let it handle the internal mechanisms and focus on providing the content. It means that much of the preparatory work is already in place, which makes it easier to effect changes such as those done in the `index.js` file.

Let's stay with this theme – now that we have our `index.js` page updated, it's time to alter the layout template that we will use across the site. We will use `index.js` from within the `\src\layouts` folder to manage it – go ahead and crack it open, ready for our next set of changes.

Altering the Site Layout

It goes without saying (and as if I hardly need to say in any case) that the layout is critical to the success of any website – something that looks a mess will quickly fail!

Fortunately, our chosen theme already provides a template file for this purpose – most of what is in the `\src\layouts\index.js` file will remain, but we still need to effect some changes for our site. We only have a handful of changes to make, so let's keep that momentum going and add them to our file as part of our next exercise.

REWORKING THE LAYOUT PAGE

Let's work through the steps to get the layout file updated for our site:

1. First, go ahead and crack open the `index.js` file from the `\src\layouts` folder in your text editor.

2. Next, we need to adjust the import references – edit the ones shown to match this block of code:

    ```
    import React from 'react'
    import PropTypes from 'prop-types'
    ```

```
import { StaticQuery, graphql } from 'gatsby'
import styled from '@emotion/styled'
import Copyright from "../components/copyright"
import Subscribe from "../components/subscribe"
import CustomerServices from "../components/customerservices"
import Connect from "../components/connect"
import SiteNavigation from "../components/sitenavigation"

import ContextProvider from '~/provider/ContextProvider'

import { GlobalStyle } from '~/utils/styles'
import Navigation from '~/components/Navigation'
import "./layout.css"
```

3. We can now focus on the main part of this page – the next change to make is to add in a call to what will be the SiteNavigation component. Add the following line in immediately before the opening `<Wrapper>` entry, as indicated:

```
<SiteNavigation />
<Wrapper>
    {children}
```

4. The next task is to update the footer – this will be handled by some components we will create later this chapter. For now, go ahead and add in or adjust the following component names, as indicated:

```
<footer>
            <CustomerServices />
            <Subscribe />
            <Connect />
    </footer>
            <Copyright />
    </Wrapper>

    )
}
```

5. The rest of the file can remain unchanged, so at this point, save the file so that Gatsby can rebuild the website for us.

At this stage, we will still likely see errors appearing, but this is something we should expect to see; many of them will be around the data that we have yet to add. That said, we've made some significant changes to this file, so let's pause for a moment to review what we've updated so you can see how it fits into our site.

Exploring the Code Changes

For this file, you will very likely begin to see a bit of a theme – many of the changes we need to make are to update the import statements, followed by alterations or additions to the components and content we use in each file.

The `index.js` file from the `layouts` folder is no exception – we began by adding statements to import several components, such as the `Customer Services`, `Subscribe`, and `Connect` modules. We followed these imports with the addition of a call to the `SiteNavigation` module; as this is the layout template, it will add in the navigation menu across the site for us.

We then added in calls to each of the blocks that we will display in the footer – this includes the `Customer Services` section, followed by the `Subscribe` block and `Connect` (or social media) module.

Hopefully, you will agree that the last two exercises have been pretty straightforward – certainly nothing to stress us out at this stage! The next task, though, will start to make things more interesting – remember that navigation block I mentioned just now? Yes, that's next: let's take a look at what's involved in getting this set up across our site in more detail.

Adding a Navigation Menu

Navigating any site is arguably just as important as the layout – a clean website without any decent navigation is just as bad as a messy site with excellent navigation. It's for this reason that our navigation has to be consistent across the site. It also must make sense to customers and not be something that requires a doctorate-level degree to work out where one needs to be!

Gatsby doesn't provide a navigation option out of the box, so this is something we need to create ourselves; for this, we will make use of the Gatsby Link component to build a simple navbar to sit just underneath our header. Let's take a look at what's involved in our next exercise.

ADDING IN NAVIGATION

For this next exercise, we will build this component from scratch – it will add in a simple navigation bar, below the main header. Let's make a start:

1. First, crack open your text editor and create a new file as sitenavigation. js in the \src\components folder.

2. Next, add in this code – we will go through it block by block, beginning with some import statements:

```
import React from "react"
import { Link } from "gatsby"
import { useStaticQuery, graphql } from "gatsby"
```

3. The real meat of this component starts with this const definition – go ahead and add in these lines next, leaving a line blank after the last import statement:

```
const SiteNavigation = () => {
{/*[...INSERT DATA CALLS HERE...]*/}
  return (

  )
}
```

4. Inside of the React fragment (. . .), go ahead and add in these statements – they won't show anything for now, but this will be fixed in Chapter 3 when we cover the data requirements for the site:

```
    <nav>
        <div>
        <Link to={`${data.datoCmsNavigation.homeLink}`}
        activeClassName="active">{data.datoCmsNavigation.homeText}</Link>
            <Link to={`${data.datoCmsNavigation.aboutLink
}`}>{data.datoCmsNavigation.aboutText}</Link>
            <Link to={`${data.datoCmsNavigation.
productsLink}`}>{data.datoCmsNavigation.productsText}</Link>
            <Link to={`${data.datoCmsNavigation.blogLink
}`}>{data.datoCmsNavigation.blogText}</Link>
            <Link to={`${data.datoCmsNavigation.helpLink
}`}>{data.datoCmsNavigation.helpText}</Link>
```

```
        </div>
      </nav>

export default SiteNavigation
```

5. Go ahead and save the file to allow Gatsby to rebuild the site content.

At first glance, this page may not make sense, unless you are already familiar with Gatsby to some degree; we've already added in import statements in previous demos, but what about this `<Link>` component I see in use in our code...?

Understanding the Changes Made

Aha, let me explain! For those of you not familiar with Gatsby, the `<Link>` components we've used in this demo are the equivalent of `<a href="..">` tags, but with one crucial difference. They should be used for internal links within a site, **not** for linking to external resources such as manufacturer or supplier sites.

The use of the `<Link>` element was just a small part of what we had in the site; we kicked off its creation by bringing the standard React `import` statement, plus one for the Link component. The last `import` statement relates to the data calls we will make in the next chapter.

Next up, we inserted a placeholder as a reminder for us to add in the data query; we then added in some statements that make use of the `<Link>` component to create our navigation. This component takes a single parameter, which is the link of our target page; in this instance, we're using a JSON object reference for each site link. It will make more sense in the next chapter, but for now, let's see how it is transformed once we compile the code (Figure 2-3), where I've taken a screenshot grab of what to expect. Feel free to take a look in your browser console if you want to see it in action.

```
▼ <nav>
  ▼ <div>
      <a aria-current="page" class="active" href="/">Home</a>
      <a href="/about/">About</a>
      <a href="/blog/">Blog</a>
      <a href="/gallery/">Gallery</a>
      <a href="/help/">Help</a>
    </div>
  </nav>
```

Figure 2-3. *The links produced from the compiled code in our site*

Okay, let's move on: we have our `index.js` and `layout.js` with updates in place, so it's time to start fleshing out the website by building or updating some of the components referenced in our code. There's no better way to start then with a top-down approach, so let's take a look at the header and see what needs to be updated to bring it in line with our site vision.

Updating the Header

For these next few pages, we'll be constructing some additional components and pages – one of the most important (I think) is the header. A suitably labeled header is key to showing off that visitors have hit the right site – a no-name site might make people wonder unless your brand happens to be so well-known that it doesn't matter!

But I digress. Thankfully for us, our theme already includes a header component – it means that rather than having to create this one from scratch, we can modify the file to suit our needs. There are a few changes we need to make, so without further ado, let's get stuck into making our changes and bringing the header up to date.

CREATING THE HEADER

To get our header up to scratch, go ahead and follow these steps:

1. First, go ahead and open the `index.js` file from our project folder in your text editor – it's in the `\src\components\Navigation` folder.

2. We have a few changes to make – the first one is to add in two imports, for images we will use in our header component. Add these lines in after the last import statement, leaving a line blank first:

   ```
   import shoppingcart from "../images/shoppingcart.svg"

   import headerImage from "../images/gatsby-icon.png"
   ```

3. The next change is to delete the code inside the `<Wrapper>`...`</Wrapper>` tags. We need to replace it with a good chunk of code, so go ahead and add in the first block:

   ```
   <header
     style={{
       background: `#a49696`,
   ```

```
        display: `flex`,
        justifyContent: `space-between`,
        padding: `20px 30px`
      }}
    >
```

4. Leave a line blank, and then add in this block:

```
        <div style={{ display: `flex`, alignItems: `center` }}>
          <img src={headerImage} alt="site header" style={{
          marginBottom: `0`, width: `100px`, height: `auto`,
          paddingRight: `15px` }} />
          <MenuLink to='/'>
            <h1 style={{ margin: 0,  font: `400 50px/0.8 'Great Vibes'` }}>
              {siteTitle}
            </h1>
          </MenuLink>
        </div>
```

5. We have one more block to add in – leave a line blank after the last block, and then add in this code:

```
        <div style={{ color: `#ffffff`}} >
          <p>help@havecakeeatcake.com | +1-800-765-4321</p>
          <div style={{ display: `flex`, justifyContent:`flex-end`}}>
            <MenuLink to='/cart'>
              <img src={shoppingcart} alt="shoppingcart"
              style={{width: `40px`, height: `auto`, fill: `#ffffff`,
              marginBottom: `0`, marginTop: `0.5rem` }} />
              {hasItems &&
                <CartCounter>
                  {quantity} items
                </CartCounter>
              }
            </MenuLink>
          </div>
        </div>
      </header>
```

6. The rest of the file can remain unchanged, so go ahead and save it before closing the file.

It's fair to say that by the time we finish building our site, it's doubtful that we will have a single page that we've not had to modify in some respect! The header.js file is no exception – in the exercise we've just completed, we've made quite a few changes throughout the component, so let's review those changes in more detail.

Understanding What Happened

To update our header component, we started by adding in two import statements. These reference two images used; one is the shopping basket, and the other is the mini header image to the left of the main site title. This was complemented with the addition of a <header> tag – for this, we've used standard HTML5, as there is no benefit in creating a separate component for it!

We then moved on to updating a <div> that's acting as a container – this contains an instance of the <Link> component that we've used before, this time to style the main header title and provide a link back to the homepage.

Next up, we then added in a block to the right of the header – this stores the contact details and a mini shopping cart summary. We will use it once we implement the cart and checkout features, later in Chapters 4 and 5. The rest of the file remains unchanged – it contains definitions for the propTypes used in this component, as well as setting a default title for our site. One function of particular note though is the useQuantity function – this is used to update the quantities displayed in the cart within the header. This makes use of a React context within Gatsby, to maintain the state of the count displayed on-screen.

Okay, let's crack on: we need to add the remaining pages for our site, such as about and help. For this demo, I've kept them reasonably lightweight – the focus of this book is more on the technical process of setting up an e-commerce site. We should assume that we would have someone suitably skilled to help with providing copy for our site!

Creating Site Components and Pages

For this next exercise, we're going to create not one but five different components – all of them are mostly identical, with the exception of some minor tweaks for each component.

With that in mind, we'll work through one as our starting point; I will give you the directions needed to add in the remaining ones. Let's take a look at the code required in more detail, starting with the about component.

CREATING ANCILLARY PAGES

For this exercise, you will see that I've omitted some of the placeholder text for reasons of space – the full version is available in the code download that accompanies this book.

Feel free to add in the remaining placeholder text if desired – it's not obligatory, and the code will run fine without it.

Let's work through the steps required to get the components set up:

1. Fire up your text editor; then in a new file, add in the following code:

```
import React from "react"
const AboutPage = () => (
  <div>
    <h1>About Us</h1>
    <p>Lorem ipsum dolor sit amet, consectetur adipiscing elit.
    Pellentesque scelerisque, libero ac sodales porta, sapien massa
    imperdiet dolor, non sodales sapien augue ac nulla.
    [rest omitted for brevity]

    </p>
  </div>
)

export default AboutPage
```

2. Save the file as about.js in the \src\pages folder.

3. Next, save a copy of the component as delivery.js into the same \src\pages folder; change the word "About" to Delivery.

4. Alter the title of this component to "Delivery, Exchanges and Returns," and then save the file.

5. For the next one, save a copy of `delivery.js` as `gifts.js`. Change all instances of the word "Delivery" to "Gifts" and replace the existing title with "Gift Vouchers." Save the file.

6. For the next one, save a copy of `gifts.js` as `help.js`. Change all instances of the word "Gifts" to "Help" and replace the existing title with "Help."

7. For the next one, save a copy of `help.js` as `terms.js`. Change all instances of the word "Help" to "Terms" and replace the existing title with "Terms and Conditions."

8. Save all of the remaining files, and then close them.

Excellent, we now have our ancillary pages in place; we can move on to creating the more important pages that we will focus on for this book.

The exercise we've just completed might have seemed a little mundane, but it goes to show that with some care and forethought, we can reuse a lot of code when working in a suitably componentized environment. We've created mocked-up versions of some of the key supporting pages you might find on any e-commerce site; for this book, they are there to provide a little more realism to our website than just having the gallery and checkout pages.

It is, however, in the next section where things will get a little more complicated – we have two more pages to create: the gallery and blog! Yes, we indeed need somewhere to display our products and talk about them; let's dive in and take a look at what is involved in more detail.

Adding in the Gallery and Blog Pages

This next exercise is probably one of the more important ones in this chapter; the remaining two pages will form the basis for more involved development later in this book, as part of mini-projects in their own right.

We will keep the design for both fairly minimalist; each will use a design that covers the basics, but in a suitably styled fashion that we can use as a basis for more complex projects in the future. For now, let's go ahead and create the placeholder pages for both in the next exercise.

ADDING IN THE GALLERY AND BLOG

To make a start on setting up our project pages, follow these steps:

1. We'll start by cracking open our text editor – create a new file.

2. Next, go ahead and add in this code – this will form the basis for our product gallery, which we will expand in Chapter 4:

```
import React from 'react'
import SEO from '~/components/seo'
import ProductGrid from '~/components/ProductGrid'

const CatalogPage = () => (

  <SEO title="Home" keywords={[`gatsby`, `application`, `react`]} />
  <h1>Products available for sale:</h1>
  <ProductGrid />

)

export default CatalogPage
```

Save the file as `products.js` in the `\src\pages` folder, then close it.

We will work on additional components to help with rendering data for the gallery in Chapter 5.

---

3. We have one more page to create, which is a placeholder for the blog – go ahead and add the following code to a new file, saving it as `blog.js` in the `\src\pages` folder:

```
import React from "react"
import Layout from "../components/layout"

const BlogPage = () => (
  <div>
    <h1>Blog</h1>
  </div>
)

export default BlogPage
```

4. Close both files – neither is needed for the remainder of this chapter.

5. There is one more change we need to make, which is to the `cart.js` file in the `\src\pages` folder. Go ahead and open this file in your text editor.

    Find the opening `<Container>` tag, and modify it thus: `<Container `**`id="cartpage"`**`>`.

6. Save the file, and close it – the remaining three pages are now complete.

Hopefully, in this last exercise, you have seen some similarities to earlier pages. Although the process for creating both is almost identical to other pages, they have the most value and will be developed in greater detail later in the book.

For now, we've set up simple placeholders: both start with imported references to React and the layout components, which we will use to render the content. Next, we initiate objects – one each for `BlogPage` and `GalleryPage` – before using the `<Layout>` tag to render a Container `<div>` element on the page.

Let's crack on – the eagle-eyed among you will have spotted that we've referenced several components, but haven't yet created them! It's time to fix that as part of the next exercise; we'll source some from the code download that accompanies this book but focus on three of the more complex ones in more detail.

Implementing New Components for Pages

We've almost finished constructing the various elements required for our site. However, as we've just alluded to, we have some components we still need to add for our website to be "feature complete":

Fortunately, that's an easy thing to fix – we need to add a total of nine components and remove one which is no longer needed. These changes are something we will do as part of our next exercise.

CREATING REMAINING COMPONENTS

For this next exercise, I'm going to take a different route – I've picked out two of the eight components, as they contain features of particular interest. These we will go through in detail.

The remaining ones consist mainly of HTML markup so that we will source them directly from the code download. Let's make a start on getting our remaining components together:

1. The first step is to extract copies of those components we will source directly from the code download – for this, save copies of the following from the code download into the \src\components folder of our project site:

   - Connect.js

   - Instagram.js, Facebook.js, Pinterest.js, and Twitter.js

   - Copyright.js

   - Customerservices.js

2. All of the components we've covered thus far are very simple units; there are two remaining that are a little more complex. These we will create from scratch, starting with newarrival.js, which will take care of the New Arrivals block on the homepage. In a new file, add the following code – save it as newarrival.js in the \src\components folder:

```
import React from "react";
import { Link } from "gatsby";
import Img from "gatsby-image";

const newArrival = (props) => {
  return (
    <li key={props.id}>
      <Link to={`/product/${props.slug}`} className="newarrival">
        <Img fluid={props.image} />
        <h4>{props.name}</h4>
      </Link>
    </li>
  )
}

export default newArrival;
```

3. The last component we need to create will display an option to subscribe for an email newsletter – this isn't functional but will be enough to simulate the feature. In a new file, add the following code – save it as subscribe.js in the \src\components folder:

```
import React from "react"
import { useStaticQuery, graphql } from "gatsby"
```

```
const Subscribe = () => {

  {/*[...INSERT DATA MAP HERE...]*/}

  return (

      <div>
        <p>{data.datoCmsHomepage.subscribeFooter}</p>
        <p>{data.datoCmsHomepage.subscribeTextFooter}</p>
        <form className="SubscribeForm">
          <div className="field">
            <input name="email" placeholder="Your email" />
          </div>
          <div className="field">
            <button type="submit" style={{ marginTop: `20px`}}>{data.
            datoCmsHomepage.subscribeButtonFooter}</button>
          </div>
        </form>
      </div>

  );
}
export default Subscribe
```

We will add in the data requirements later in Chapter 3.

---

4. Go ahead and save the file – close any that are still open, as we don't need
    them in this chapter.

Although this was a reasonably short exercise, we've covered some useful tips – let's take a moment to review the code in more detail, as a precursor to the work we will complete in the next chapter.

Exploring the Code in Detail

We kicked off by first removing a redundant component; it was no longer needed, so it served no purpose to keep it.

We then extracted a number of the missing components from the code download that accompanies this book; this we did for reasons of space and that these components are primarily just markup.

Once done, we then created two components – each had the relevant import statements added (primarily as references for React and Gatsby). First, for the `newarrival.js` component, we pass in standard React props, before setting it to return an unordered list containing (a prop-driven placeholder for) the name and the product slug (which we used as a link to the product page).

The second and final component, Subscribe, is a little more complicated – here we have similar import references, but this time to React and GraphQL (the latter of which will make more sense once we cover the data requirements in the next chapter). We then set this component to return not an unordered list but a set of nested `<div>` tags that form a mocked-up form for submitting email addresses for a newsletter. Here, we use standard form markup, but what makes it more special is that we have JSON-based object references to what will be our data (that we add in the next chapter).

One thing worth pointing out for those of us who might have some familiarity with Gatsby: when we get to start adding in data, we would typically add import references for GraphQL. As outlined back in Chapter 1, this will be our primary mechanism for retrieving data from the CMS. We've, however, also used the `useStaticQuery` method – this has the same effect as the `graphql` reference, but we should use this in components (the `graphql` one is for use from pages). It won't make sense just yet, but hang in there – I promise all will come clear once we start dealing with data!

Summary

When building a site, and particularly one that could (or will?) earn money, we should always consider it a journey and one that will evolve. We began that journey back in Chapter 1, where we explored the basic concept behind the site we're developing throughout this book; Chapter 2 saw us start to turn this into a reality. We've covered a lot of code in this chapter, so let's take a moment to review what we have learned.

We began with some necessary housekeeping, before quickly running through the technical architecture; the latter was something we covered back in Chapter 1, but this gave us a chance to explore the page makeup of the site in more detail.

Next up, we moved on to updating the main homepage, before refactoring the layout used for the site; this included adding site navigation at the same time. We then tweaked the header before beginning to create the additional pages and components required for the site.

We then picked out two pages in particular – the product gallery and blog – before creating placeholders for both; we noted that these would be developed further later in the book.

Phew! We've covered a lot of code – admittedly, if we run it now, it is likely not to work, but this we should expect to happen. It is something we will fix once we add in the data in Chapter 4; for now, we need to add some styling, so the site will at least look presentable. We will work on this in the next chapter, so stay with me as we begin to turn this ugly duckling into something more akin to a graceful swan!

PART II

CHAPTER 3

Styling the Shop

In Chapter 2, we focused on creating the barebones of our shop – adding in pages for a blog, a product catalog, and the like. The trouble is if we were to run our code now in a browser, I can pretty much guarantee two things: 1) it wouldn't look that great – if indeed it ran – and 2) it wouldn't show anything as we don't yet have any data!

It's time to fix the first problem – we can do that by adding in some styling across our shop. However, the sharp-eyed among you will have noticed that we've already added some styles into the code!

Yes, it's one of those things we indeed have to bear in mind when using Gatsby: there are several ways to add in styling to our code. (It's also the same with other libraries and vanilla JavaScript too.) In this chapter, we'll look at some of the key styling concepts I've used to style the shop, starting with deciding on the approach to how we will style our shop.

Deciding on the Approach

Decisions, decisions – how will we style our shop? I wonder…

It's a good question: one to which there isn't necessarily one right answer. Gatsby allows us to style in several different ways; there are advantages and downsides to each approach.

For example, we can style using the traditional method of adding a class name to our code and centralizing those classes in one or more style sheets. It's a perfectly adequate approach, but one where the pressure is on us to apply suitable classes, and that might not always be possible. Instead, we could in-line our styles; this means there is one less resource to call from the server (i.e., the style sheet), but we can't necessarily compress the code.

© Alex Libby 2021
A. Libby, *Gatsby E-Commerce*, https://doi.org/10.1007/978-1-4842-6692-2_3

For this book, I've decided to take something of a hybrid approach – this satisfies a desire to follow old-school methods (yes, I am a little traditional when it comes to styling). We use the gatsby-shopify-starter theme, which already uses the @emotion library (available from `https://emotion.sh/`), plus some individual style sheets formatted as Gatsby style files. At the same time, I will add some styles to individual components, using a mix of vanilla CSS and Sass styling (the latter to show how such a tool might be used in our projects). I suspect there will be areas for improvement in terms of where we place styles, but hey, isn't that part of continuous improvement?

Leaving aside the intricacies of styling in Gatsby, let's move on – before we can apply any color, we need to choose a suitable palette. I've already done this in the demo, but it's worth taking a look at how I did this in a little more detail.

Choosing a Color Theme

The first task for our site is to work out what colors we should use – the color we have from the starter theme ("rebecca purple") wouldn't be my first choice!

We could indeed choose any one of hundreds of different colors or even shades of colors; the choice of color can have a positive or negative impact on the success of our site. At this point, it's important to note that choosing the right color palette means having at least an understanding of color psychology; that's something which is a little too far outside the scope of this book, but there is a simple trick we can use to give us a starting point.

DEMO: CHOOSING OUR COLOR SCHEME

An easy way to create a palette as a starting point for our site is to sample a photo of a product we would be selling to get the dominant color (or colors) from that image. We can then make use of something called color harmonies to create our palette. Let's work through the steps required:

1. The first task is to choose the image. For this demo, I used the fairy cakes image; I used a color picker plugin for Chrome, to sample and choose an initial color that I felt best suited the overall theme of our shop.

2. Next, browse to `https://mycolor.space` and enter the number in the grayish-red pill and then click Generate – this generates a list of several themes, all based around different types of color harmonies.

I've chosen to use the one shown in Figure 3-1 – you can also see it and other options generated by the MyColor website at `https://mycolor.space/?hex=%23A49696&sub=1`:

Classy Palette

#A49696   #574142   #D19FA0   #9A9B81   #676850

Figure 3-1. A screenshot of our chosen color palette

Okay, I'll admit (and before you ask): the name of this palette didn't sway me! It does serve to illustrate an important point, though: the colors chosen by this site are all based on the use of different color harmonies. The harmony names used might range from names such as triadic to analogous or complementary – in short, each uses a different formula to work out colors that best fit your starting color.

You can see the original palette at `https://mycolor.space/?hex=%23A49696&sub=1`; for those of you interested in learning more about color harmonies (and some theory), then the Tiger Color website has a useful article at `www.tigercolor.com/color-lab/color-theory/color-harmonies.htm`.

The great thing about using this approach is that we can be sure of one thing. It doesn't matter what our base color is, as formulae work out which colors to use automatically, so the resulting colors will always work together based on the palette type we use. It takes out the guesswork behind what colors to use – not everyone might like our chosen palette, but then we can't please everyone!

Adding Custom Fonts

With our color palette finalized (at least for now), the next task is to choose the fonts we want to use for the site. As before, we could elect to use any one of thousands of different fonts – free or commercial. There is something to be said for keeping the choice simple, although choosing fonts can have an equal impact on the success of our site. There is one more choice we need to make, though: do we go local or remote?

Aha, that was admittedly a somewhat cryptic comment, so let me explain what I mean: we'll do both! Huh, I hear you ask: how can we do both? Well, the answer to that lies in a great little NPM package created by Kyle Matthews, hosted at `https://github.com/KyleAMathews/typefaces`. It allows us to have the best of both worlds, by using Google Fonts, but hosting them locally.

The use of remotely hosted fonts can be a bit of a minefield – while it can make it very quick to retrieve them (as they are hosted via a CDN), it can mean that if they become unavailable, it will affect how our site looks. Kyle's project allows us to install Google Fonts (and others too), using NPM. It means that fonts are always available (even offline) and are loaded significantly faster than through CDN and we can manage dependencies through NPM.

ADDING CUSTOM FONTS

Let's take a look at the steps I used to add them into our site – we're going to use two, namely, Open Sans and Great Vibes:

1. First, fire up a Node.js terminal session, and then change the working folder to our project folder.

2. At the prompt, enter the following commands, in turn, pressing Enter after each:

   ```
   npm install typeface-open-sans typeface-great-vibes --save
   ```

3. Once done, go ahead and add the following lines to `\src\layouts\index.js`, immediately after `import "./layout.css"`:

   ```
   require("typeface-open-sans")
   require("typeface-great-vibes")
   ```

We should have two import statements in our code, as indicated in this code block:

```
Import { Global Style } from '~/utils/styles'
Import Navigation from '~/components/Navigation'
Import "./layout.css"
Import "typeface-open-sans"
Import "typeface-great-vibes"
```

4. The last step is to amend the site's style sheet to reference the new fonts – for this, go ahead and create a new folder called styles within the \src folder of our site.

5. Next, extract a copy of the global.css file from the code download that accompanies this book; drop that file into the styles folder created in the previous step. This contains some predetermined styles for our site, as well as updated references for the new fonts we've installed in this demo.

Setting up each font package is a simple change, but one that opens up some real possibilities – at the same time, it has some implications in terms of how we use this new feature. Let's take a quick look at the steps in more detail.

Understanding What Happened

When working with custom fonts, one of the steps we would take is to add the appropriate @font-face declaration into our CSS style sheet, right?

In this case, that's something we don't need to do – instead, we installed the packages in the same way we would do with any NPM-based package. We then added two declarations to index.js in the layouts folder, which we use throughout the site; it ensures the fonts will be available across the site.

For the last step, we then introduced a declaration for the body to call the Open Sans font. We did something similar for the Great Vibes font that we use to style the header title; we reference that one as an in-line call from the navigation.js file.

The best part though is that we've avoided the need to add in any @font-face declarations – if we take a look at the contents of the typeface-great-vibes or typeface-open-sans folder in the node_modules folder (Figure 3-2)...

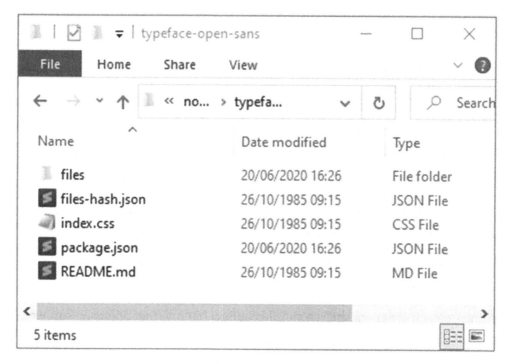

Figure 3-2.   *The contents of the typeface-open-sans folder*

...we will find inside an `index.css` file that contains the appropriate font declarations and which will be subsumed during the Gatsby build process automatically. Neat, huh?

Okay, let's crack on: it's time to get a little visual! The next task isn't strictly a styling issue, but one that does affect styling the site. I'm talking about SVG images and refactoring them – I'll bet that you're probably asking how that affects our style sheet, right?

Refactoring the SVG Images

Go ahead and crack open the `connect.js` file inside the `\src\components` folder – noticed anything about how we're calling in the social media icons for our site?

Granted, you won't be able to tell what they look like (at least not yet!) – but you should at least see the names of four components we're using to display the social media icons, as shown in this (partial) example:

```
<section className="SocialIcons">
  <div className="level-item">
    <a href=https://www.facebook.com/havecakeeatcake tar...
```

```
      <Facebook />
    </a>
  </div>
```

While researching and developing code for this book, the original version of that block of code looked something like that shown in this code extract:

```
<section className="SocialIcons">
  <div className="level-item">
    <a href ="https://www.facebook.com/havecakeeatcake" target="_blank"
    rel="noreferrer">
    <svg className="svg-inline--fa fa-facebook-square fa-w-14" aria-
    hidden="true" data-prefix="fab" data-icon="facebook-square" role="img"
    xmlns="http://www.w3.org/2000/sv viewBox="0 0 448 512" data-fa-
    i2svg="">
      <path fill="currentColor" d="M448 80v352c0 26.5-21.5 48-
      48 48h-85.3V302.8h60.618.7-67.6h-69.3V192c0-19.6 5.4-32.9
      33.5-32.9H384V98.7c-6.2-.8-27.4-2.7-52.2-2.7-51.6 0-87 31.5-87
      89.4v49.9H184v67.6h60.9V480H48c-26.5 0-48-21.5-48-48V80c0-26.5 21.5-
      48 48-48h352c26.5 0 48 21.5 48 48z"></path>
    </svg>
    </a>
  </div>
```

I have one word for that – awful! And that's for several reasons:

- Take a look at the in-line style classes we use – if you're familiar with a particular icon library, you should immediately spot which one! The trouble is the classes we have here are clumsy at best: we can do better.

- As SVG images aren't images in the true sense, but HTML markup, we can treat them differently – it means we can apply shared classes against each for properties such as background color.

- The code alone is not very readable: this makes it less reusable and harder to debug!

Fortunately, there is an easy fix for this – we can turn all four icons into Gatsby components that can be referenced directly from our code. Turning them into components is something I've already done in the version of the code that accompanies this book; let's work through how I made these changes in more detail.

REFACTORING THE SVG IMAGES

To effect the changes, I worked through these steps:

1. First, I navigated to `https://transform.tools/` – it's an excellent site for turning SVG markup into JSX code, as long as you can live with the adverts.

2. Minimize this for a moment – next, go ahead and open any one of the four SVGs from the code download that accompanies this book in your text editor. I will assume for this exercise that you start with the Facebook icon.

3. Copy and paste all of the code from your editor into the left-hand pane, marked SVG.

4. Copy the transformed code from the JSX pane into your editor – it will look like the code shown in in the following, once you save it to the file:

```jsx
import * as React from "react";

function SvgComponent(props) {
  return (
    <svg
      aria-hidden="true"
      data-prefix="fab"
      data-icon="facebook-square"
      viewBox="0 0 448 512"
      {...props}
    >
      <path
        fill="currentColor"
        d="M448 80v352c0 26.5-21.5 48-48 48h-85.3V302.8h60.6l8.7-
67.6h-69.3V192c0-19.6 5.4-32.9 33.5-32.9H384V98.
7c-6.2-.8-27.4-2.7-52.2-2.7-51.6 0-87 31.5-87 89.4v49.9H18
4v67.6h60.9V480H48c-26.5 0-48-21.5-48-48V80c0-26.5 21.5-48
48-48h352c26.5 0 48 21.5 48 48z"
      />
    </svg>
  );
}

export default SvgComponent;
```

5. In each of the files, replace SvgComponent with the name of the social media platform – for example, the SvgComponent shown in Figure 3-6 should be changed to Facebook.

6. Repeat steps 2–4 for each of the other SVG icons – name them as per the social media platform name, that is, twitter.js, instagram.js, and pinterest.js for Twitter, Instagram, and Pinterest, respectively. Make sure you rename the SvgComponent name accordingly too!

Hopefully, you will agree that this is far more legible! If we rewrite each of the original SVGs as components, we can make our component reusable, both for this project and future projects, as well as bringing it more in-line with the Gatsby/React philosophy. This refactoring has also highlighted some key features that we should cover before continuing – let's take a moment to consider the code changes in more detail.

Breaking Apart the Changes

Although this was a short exercise, it was nevertheless an important one – Gatsby is pretty forgiving about code styles used, but it does pay to use a React style of writing where possible! It might require a little more writing of code, but this is a trade-off with ensuring both legibility and reusability, two of the central tenets of Gatsby.

To get there for this demo, we kicked off by taking the Facebook icon and dropping the contents into the transform website. There, it reformatted the code into a React-based component, by realigning each property. At the same time, it inserted a spread operator (the {...props} statement), to allow us to pass in any other properties defined for this component.

We then renamed the SvgComponent name to better represent the social media icon we used, before repeating the process for the other icons. We then rounded out this exercise by saving each to disk – the calls to each component already added in an earlier activity.

Okay, let's move on: there are still a few things we can do to take our styling further, so it's time to get a little sassy! No, it's not a reference to being impudent or taking a spirited approach to coding, but making use of the Sass preprocessor to help better organize our style sheet code! It's a great tool to use and an easy one to implement if you've not used it before – let's dive in and take a look in more detail.

Taking Things Further

It's at this point we could say we're done and dusted with styling and that it's time to move on to the next part of the site, right?

Well, perhaps not. There are a few more things to consider: What if you happen to be one of those developers who are a fan of using preprocessors, such as Sass, or have heard about using it? We decided to develop from the ground up; could we have done things differently? What other areas could we have also looked at styling or perhaps refactored to help optimize our code?

These are all valid questions – I know we won't be able to cover all of the possible changes we could make in this chapter, but there's some food for thought! To see what I mean, let's start by exploring how we might make a conversion to using a preprocessor – I will use the all-popular Sass as my example, but the principles will be similar for tools such as Less or Stylus.

Converting Styling to Use CSS Preprocessors

For those of you not already familiar with Sass, it's a great tool to help with organizing and writing a shorthand form of code that will transform into valid CSS.

Sass is a superset (or extension) of CSS – in short, it combines the best parts of simple JavaScript functions with CSS to help facilitate writing styles. For example, you might use a background color of #f4f4f4 throughout your code. What if you wanted to change it? Sure, you can do a search and replace, but that's tedious at best: instead, you can set a variable such as `$primary-color: #f4f4f4`. We can then use a statement such as `background-color: $primary-color` in the main part of the style sheet. When you come to transform your code (which is done automatically for us), it will automatically replace any instance of `background-color: $primary-color` with `background-color: #f4f4f4.` Neat, huh?

Okay, so there's a lot to Sass than just setting simple variables! The critical point to note, though, is that Sass historically came with two different syntaxes – I will use the current syntax, which uses file extensions ending in `.scss`. At the same time, you might hear of various incarnations of Sass, such as Ruby Sass, LibSass, or even Node-Sass; all do similar things, but we will use Dart Sass (considered to be the primary version of Sass).

Enough chitchat. Let's get stuck into writing some code! To use Sass, we have to alter how we generate our CSS file at build time; it requires a little work, but nothing too heavy. At the same time, we'll begin to convert the existing CSS to use Sass equivalents – there's a lot we can do to switch over to using Sass completely, but at least this will give you an indication of the types of changes we can effect as part of converting the style sheet.

CONVERTING TO USE SASS

To switch over to using Sass, follow these steps:

1. The first task is to install Sass – for this, go ahead and fire up a Node.js terminal session, and then change the working folder to our project folder.

2. At the prompt, enter this command and press Enter to install Sass:

```
npm install sass -save-dev
```

3. Once done, we need to install the `gatsby-plugin-sass` plugin, as a wrapper for Sass – go ahead and run this command at the prompt:

```
npm install Gatsby-plugin-sass -save-dev
```

4. We need to include the plugin in the `gatsby-config.js` file – crack that file open in your text editor (it's at the root of the project folder), and then add in this code before the call to `gatsby-transformer-sharp`:

```
{
    resolve: `gatsby-plugin-sass`,
    options: {
      implementation: require("sass"),
    },
  },
  `gatsby-transformer-sharp`,
  `gatsby-plugin-sharp`,
  {
```

5. Next up, we need to alter `gatsby-browser.js`, to reference our new Sass style sheet. Change the extension of the imported file thus:

```
import "./src/styles/global.scss"
```

6. Save and close this file – we can now start editing our style sheet! Save a copy of `global.css` as a backup; then as our first change, replace the `nav`, `nav div a`, and `nav div a:hover` style rules with this block:

```
nav {
    background-color: $nav-background-color;
    display: flex;
    justify-content: center;
    padding: 10.56px 11.2px;
    margin-bottom: 50px;

    div a {
        color: $nav-text-color;
        cursor: pointer;
        padding: 11.2px 12px;
        letter-spacing: 0.03rem !important;
        text-decoration: none;
        text-transform: uppercase;
    }

    div a:hover {
        background-color: $nav-hover-color;
        padding: 11.2px 12px;
    }
```

7. Next, add in these lines at the very top of the file, before the body rule declaration:

```
$newarrivals-border-color: #cccccc;
$nav-text-color: #4a4a4a;
$nav-hover-color: #f4f4f4;
$nav-background-color: lighten( $nav-text-color, 62.6 );
```

8. Go ahead and save the file – at this point, Gatsby will transpile (or convert) our Sass style rules into valid CSS for us. We will see this in action in the next chapter when we do our first real test of the site, but for now, Figure 3-3 shows a screenshot of what to expect.

```
nav div a {                                      global.scss:28
  ☑ color: ■ #4a4a4a;
  ☑ cursor: pointer;
  ☑ padding: ▶ 0.7rem 0.75rem;
  ☑ letter-spacing: 0.03rem !important;
  ☑ text-decoration: ▶ none;
  ☑ text-transform: uppercase;
}                                                        ⋮
```

Figure 3-3. *An example of Sass code transpiled to CSS*

If you want to take a look, open your browser's Developer Console area – you will see this under the Elements tab (assuming use of Chrome).

9. If you don't see `global.scss` (shown in the top-right corner of Figure 3-7), then you may need to enable CSS source maps. It will vary between browsers, but as an example, it's available from within Google Chrome's Developer Console by clicking the three vertical dots and then More tools ➤ Settings. Figure 3-4 shows what to look for, once you have the Settings page displayed.

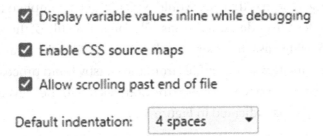

Figure 3-4. *The CSS source maps option from Chrome*

Although we've only made one change to our style sheet, this isn't the end of it – not by a long shot! There are lots of more examples in this style sheet where we can perform similar changes – or nesting, to give it its proper name.

Making use of Sass in our demo does raise some valuable opportunities, so let's take a moment to examine the code changes in more detail and cover off some more examples of where we could update our code.

Breaking Apart the Code Changes

This option may not be for everyone, but it is one I definitely would recommend considering – Sass is a great tool to help organize and reduce the amount of CSS you have to write when styling a site.

One of the ways it does this is by allowing us to nest styles within another – it might seem a little alien, but ideal if you think of instances where you might find you have a lot of duplicated rule names. Navigation styling is one of the worst offenders for this; I've lost count of the number of times when I have to write something like `nav ul li ul li li` or similar!

For this example, we focused on implementing Sass as a tool – we kicked off by installing the main Dart Sass plugin, followed by a wrapper plugin to allow Gatsby to interface with (and compile) Sass code from within its build process. We then rejigged the `nav div a` rule, to first remove the `nav` part of the element, before moving it inside the `nav` rule. Sass then takes the `nav` rule and compiles that as is, before transpiling the `div a` into `nav div a`. It takes a little getting used to but is ideal where you see common elements between two different rule types.

The critical thing to note is that you would typically get a compiled file when using Dart Sass – it transpiles the code from the Sass file into a CSS file of the same name. You don't get that when using Sass in Gatsby; it will produce a file with a randomly generated name, in much the same way as other files from the Gatsby build process. The only way to prove it is using the Sass code is to check the Sources tab in the Developer Console – you can see an example, as indicated in Figure 3-5.

```
nav {
  background-color: ■#D19FA0;
  display: flex;
  justify-content: center;
  padding: 0.66rem .7rem;
  margin-bottom: 50px;

  div a {
    color: ■rgb(74, 74, 74);
    cursor: pointer;
    padding: .7rem .75rem;
    letter-spacing: 0.03rem !important;
    text-decoration: none;
    text-transform: uppercase;
  }
}
```

Figure 3-5. *A partial example of our Sass file from the Sources tab in Chrome*

Okay, let's move on: I mentioned that there are other examples of Sass we could implement in the style sheet. These are easy to apply, so let's take a look at them in more detail.

Implementing More Changes Using Sass

Working with the Sass toolset can be something of a double-edged sword – when used with care and consideration, it can be an immensely powerful tool. However, if we haven't planned things well, it might end up not being as useful as it could be!

In this next demo, I'm going to work through a couple more examples of how we can tweak the Sass file we created in the previous exercise, so you can get a flavor of the type of improvements we can make when working with Sass. At the same time, we will make use of the Sass Color Calculator tool at https://sasscolorcalculator.com/, to help calculate some of the color values we will use in this demo. Let's take a look at the changes in more detail.

DEMO: TWEAKING THE SASS CODE

For this next exercise, we'll make a couple of small tweaks to give you a feel for how we can improve our code – to do so, work through these steps:

1. Crack open your copy of `global.scss` from the project folder, and add in this block of code at the very top of the file, before the body `{...}` rule:

```scss
@mixin SocialIcons {
  color: #ffffff;
  text-decoration: none;
}
```

2. Next, scroll down a little, and then modify the rules shown in the following, as indicated:

```scss
main div ul li, main ul li {
  padding: 5px;
  border: 1px solid $newarrivals-border-color;
  margin-right: 20px;
}
```

3. We need to do it with one more block – go ahead and edit the code as highlighted:

```scss
nav {
  background-color: $nav-background-color;
  ...

  div a {
    color: $nav-text-color;
  ...
  }

  div a:hover {
    background-color: $nav-hover-color;
  ...
  }
}
```

4. A little further down, we have a rule for `main button` – toward the end of the rule, alter the code to bring the `hover` rule inside the `main button` rule, as indicated:

    ```
    background-color: #450b40;
    background: linear-gradient(131deg, #450b40, #702069);

    &:hover {
      opacity: .9;
    }
    }
    ```

5. There's one more change we can make – scroll down to this rule: `footer > div:nth-child(3) > section > div > a`.

6. Go ahead and replace the contents of that rule with this line:

    ```
    footer > div:nth-child(3) > section > div > a {
      @include SocialIcons;
    }
    ```

7. Do the same for the hover rule too, immediately below it:

    ```
    footer > div:nth-child(3) > section > div > a:hover {
      @include SocialIcons;
    }
    ```

8. Go ahead and save the file – Gatsby will attempt to build, but we will likely see errors from missing data. We will thoroughly test our solution in the next chapter!

In this exercise, we've only made some small changes to keep things simple. In reality, we could easily extend the nesting changes to cover other rule definitions or potentially look at using a tool such as Autoprefixer to help manage vendor prefixes. But I digress. Even though it was a simple demo, we've covered some useful tips; let's take a moment to review the code in more detail to understand how it has helped style the site.

Breaking Apart the Changes

Mixins…variables… To quote that Spanish waiter from the British comedy *Fawlty Towers*, "¿qué…?"

Yes, I have to admit that it might sound like double Dutch for those of you not familiar with Sass, but don't worry – it's not as difficult as it might seem! Making use of variables allows us to define the colors once at the top of the file; when compiled, Sass will automatically replace any variable placeholder with the relevant value from the declarations at the top of the file. We can see an example of this taken from our code in Figure 3-6.

```
main div ul li, main ul li {                    global.scss:24
    padding: ▸ 5px;
    border: ▸ 1px solid ▢#cccccc;
    margin-right: 20px;
}
        24  main div ul li,
        25  main ul li {
        26      padding: 5px;
        27      border: 1px solid $newarrivals-border-color;
        28      margin-right: 20px;
        29  }
        30
```

Figure 3-6. *Tracing a compiled style to its Sass equivalent*

We then refactored code in the next two steps – we swapped the original colors for relevant variable declarations. We then inserted the hover rule for the main button element inside its parent element – this uses the principle of nesting, which is something we touched on in the first Sass exercise. We then introduced another technique, which is to create a **mixin** – this is simply a block of reusable code that we set up at the start of our code, and we called it in as part of the rule for the Social Icons block. From a code perspective, it looks like the code displayed in Figure 3-7, which is taken from my browser console area.

```
159  footer > div:nth-child(3) > section > div > a {
160      @include SocialIcons;
161  }
162
163  footer > div:nth-child(3) > section > div > a:hover {
164      @include SocialIcons;
165  }
```

Figure 3-7. *Using a mixin when styling our shop*

We will put these changes to a proper test when we use Netlify in the next chapter to do a dry run test of our site.

If you would like to learn more about the principles of using Sass, and in particular Dart Sass, then you might want to refer to my book *Introducing Dart Sass*, published by Apress.

Okay, enough of being sassy (if you pardon the pun). Let's change tack and take a look at something else! Throughout this chapter, we've covered some of the techniques I've used to style our shop. However, I know that the styling may not be perfect; there will always be room for improvement! Before we round out this chapter and move on to tackling data, let's take a moment to explore some of these areas that might benefit from tweaking in more detail.

Taking Things Further

When constructing a site, we should never assume it is complete – a site should grow and evolve and only die a death when circumstances mean we no longer need it. The same applies to styling: styles become passé and outdated, so keeping them fresh should always be a priority.

Keeping this idea in mind, I know there are a few areas of our shop that could well benefit from being tweaked as part of ongoing development. Making these changes is something I could do, but then I wouldn't have anything for you to do as my audience, right? Instead, let me give you a few pointers where we could improve our code (and these are in no particular order):

- We've used a mix of in-line and global styles (the latter for want of a better way to describe it) – should we be using more localized styles in components, or can we introduce more styles into the `global.scss` file (or `global.css` file, for those of you not using Sass)?

- We're using the original layout.css file from the `gatsby-shopify-starter` template, but this contains a lot of extra redundant styles; this is ripe for pruning if you pardon the gardening pun! We can easily trim the content back, convert to Sass (if desired), and merge it in with the `global.scss` file we're also using in our demo.

- If we remain with using Sass (and why not – it's such a great tool), then we could use the Sass Color Calculator we used earlier in this chapter to generate an entire color palette. Instead of having separate base colors (and there is nothing wrong in this approach), we can automatically calculate our color palette from one base color. It means that if it should change, then everything will still work without the need for replacing lots of values. We will need the likes of black and white as colors, but it's one way to simplify our use of colors!

- We talked about the use of Autoprefixer for adding vendor prefixes where needed – although this is becoming less of a need, there are still some rules that need it. We would need to add this in as part of webpack, or perhaps as a stand-alone tool, and set it to monitor for changes; Gatsby doesn't have a dedicated plugin – at least not for now. Who knows? Maybe there is scope to write something.

- As a simple exercise, and for those who want to use Sass, the global. scss file has plenty of scope for improvement, particularly around nesting. It might seem a simple change, but it's a good one to help group together common styles and make it easier to update the file in the long term.

- We're also using styles from the emotion library – these are coming in by default from the starter theme used in our project. While this works technically, it does raise a question – are we happy with mixing in three different sets of styling? We have the standard CSS style files, along with (now) Sass and the emotion styles from the theme – I don't know about you, but that seems a little excessive, and perhaps we should consider rationalizing what we use!

These are just a few ways we could improve the styling for this shop – I'm sure there will be more, but that all depends on the direction we want to take it! We will, however, come back to styling later in this book: once we've added in the cart and blog, there will be changes we need to make to style the new areas of the site.

Summary

We began our journey through this chapter by deciding on the approach we would use to style our shop – this settled on a hybrid approach, where we can use a mix of in-line CSS-in-JS styles, along with the more traditional use of classes and a separate style sheet.

Next up, we then explored a simple method for choosing the color scheme for our shop; at the same time, we added in some custom fonts to style both the header title and remaining text throughout the shop. We then moved on to understanding some of the improvements we could make to the SVG images in the demo. We examined how this isn't directly related to styling, but that reformatting the SVGs as components allows us to implement more consistent and reusable styling.

We then explored a useful technique to help take styling a little bit further – this involved the use of preprocessors (in our case, Sass) and understanding how we can implement such tools with little difficulty. We finally rounded out this chapter with a look at some of the areas we could improve in terms of styling – space constraints meant we couldn't cover them all in this chapter, but it would at least give us some food for thought!

Okay, onward we go: we've created the basis for our shop and applied some basic styling, so it's time to bring it to life! I'm sure you have heard of the statement "content is king" – or should that be "data is king"? It's a good clue as to what we need to do next: yes, it's time to add in data to our shop. Stay with me, as we will add in the content for our shop and finally test it to ensure it all works as expected...

CHAPTER 4

Sourcing Data

At this stage, we have a site in place, but there is one key element missing: data!

Yes, a shop isn't any good without products (i.e., data), so throughout this chapter, we will work through what is required to set up our data and hook it into our shop. We'll take a look at what options we have when it comes to implementing the checkout and payment process so that we can be sure our data needs are satisfied from the outset.

We'll also do something I know you will be itching to do – test our shop! Indeed, we've not been able to do this until now, given that for it to work, we need to have data, markup, and (to a greater or lesser extent) styling in place. However, we will fix that at the end of this chapter; we will use Netlify to host a test version of our shop. So, folks, plenty to do: let's make a start with getting data set up, using the DatoCMS system.

Getting Started with DatoCMS

Any site needs content – be this descriptive content, product information, or labels to operate the website. It doesn't matter.

Historically, this is something we would have done using a database such as MySQL (or perhaps something a little beefier, depending on the site of the shop). However, this is not without its problems: databases pose an inherent security weakness for any website, and data has to be sourced each time customers request it. This security risk makes sites slow and vulnerable to hacking – indeed, the more substantial the website, the bigger the potential risk!

Thankfully though, when using Gatsby, we can take a completely different approach. Gatsby compiles site pages into static content during the build process; we request data at this point only and not while the site is running, which helps make the site superfast.

© Alex Libby 2021
A. Libby, *Gatsby E-Commerce*, https://doi.org/10.1007/978-1-4842-6692-2_4

By default, Gatsby uses GraphQL: this allows us to source content from any system which supports this technology. We could use the version of GraphQL that comes with Gatsby, but to make things more interesting, why not use an external system? As a JAMStack tool, Gatsby can source data from a wide variety of sources, such as APIs, YAML files, JSON, CSV, and, of course, traditional databases…but that last way is old school and serves no real benefit nowadays!

For this project, we're going to use data from two different (external) tools. The first is DatoCMS (hosted at `www.datocms.com`) – it's a headless CMS that allows us to decouple the presentational layer (i.e., what you see on the site) from the data storage. Separating the presentational layer means we can use all manner of different means to get at it; the CMS works by exposing data through an endpoint, in JSON format:

- We're not "dropping all of our eggs in one basket" – so if Gatsby stopped working, then at least we wouldn't lose everything!

- Using a headless CMS such as DatoCMS gives us a flexible GUI to manage our data; security is handled for us by Dato, so there is one less thing to worry about.

- We can consume data exposed in JSON format, using all manner of different frameworks, so if we decided to change tools in the future, the switchover would be more straightforward.

The second is to use the GraphQL data source from within our checkout and payment provider, Shopify. This exposes all of the products we want to sell from our shop in a convenient format that can be consumed in the same GraphiQL front-end explorer application.

Now, it might seem a little odd to use data from two different sites for a small project such as ours; there are several reasons why we're taking this approach:

- Why not? I know it might seem odd, but one of the great things about Gatsby is that it can aggregate data from different sources using GraphQL, so here's a good opportunity to prove this is possible!

- Shopify requires us to add the products we want to sell into the dashboard of our account on the Shopify website; it does mean though that we can use it to manage options such as variants, as well as display information such as stock levels.

- Shopify doesn't make it so easy to expose entries such as identifying labels (e.g., to indicate new arrivals). To keep things simple for now, we will use DatoCMS to handle this part, but it's a perfect opportunity to move the data for this into Shopify.

- Shopify can't handle labels for features such as navigation, so we need to use an alternative source. We could use the internal GraphQL client, but that would be boring – adding in DatoCMS gives us an extra "edge" to sourcing data for our project.

Okay, enough chitchat. Let's crack on with getting our data set up! Over the next few pages, we will work through a multi-part exercise; when finished, we will have access set up, DatoCMS integrated into our shop, fields created, and content added to the CMS.

We will also set up an account for Shopify, and complete a similar exercise later, in Chapter 5, to get products added to our store.

Don't worry, though – we will pause to recap content before moving on to the next exercise!

With that in mind, let's make a start on our mega exercise: the first step is to get a database set up in DatoCMS and add in the media for our site.

Throughout this book, I will assume the name of the database we use is havecakeeatcake. However, you may find you need to change it if DatoCMS flags the name as already in use or if you prefer to use something else. If so, please change it accordingly.

Setting Up the Database and Adding Media

The first task in getting content set up and available for use in our shop is to get a database configured for use in DatoCMS.

At this stage, it's important to note that the use of the word database is in the generic sense only – DatoCMS uses CRUD techniques to create and access database content, but much of the hard work is abstracted away from us.

Instead, we will use a GUI-driven approach to create the storage and set up fields; it makes it much easier to configure and tweak the content. With this in mind, let's take a look at the steps required to get the initial database area set up in more detail.

DATOCMS PART 1: THE INITIAL SETUP

To get our storage area set up, follow these steps:

1. Browse to www.datocms.com, and then click the Enter dashboard at the top right.

2. Click New project ➤ Blank Project – enter havecakeeatcake as the name.

3. Click the name on the next screen and then Enter project.

The project will appear in a new tab, ready for us to use. We need to set up both fields and media, so proceed with these steps:

4. Download and extract a copy of the images from the code download that accompanies this book – save them to the project folder, inside the \src\ images folder.

Storing the images in this location is a temporary measure until we can get them into DatoCMS.

---

5. Click Media and then Upload New Assets.

6. Navigate to where you stored the images, then hold down Ctrl (PC/Linux) or Cmd (Macs), and click each in turn. Select Open.

7. All images will be uploaded to DatoCMS – if you prefer, you may do steps 2–4 in smaller batches, if it is easier.

8. Leave the window open as is, but minimized – we will come back to it shortly.

If all is well, we should now have a project set up, ready for us to start adding records; we also have the media in place that we will use in our shop. The next stage of this mega demo is where things start to get interesting; we need to create our database or storage area for the records that we will access from our shop. There are quite a few steps involved, so let's dive in and take a look in more detail.

DATOCMS PART 2: SETTING UP THE DATABASES

To get the database set up with the appropriate fields, go ahead with these steps:

1. Click Settings – we need to add a new database.

2. At the bottom of the page, click the + sign, and then make sure you are on the Basic Info tab.

3. In the Name field, enter Cupcake (note the case and spelling!) – you should see cupcake appear in the Model ID field. If not, go ahead and enter it here too (in lowercase). Click Save Model.

4. Repeat steps 1–3, but this time, use HomePage as the Name and homepage as the Model ID.

5. Repeat steps 1–3 for the third time, but this time use Navigation as the Name and navigation as the Model ID.

We will come to the latter two later in this chapter.

---

6. Once done, click the Content tab and then Add menu item.

7. In the Label field, enter Products, and then click Save Item.

8. Click Add menu item again, then enter Cupcake as the label, and change Point this to Model with the Connected model as Cupcake. Click Save Item when done.

9. Repeat step 8, but this time replace the word Cupcake with HomePage.

10. Repeat step 8, but this time use the word Navigation instead of Cupcake.

11. Once back at the Settings tab, drag the Cupcake entry over Products; Products should turn into a drop-down menu.

12. Minimize the window, but leave it logged in on the Settings tab – we will revert to it shortly.

It might seem like quite a few steps to work through, but organizing content is critical to the success of any database! We still have more to do, though, but before we do, let's take a moment to review what we've done so far. Go and grab a drink, and take a few minutes to step away from your computer – when you're ready, we can review the demo in more detail.

Breaking Apart the Changes

We kicked off part 1 of our demo by setting up a new project on the DatoCMS site – this will act as the data source for our project. At the same time, we then uploaded the images that we would later use to create the product gallery for our shop.

We then moved on to part 2; this involved setting up the three databases for our shop; this included the main Cupcake database, along with ones for Navigation and HomePage. We followed this with several steps to create and organize the menu displayed within DatoCMS's admin area; it's a small change, but one worth doing to maintain an orderly system in DatoCMS! At the end of setting up links, we ended up with the menu displayed in Figure 4-1.

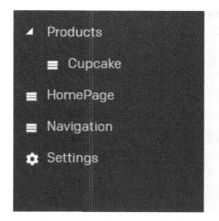

Figure 4-1. *The menu structure for the admin area in our DatoCMS account*

Okay, let's move on: we have set up an account with DatoCMS, added three databases, and organized how they appear in the admin area of our account. The next task is to add in the relevant fields for each database – this isn't the most exciting of tasks, so let's get to it without delay.

Creating the Database Fields

I know you're going to hate me for this next exercise, but it's one we have to complete – adding all of the fields into our databases. Let's just say it's a necessary evil if we want to get data displayed in our shop…

But I digress. We have three sets of data fields to add in: products, homepage labels, and navigation entries. Let's take a look at what's involved in more detail, starting with the products.

DATOCMS PART 3: SETTING UP THE FIELDS

To get the fields set up, let's work through these steps:

1. Click Cupcake in the L/H menu and then cupcake next to the Cupcake collection.

2. At the bottom, click Add new field – it will display a set of choices. Click Text ➤ Single-line string.

3. On the Settings tab, enter Stock ID in the Name field and `stock_id` in the Field ID field, and then click Save Field.

4. We have another nine fields to add in, so go ahead and repeat steps 2–3 to add in each of these fields, but this time, use the information provided in Table 4-1.

Table 4-1. *Field values to use for the Cupcake database*

Name of Field	Of Type	Field ID
Name	Single-line string	name
Description	Multiple-paragraph text	description
Product Image	Single asset	product_image
UOM	Single-line string	uom
Price	Floating-point number	price
New Arrival	Boolean	newarrival
Slug	Slug	slug
Product URL	Single-line string	product_url

5. We have two more sets of fields to add in – the next one will cover the navigation entries. In the center list, click Navigation.

6. Go ahead and follow the same steps 2–4 from this exercise, but this time, use the field values shown in Table 4-2.

Table 4-2. *Field values to use for the Navigation database*

Name of Field	Of Type	Field ID
Home Text	Single-line string	home_text
Home Link	Single-line string	home_link
About Text	Single-line string	about_text
About Link	Single-line string	about_link
Blog Text	Single-line string	blog_text
Blog Link	Single-line string	blog_link
Products Text	Single-line string	products _text
Products Link	Single-line string	products_link
Help Text	Single-line string	help_text
Help Link	Single-line string	help_link

7. There is one more set of fields to add in, which is for the homepage labels – click HomePage in the center pane.

8. Go ahead and add the fields in, using the same method as before, but this time use the values shown in Table 4-3.

Table 4-3. *The fields to use for the HomePage labels*

Name of Field	Of Type	Field ID
Site Label	Single-line string	site_label
Contact Address	Single-line string	contact_address
Telephone	Single-line string	Telephone
New Arrivals	Single-line string	new_arrival
About Us	Single-line string	about_us
Customer Service	Single-line string	customer_service
Help	Single-line string	Help
Delivery	Single-line string	Delivery
Gifts	Single-line string	gifts
AboutUs	Single-line string	about_us_footer
Terms	Single-line string	terms_footer
Subscribe	Single-line string	subscribe_footer
Subscribe_text	Single-line string	subscribe_text_footer
Subscribe_button	Single-line string	subscribe_button_footer
Social Media	Single-line string	social_media_footer

9. We can minimize the browser window for now – we are done with adding fields to our databases.

Phew, got that task out of the way, *chuckle!* Okay, so I might have been a little dismissive there, as merely inputting data isn't everyone's cup of tea. However, it is a valuable exercise – adding in the right fields can help or hinder in how our information is stored and ultimately the success of the database and our site.

In this case, we've created three separate databases, inside of which, we've added fields appropriate for their usage. We specified the name of the field (as shown in DatoCMS), along with the field ID (used for querying the data) and the field type. The latter is essential, as we don't need to specify a multiline field for something that will always be one line of text, for example.

Okay, let's move on to the penultimate part of this mega exercise; it's time to add in product details, navigation links, and homepage links to our databases. It's not the world's most exciting task, but hey, someone's gotta do it!

Adding Data to Our Shop

Now that we have the fields set up in each of the databases, it's time to fill them with content; the downside of using DatoCMS is that there is no easy way to do this without code.

We could spend time writing an import function, but this is overkill for our needs; by the time we've tested it, you would very likely have gotten all of the data into the system! The best way to add it in is manually – let's take a look at what's involved, as part of our next exercise.

DATOCMS PART 4: ADDING DATA TO THE CMS

To add data into DatoCMS, make sure you are logged in from the homepage, and then follow these steps:

1. Browse to `https://XXXXX.admin.datocms.com/editor`, where XXXXX is the name you gave your site at the start of this chapter.

2. Click the Content tab and then Cupcake.

3. Click NEW RECORD on the right.

4. Go ahead and fill in the details for the first cupcake, using data from the spreadsheet in the code download – it's saved as `Field data to use for site.xls`, on the Products tab.

5. Repeat the process until all six cupcake products have been added – make sure you click SAVE after each one!

6. Click HomePage, and then add in the fields for this using the same spreadsheet from step 4. The entries are on the HomePage tab; again, make sure you click SAVE after adding the entries.

7. Click Navigation on the left, and then use the same spreadsheet to add in the entries for this database from the Navigation tab of the same spreadsheet.

8. You can now minimize the browser window – all of the data is now available for us to use from the DatoCMS system.

I know that last exercise was what some might call a real ball-ache of a task, but it's still an important one: without it, we wouldn't have any data to use in our shop. With that done and dusted, we can now focus our attention on the final part of this process, installing the DatoCMS plugin into the shop.

Integrating DatoCMS

We've almost completed the integration of DatoCMS into our shop – there is one last task to do, which (ironically) is to install it. Fortunately, it's a straightforward plugin to set up, so without further ado, let's crack on and get it installed into our shop.

To learn more about the plugin, head over to the main documentation page on the Gatsby site, available at `www.gatsbyjs.org/packages/gatsby-source-datocms/`.

| DEMO 5: INTEGRATING DATOCMS INTO OUR SHOP |

To integrate DatoCMS into our shop, run through these steps:

1. First, fire up a Node.js terminal session, and then change the working folder to our project area.

2. At the prompt, enter this command and press Enter to install the plugin for DatoCMS:

```
npm install --save gatsby-source-datocms
```

3. Next, crack open the `gatsby-config.js` file at the root of our project folder, and scroll down to the end of the file.

4. Just before the final closing bracket, add in this code – it should look similar to this:

```
    {
        resolve: `gatsby-source-datocms`,
        options: {
            apiToken: `<ADD YOUR API KEY HERE>`,
            preview: false,
            disableLiveReload: false,
        },
    },
  },
],
}
```

5. There is one last thing to do, which is to get the API key – for this, make sure you are in the project area, at `https://havecakeeatcake.admin.datocms.com/editor`.

6. Click the Settings tab and then API Tokens ➤ Read-only API token. Click the Copy option against the API key, and then paste it in to replace the text <ENTER YOUR API KEY HERE>, shown in the previous step.

7. Save the file and close it – we've completed the installation of DatoCMS into our shop.

Another quick exercise, but probably the most important one – without it, we clearly can't communicate with the DatoCMS system, let alone our databases! The installation process for this plugin follows mostly the same steps as any NPM-based plugin; the only additional step we had to do was to add in the configuration settings for DatoCMS into the `gatsby-config.js` file. At the same time, we also added in the API key for the project hosted on the DatoCMS site; the read-only key is perfectly adequate here, as we're not changing any data that we fetch from DatoCMS.

A quick check in the `package.json` file will also confirm that we have the DatoCMS plugin installed – you should see an entry similar to this one:

```
"react-datocms": "^1.2.5",
```

It might be a higher version number by the time this book is published; as long as it is 1.2.5 or higher, then this is fine.

Okay, let's crack on: we've done the hard work in getting DatoCMS set up and the databases created, so we can now have some fun in creating our queries!

Before we do so, I want to quickly cover off a few points of note around using DatoCMS as a tool. Sure, we can use the bundled GraphQL tool from within Gatsby – it's a perfectly adequate tool. However, using a headless CMS does open up some useful options for us, plus raise some security concerns; let's take a moment to explore what this means for our site.

Implications of Using DatoCMS

Over the last few pages, we've talked about using DatoCMS and extolled the virtues of having a system where we can decouple the presentational layer. However, have we thought about what this might mean for us?

There are some advantages to using a headless CMS: it gives us flexibility about how we get the data. We can switch between different frameworks, yet our data will remain consistent throughout; as long as that framework supports JSON (which most do), then we won't have any issues.

Making use of a headless CMS such as DatoCMS means that we don't have to worry about how it displays content; we can fetch all of the content from a JSON object, so we can control how it renders on-screen. At the same time, we can deliver it to multiple devices, including mobiles and tablets; the separation makes it easier to maintain, more secure, and scalable across our website.

A drawback of using a headless CMS is that we have to handle how the content appears; it does mean extra pressure on us to get it right, but at least it is in our control. At the same time, using a headless CMS implies that we won't be able to preview how it displays the content on-screen; this isn't an issue though, as long as we factor in suitable checks and time to verify it looks OK on-screen. We do have to make sure that the right people have the proper access – that is going to be a requirement, though, no matter which CMS we use!

Constructing Data Queries for Our Shop

Now that we have DatoCMS set up and plugged into our site, it's time we started using it! Throughout the rest of this chapter, we will be creating various queries to retrieve data for our shop.

To help get accustomed to using DatoCMS and prove everything is working as expected, we will run a quick test by creating a query directly into the admin GUI. We'll go through the details of the query in more detail at the end of the demo, but for now, let's crack on with creating that query.

QUERYING PRODUCTS

To get set up, ready to enter queries, please run through these steps:

1. First, fire up your browser, then navigate to `https://dashboard.datocms.com/login`, and click Login.

2. Next, click havecakeeatcake and then Enter project.

3. Switch to the API Explorer tab – it is here where we will enter our queries.

4. The first query we will test is to retrieve a single product from the database – go ahead and copy this into the left-hand pane, and then click the button with the big black right arrow to execute the query:

```
query WorkQuery {
  cupcake {
    stockId
    name
    price
    productImage {
      responsiveImage {
        alt
        base64
        bgColor
```

```
        title
      }
    }
  }
}
```

Tip   Don't worry too much about formatting: there is a Prettify button you can use to format the query correctly.

---

5. If all is well, you should see what appears to be random product details appear on the left, as shown in Figure 4-2.

```
1 ▼ query WorkQuery {
2 ▼   cupcake {
3       stockId
4       name
5       price
6 ▼     productImage {
7 ▼       responsiveImage {
8           alt
9           base64
10          bgColor
11          title
12        }
13      }
14    }
15 }
16
```

```
▼ {
▼   "data": {
▼     "cupcake": {
        "stockId": "DCS0003",
        "name": "Heritage cupcakes - assorted",
        "price": 1.2,
        "productImage": {
▼         "responsiveImage": {
            "alt": null,
            "base64":
  "data:image/jpeg;base64,/9j/4AAQSkZJRgABAQAAAQABAAD/2wCEAAo
  HBwgHBgoICA4TDQ4LFRgNDQ0PCxEJDQ0YFxUZGBYTIhUaHysjGh0oHRUiJD
  UlKC0vMjIyGSI4PTcwPCsxMi8BCgsLDg0OHBAQHDscIhw1Ly8vLzUvLy8vL
  y8vLy8vLy8vLy8vLy8vLy8vLy8vLy8vLy8vLy8vLy8vLy8vLy8vL//AABEI
  ABAAGAMBIgACEQEDEQH/xAAYAAACAwAAAAAAAAAAAAAAAADBAABBv/EAB0
  QAAICAQUAAAAAAAAAAAAACAQQFAxESFTH/xAAWAQADAAAAAAAAAAAAAAAAA
```

Figure 4-2.   *The results of running the single product query*

At this point, things are starting to come together – we've set up DatoCMS, integrated it into our site, created the back-end databases, and written a test query.

However – to quote an old saying – the "proof is in the pudding"; writing a test query is a good start, but it will only be of any use once we add it into our site as proper code! In our case, the query we created returned the first product available in the database; we could easily add in a filter to retrieve a specific item, based on details such as its SKU (or stock ID) or the image assigned to the product.

Okay, cracking on, we can now focus on setting up the data queries for the various pages that need to request data from the DatoCMS system. We have a few changes to make, so let's dive in and take a look at what is required in more detail.

Setting Up the Site Pages

So far, we've set up DatoCMS, plugged it into our site, and ran some queries – it's time to make use of those queries and create some others for our site!

Over the next few pages, we will run through each instance where GraphQL is used to query the database and return data for the site. At the same time, we will plug the missing queries into the code from Chapter 2, so that all of the pages should be feature complete by the end of this chapter.

Let's make a start with the main index page – there's a good chunk of code to cover, but we will go through it all at the end of the exercise.

Updating the Main Index Page

The first step in integrating data to our site is to update the index page – this contains the New Arrivals block, for which we will source three products from the database.

In the interests of space, I will only highlight the areas that need changing – you may like to refer back to Chapter 2 or review the index.js file before making any changes!

UPDATING THE INDEX PAGE

To update the `index.js` page, follow these steps:

1. Crack open `index.js` in your text editor – it's in the `\src\pages` folder.

2. Scroll down the page until you see this line:

    ```
    export default IndexPage
    ```

3. Leave a line blank, and then add in this query:

```
export const NewArrivals = graphql`
  query NewArrival  {
    allDatoCmsCupcake(filter: {newarrival: { eq: true }},
    sort: { fields: [stockId], order: ASC }) {
      edges {
        node {
          id
          stockId
          name
          newarrival
          slug
          productImage {
            width
            height
            fluid(imgixParams: { fm: "jpg", auto: "compress"}) {
              ...GatsbyDatoCmsFluid
            }
          }
        }
      }
    }
  }
`
```

4. Go ahead and save the file, and then close it.

At face value, this might have seemed like a short exercise, but it shows a few important points about how GraphQL and DatoCMS work. There are enough differences in it that will confuse you when it comes to working with DatoCMS, so let's take a moment to review these steps in closer detail.

Understanding the Changes

If you've already used GraphQL before, then the format of the query we've used will look familiar. For those of you not so familiar with GraphQL, let's work through this query.

We wrap each query in an `export` statement, which tells Gatsby to query our database and return data available via (in this case) the `NewArrivals` constant:

```
export const NewArrivals = graphql`
...
`;
```

Inside the query (called `NewArrivals` – each must have a unique name), we reference the `allDatoCmsCupcake` object. We pass into it two properties: the first is the `newarrival,` which must equal true, and the second is to sort all three products by the `stockId` field. We've only specified three products for this demo, but in practice, we might well set the `newarrival` field to `true` for a more significant number of products.

Although the original query we created at the start of this chapter used `allCupcake` as the object name, `allDatoCmsCupcake` is the name we have to use, when referenced outside of the API Explorer.

Next up, we specify edges. This is in effect an array of records within our database; each is available via the node property. We then request data from several fields, such as `id`, `stock id`, `name,` and `newarrival`, before retrieving the product's image via the `productImage` property.

If you're curious about the various fields specified under `productImage`, these are from the imgIX image processing API; DatoCMS supports this as a means of processing images retrieved from its database.

You can learn more about imgIX from `www.imgix.com`.

The values that we retrieve from the database we then pass into the `Newarrival` component as props – we can see them displayed from within that component:

```
import React from "react";
import { Link } from "gatsby";
```

```
import Img from "gatsby-image";

const newArrival = (props) => {
  return (
    <li key={props.id}>
      <p>{props.name}</p>
      <Link to={`/product/${props.slug}`}><Img fluid={props.image} /></Link>
    </li>
  )
}

export default newArrival;
```

Okay, let's crack on: the new arrival products are now displayed, but before we can move on, there is one more change we need to make.

To get around the site, we need some form of navigation; instead of having hard-coded values, we will add suitable links into the Navigation database we set up earlier in this chapter. Let's take a look at what is needed to allow customers to navigate around our site in more detail.

Adding Entries to the Navigation Menu

Our next query is much simpler; it only has one level of data to return, unlike the (part) nested query used for the new arrivals!

In this instance, we simply return all of the labels and links required to form the navigation for our site – the code we created back in Chapter 2 will handle the rendering of the text and links into the appropriate slots on the page.

ADDING IN NAVIGATION

To update sitenavigation.js, follow these steps:

1. Crack open a copy of sitenavigation.js in your text editor, and then find this line:

    ```
    const SiteNavigation = () => {
    ```

    Immediately below it, add in this query:

```
const data = useStaticQuery(graphql`
  query NavQuery {
    datoCmsNavigation {
      homeText
      homeLink
      aboutText
      aboutLink
      blogText
      blogLink
      galleryText
      galleryLink
      helpText
      helpLink
    }
  }
```

2. Save the file and close it.

That was probably one of the most straightforward exercises we did and will do in this chapter – and the rest of the book! By now, the format of each query should start to look a little more familiar; let's take a quick look at what we did in this exercise in more detail.

Understanding the Changes Made

In the exercise we've just completed, we started by defining a constant named data; this time around, we used the useStaticQuery method to trigger our GraphQL request to DatoCMS.

For the uninitiated, you might be wondering why we use this one and not the graphql`...` query we used in previous examples. The answer to this is simple: they both do the same thing, but we must use useStaticQuery when triggering queries from a component, whereas graphql`...` is for pages.

Inside the query, we've requested that DatoCMS return all of the fields needed for our navigation; I've used the format ...Text and ....Link to help organize each pair of values required for each navigation link in our demo.

Looking further afield, you may remember from Chapter 2 that we included a list of Link components; here's a brief extract/recap of that code:

```
  return (
     <nav>
       <div>
         <Link to={`${data.datoCmsNavigation.homeLink}`}
         activeClassName="active">{data.datoCmsNavigation.homeText}</Link>
...
       </div>
     </nav>
   </>
  )
}
```

Now that we have the query set up and added to the SiteNavigation component, it means that Gatsby can replace the placeholders with the proper values from DatoCMS, at the point of building the site and displaying it in the browser.

Reviewing Data for Page Layout

So far, we've made good progress with adding queries to the relevant pages in our site. This next one is something of an oddity, though: the query we need is already present in our code!

Yes, this is indeed the case; by default, Gatsby's starter theme includes a call to the siteMetadata reference within GraphQL. It's important to note that this is **not** being sourced from DatoCMS, but from within the version of GraphQL that comes bundled with Gatsby:

```
const Layout = ({ children }) => {
  const data = useStaticQuery(graphql`
    query SiteTitleQuery {
      site {
        siteMetadata {
          title
        }
      }
    }
  `)
```

```
return (
  <Header siteTitle={data.site.siteMetadata.title} />
  <SiteNavigation />
```

It works in the same way as the queries we've created thus far; the only difference is that we don't include the DatoCMS tag, which means we can call in data from multiple GraphQL sources – one of the key strengths of Gatsby!

Okay, let's continue: we still have queries we need to add in for two more pages. The pages that remain are `subscribe.js` and `customerservices.js`; once we've completed them, we will have a working site with data sourced from DatoCMS. Let's take a look at the code required for these two queries in more detail.

Hooking in Data for Pages and Components

Although we've created several pages and components for our shop, there are only two which need adjusting. Both of them are components, and both sit in the footer – they are `customerservices.js` (or Customer Services block) and `subscribe.js`, or the Social Media component.

All of the other pages can remain as is; some of you may notice that `seo.js` does indeed have a GraphQL query, but that one doesn't need changing for this exercise. Let's take a look at what we need to do to retrofit the GraphQL queries for these two components in more detail.

ADDING DATA TO COMPONENTS/PAGES

We have several components to edit, so let's crack on with the first one, which is `subscribe.js`:

1. In your text editor, go ahead and open subscribe.js, and then look for this line:

    ```
    const Subscribe = () => {
    ```

2. Immediately below it, add in this query:

    ```
    const data = useStaticQuery(graphql`
      query SubscribeQuery {
        datoCmsHomepage {
          id
          subscribeFooter
    ```

```
            subscribeTextFooter
            subscribeButtonFooter
        }
    }
  `)
```

3. The rest of the code can remain as is, so go ahead and save the changes and then close the file.

4. Next, go ahead and open the `customerservices.js` file, and look for this line:

```
const CustomerServices = () => {
```

5. Immediately below it, add in this query:

```
const data = useStaticQuery(graphql`
  query CSQuery {
    datoCmsHomepage {
      id
      customerServiceFooter
      helpFooter
      deliveryFooter
      giftsFooter
      aboutUsFooter
      termsFooter
    }
  }
`)

return (
```

6. Go ahead and save that file too – we can close it as it is no longer needed for this exercise.

Yay! We now have all of the queries in place! Adding in these two final queries means that we now have a working basis of a site, ready for us to add in the cart (which we will do in the next chapter). In the meantime, let's quickly review the changes we made in this exercise in more detail.

Exploring the Code in Detail

Unlike some of the earlier queries we've added in, these two are very straightforward: we use the same `useStaticQuery` method as done previously. This time though, we create new queries to return the various labels and links required for the Customer Services and Subscribe components; neither requires any filtering or sorting. It is purely a case of fetching all of the data as is and using the code later in each component to render it on the screen (as shown in this partial example):

```
<ul>
  <p>Customer Service</p>
  <Link to="/help/"><li>{data.datoCmsHomepage.helpFooter}</li>
  </Link>
  ...
</ul>
</div>
```

Okay, let's crack on... Hold on a moment: can anyone spot a problem with that last paragraph and code example?

If you were paying attention (heck, that sounds awful saying that!), you should notice that we're **not** retrieving content for the links in the Customer Services block, only the labels! I've done this deliberately: can you work out what needs to change so that we can return both links and labels from DatoCMS?

Testing the Shop

Okay...wait for it... Wait for it... Yes, we can finally test our shop!

I know it's not something we've been able to do very easily up until now; running the `gatsby develop` command will more than likely generate errors! Thank you, though, for being patient – I promise you it will have been worth the wait!

To test our shop, we're not going to upload it into GitHub – this is something we will do later in the book. At this stage, that's overkill for what we need; there is a much simpler approach we can take. Let me introduce you to Netlify; for those of you who have not used it, it's a great hosting tool that will automatically build and deploy the site to a Netlify-based URL for us.

It's a useful tool to know, although there are a couple of things we should be aware of around usage – let's take a look at them and see what it means for us in more detail.

Uploading to Netlify

Netlify describes itself as "The fastest way to build the fastest sites."

It's a bold statement, but very accurate: if you want a way to host a site without the worry of costly infrastructure, servers, or DevOps, then Netlify is worth considering as a tool.

We could use it as the basis for hosting the final version of our site, but using it as a more permanent measure does have some points we need to consider – we will explore what this means at the end of the demo.

Meanwhile, there is one thing we will need to do to use Netlify – that is to sign up for a free account. We can do this in one of several different ways: GitHub, GitLab, Bitbucket, or by using email.

I've already set up a GitHub repository, which we will get back to later in this book – for now, I recommend using email. The test is meant as a temporary measure to get an initial feeling for how the site is running, so email is perfectly adequate at this stage!

Okay, with sign-up complete, let's move on and upload a copy of the site, to see what it looks like in action.

TESTING OUR SITE

To test our site with Netlify, make sure you have your project folder open in Windows Explorer (or file manager), and then follow these steps:

1. First, crack open your browser, and then navigate to `www.netlify.com`. Once there, we have several options available for signing up – choose Email.

2. At the next prompt, enter your chosen email and password, and then click Sign up.

3. Once saved, you will get a Netlify domain address assigned to you – it will look something like this, `https://app.netlify.com/sites/XXXXX/`, where XXXXX will be a random set of characters for your site.

4. Head back to the homepage, and then click Login – it will redirect you to the Sites tab. Scroll down until you see a box with the text "Want to deploy a new site…" Switch to your file manager, and then navigate to the root of your project folder.

5. Drag and drop the `public` folder only into this box, and then switch back to the browser.

6. Click the Overview tab, and wait a few minutes – Netlify will automatically build and deploy your site. Assuming we encounter no problems, you should see something akin to the screenshot shown in Figure 4-3.

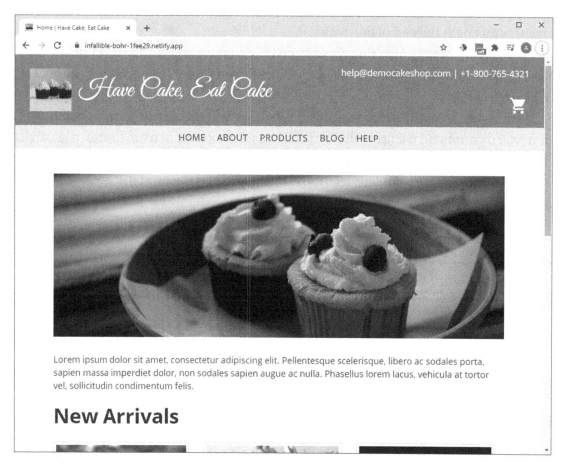

Figure 4-3. *Testing the site via Netlify*

You can see my version of this site at `https://infallible-bohr-1fee29.netlify.app/`

Yes! I'll bet you've been waiting to see it running in some form for a while – it's a good feeling to see it in the flesh, even though we've had to be patient while we got it set up. Although Netlify is only a stop-gap measure, there are a few important points we should cover off; let's take a moment to review the steps we've just completed in more detail.

Reviewing the Demo

For this exercise, we began by creating an account on the Netlify website – we covered the point that we could use logins such as GitHub or GitLab, but that email would suffice for our needs at this time.

We then received a notification on-screen of the domain that Netlify assigned to our site; we then dragged and dropped a copy of the public folder from our website into the upload area, ready for Netlify to build it as a test version of our site. This last step was completed automatically by Netlify, with the resulting website available shortly afterward, using the URL provided by Netlify.

Looking further afield, I mentioned that using Netlify does have some features that we should consider:

- Netlify can become expensive if our site gets popular or we start adding lots of updates – the free plan of 300 build minutes a month will soon get used up, and the next level up is a fair jump!

- Dragging and dropping the public folder into the Netlify site isn't a practical solution long term – there are better alternatives.

- The upload option we're using makes it easy to update, but this lacks source control – this is something we should have in place, yet this will need us to add GitHub, GitLab, or the like into the mix, making it more complex.

- GitLab and GitHub can build our site automatically and manage version control for free – there is no cost incurred for build time, although it can take a little effort to get this set up.

It's for these reasons that we are only using Netlify as a stop-gap measure – granted, sometimes we may need to incur a cost when developing a solution, but I'm very much of the view that why should we if we can do it free! GitHub may not be everyone's first choice when it comes to developing a site, but as long we don't mind open sourcing the site, then it is free for building, deploying, and hosting websites. Can you do better than that?

Summary

Another monster chapter bites the dust – we should at least have a working site now, ready for us to add in the cart! We've covered a lot of content throughout this chapter, so let's take a moment to reflect on what we've learned.

We kicked off with a look at how to integrate DatoCMS as our chosen CMS into the shop; this included setting up our account, databases, and relevant fields and adding in the content. We then moved on to creating some test queries to get used to how DatoCMS works, as well as proof we can source data correctly. At the same time, we also covered off some of the implications for using DatoCMS – we saw that using a headless CMS isn't without its concerns, but these will be less of an issue if we manage them properly.

Next up, we then started to build out the queries for the various pages and components in the shop; for reasons of space, we focused purely on the changes needed to integrate the queries within each file. At the same time, we took the opportunity to upload a copy of the site to Netlify, so we can test it works as expected, even though we are still developing the site.

We then rounded out the chapter with something that I know we've been waiting for a long time: we finally got to test the initial version of our shop using Netlify! We explored some of the reasons why using this approach was preferable to waiting for the proper deployment later and that while it is a sound approach, there are some considerations that we need to be mindful of while using Netlify.

Phew! Our shop is now operational and has data – it's time we added in the cart. For this, we will use Snipcart, which is perfect for a static site generator such as Gatsby. We'll work our way through adding in the product page and links to Snipcart, before displaying the cart itself – stay with me as I will cover this and more in the next chapter.

CHAPTER 5

Building the Catalog

So far, we've created the essential pages for our site (or most of them), set up our data sources, and hooked in data from our data sources. Our shop is beginning to take shape, but this is where things get interesting – what about displaying products in our shop, ready for sale?

Throughout this chapter, this is something we will address – we'll work our way through understanding more about the tools used to construct our shopping cart, before creating queries to source the product data and building the product gallery and pages for our products. We'll also take a look at adding product variants and discounts and touch on some simple ways to start to customize the cart to suit our needs.

Let's begin, though, with a look at the method we will use to construct the catalog and see how this approach fits into the broader picture of our site.

Exploring the Structure

When building a product gallery and individual pages, one might forgive us for thinking that we have to use individual pages for both the gallery and each product, right…? Well, perhaps not – let me explain why.

The traditional method would be to create a page per product – while this will technically work, it comes with a significant manual overhead! What happens if we need to update a specific field on the page or add in new ones? Content will quickly become out of date and begin to follow different formats; this is not something we can support long term if our site were to grow in size beyond just a few products.

The alternative to this is to use a template, which happens to be one of the critical strengths of Gatsby. Instead of creating individual pages, we can create one master page as our product gallery. We can then use one of Gatsby's core system files to pass data across to a new template file; any change made to this will automatically appear across all products at build time.

© Alex Libby 2021
A. Libby, *Gatsby E-Commerce*, https://doi.org/10.1007/978-1-4842-6692-2_5

To understand some of the specifics of how this works, take a look at the schematic in Figure 5-1.

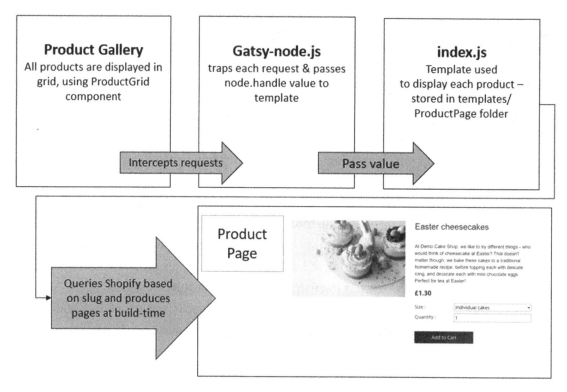

Figure 5-1. *Schematic of creating product pages dynamically*

A larger PDF version of this image is available in the code download that accompanies this book.

We begin with our gallery, `products.js`, which displays all of the products. This component renders each product using a new `ProductGrid` component.

To avoid creating separate pages, we will use the `createPages` action handler in `gatsby-node.js` to intercept requests for individual products and build them at compile time. It means that we only need one handler and a template to create a host of pages, although this isn't without its trade-offs in terms of performance! For our site, this won't be an issue, but it will be if we create something larger – let's take a moment to consider what effect these trade-offs may have on the performance of our site in more detail.

Assessing the Implications of This Approach

If we're working on creating a large site (its purpose doesn't matter – it's the size that counts here), then using the `createPages` API wouldn't be an ideal approach.

Why? Well, it has a lot to do with when we build our pages (and by this, I mean compile, not construct in an editor!). Creating them during build means all of the data is collected together. It also removes the need for GraphQL queries in the template; we can also use one query language to create these pages, even though they may come from different sources.

The trade-off, though, is that we won't know what we are querying for if we're using a template; any changes we need to make to the structure will require a full rebuild of the site (incremental builds only work for sites with physical pages).

On a more serious note, though, if we use this method, then all of the page data (and context) is stored in a redux store and therefore in the page's memory. If your site happens to be a large one, then this will cause problems with resources, owing to the amount of data passed by the page context. You will likely get out of memory errors appearing, depending on the size of your site! It's worth bearing in mind that garbage collection will happen more frequently too, particularly as pages are not stored in memory permanently, but saved to disk once we've run the initial query.

Okay, let's crack on: now that we've explored what structure we will use and are aware of the trade-offs of using this approach, let's put it into action! Fortunately, our chosen Gatsby starter already includes the relevant Shopify queries in place, so all that remains for us to do is install the Gatsby plugin for Shopify and review the GraphQL queries in place within the theme. Let's crack on by first getting that plugin installed and ready for use.

Sourcing Data for the Product Catalog

Cast your mind back to Chapter 4 – remember how we ran some test queries to confirm our data source was operating and able to return data correctly?

Well, it's time to revisit this subject, but this time around it's the turn of Shopify. As we will shortly see, the theme already does some of the heavy lifting for us, but there remains a couple of things we need to do. The first of these is to complete the setup of Shopify, so let's dive in and take a look at what we need to do in more detail.

INSTALLING AND CONFIGURING SHOPIFY

Shopify already comes part installed – it uses the `gatsby-source-shopify` plugin (specified in the `package.json` file), which we installed as part of setting up the theme. However, there is one task we need to do, which is to configure two properties:

1. Crack open your text editor, then open the `.env.development` file at the root of your project folder, and modify the values accordingly:

```
SHOPIFY_ACCESS_TOKEN=<YOUR STOREFRONT API TOKEN HERE>
SHOP_NAME=<THE SUB-DOMAIN PART OF YOUR SHOPIFY STORE URL>
```

   - SHOPIFY_ACCESS_TOKEN – You can find this by logging into your Shopify account, then clicking Apps ➤ Manage private apps ➤ name of your app, and using the storefront access token at the bottom of that page.

   - SHOP_NAME – In my demo, I'm using havecakeeatcake, but if you are using a different name for your store, then please use that instead.

Note   This should only be the first part of your Shopify store domain; in my case, as my store is havecakeeatcake.myshopify.com, I use havecakeeatcake for the SHOP_NAME property.

---

2. Save and close the file.

3. Next, browse to `www.shopify.com`, and log in with the credentials you created in Chapter 1.

4. Once at the main dashboard, we need to set up a private app for our shop – click Apps and then Create a new private app.

5. On the next page, enter the name of your shop – this is the display name for your shop.

6. Next, add in an email address for your store – it does need to be operational, as we use this to send email confirmations from your shop.

7. Shopify will generate an API key and password – **you must keep these secure**, as divulging them will leave your site at risk of hacking!

8. Scroll down to the Admin API Permissions box – you should, as a minimum, have Products set to Read access.

9. Next, tick the box against "Allow this app to access your storefront data…" and make sure you check all of the checkboxes under Storefront API Permissions.

   This last step is purely for development purposes: I would recommend removing permissions where needed once in production or at least reducing them to read-only where possible.

10. At the bottom of the page, click Save – your store's app is now set up for use.

This demo was one of those exercises where we begin to tie in Shopify to our site and prepare it for general use in our project; without it, we can't talk to Shopify and vice versa! To prove it works, we will run a test query in the GraphiQL interface, but before doing so, let's quickly cover off the changes we've made as part of this last exercise in more detail.

Understanding What Happened

Although there was very little code required for this last exercise, the steps we took were nevertheless still relevant – we kicked off by setting up the `.env.development` file to store API values needed for our shop (and so they are not exposed to prying eyes).

We then moved on to starting to configure Shopify – we had to set up a private app which is required when developing sites in Shopify that are not yet for public use. We added several configuration details such as an email address and name for our shop; Shopify then created the appropriate API and secret keys for later use if we develop our shop further using the API. We then rounded out the demo by setting permissions; it's important to note that these might seem a little lax for now, but that we should reduce them when moving the shop into production use.

Okay, let's move on: unfortunately, the next part might seem a little mundane, but it is a necessary must! We need to add some products to our shop! This adding process is an essential task, so let's get right on in and add a handful of test examples to our store.

Adding Products to Shopify

Okay, so we have the basic setup in place for Shopify; we now need to add in products! Our shop will, of course, be useless as a chocolate teapot without them, so this is something we need to address. Fortunately, Shopify makes it very easy to add them in, although I have to admit it can be a little bit of a ball-ache to do so; let's take a look at how, as part of our next exercise.

ADDING IN PRODUCTS

To add products, follow these steps:

1. First, browse to `https://XXXXX.myshopify.com/admin/products`, where XXXXX is the name of your store – go ahead and log in using your credentials, if prompted.

2. Once on the main dashboard, click Add Product.

3. Use the accompanying spreadsheet to fill out details for each product.

4. Click Save after each product, and repeat until you have all nine products in your Products list.

Thank goodness that we've completed this part! Yes, it was a pain in the neck, but at least we only need to do it once. We can, of course, add in more later if we want to, but we have a good handful now set up in Shopify, so this is more than enough for our needs.

Let's move on – now that we have the Shopify plugin set up and configured, it's time to put it to the test! This test could go perfectly or fall into a complete heap... Don't worry – I'm only joking! I'm sure it will go fine; it's a little nerve-wracking, so without further ado, let's dive in and make sure our GraphQL set up is working correctly.

Testing the Shopify GraphQL

Our starter theme may already include the GraphQL statements needed to source details from Shopify, but they will be useless if GraphQL isn't working correctly! Thankfully this is an easy test to complete – we will use one of the queries needed for our store to prove all is working as expected. Let's dive in and take a look at the steps necessary to test this connection in more detail.

CREATING A TEST QUERY

To test the GraphQL integration for Shopify, work through these steps:

1. First, crack open a Node.js terminal session, and then change the working folder to our project area.

2. At the prompt, enter gatsby develop and press Enter – this is to ensure the development server for our store is running.

3. When you see this…

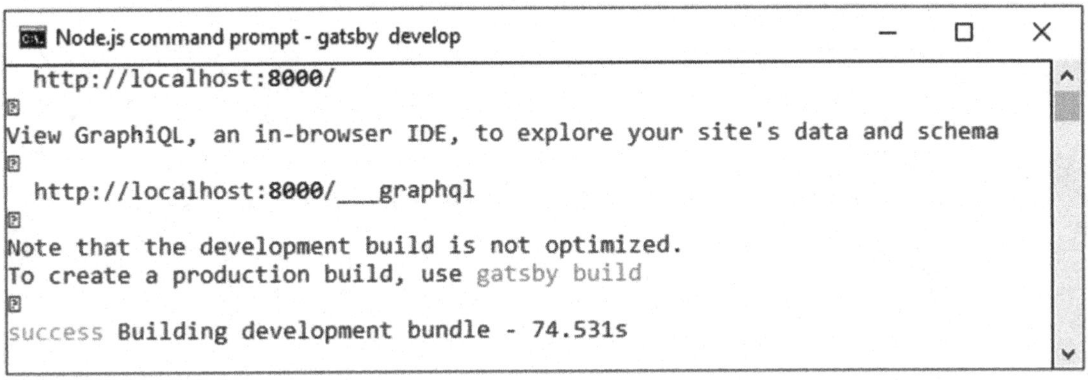

```
Node.js command prompt - gatsby develop                            —    □    ×

  http://localhost:8000/

View GraphiQL, an in-browser IDE, to explore your site's data and schema

  http://localhost:8000/___graphql

Note that the development build is not optimized.
To create a production build, use gatsby build

success Building development bundle - 74.531s
```

Figure 5-2. *Running the Gatsby dev server*

…we can now test GraphQL. For this, browse to
http://localhost:8000/___graphql in your browser, then enter this
query into the left-hand pane, and click the Prettify button to make sure it is
correctly formatted:

```
{
  allShopifyProduct(sort: {fields: [createdAt], order: DESC}) {
    edges {
      node {
        id
        title
        handle
        createdAt
        images {
          id
```

```
              originalSrc
            }
            variants {
              price
            }
          }
        }
      }
    }
  }
}
```

4. If all is well, we should see something akin to the screenshot shown in Figure 5-3.

Figure 5-3. *Running a test query for Shopify*

If you read on, you may spot similarities between this query and the one used in the "Reviewing the ProductGrid GraphQL" section; they are identical, with only minor changes to allow it to be consumed directly in code!

Excellent! With that now set up, our store should be able to query Shopify and retrieve products as needed. The starter theme we're using already contains the relevant queries to make this happen; we will review these in more detail shortly. For now, let's quickly review what we've done in this exercise, so we can see how these changes fit into the bigger picture.

Understanding the Query Used

When it comes to working with Gatsby, one of the best features is its use of GraphQL; this tool can source data from pretty much anywhere.

So far in this book, we've used it in a variety of different scenarios – the last exercise was no different. In this instance, we used the `allShopifyProduct` JSON object and specified a mix of fields, including ID, `title`, product `handle` (used to feed into the product pages), and `images`. We also set it to show all products in descending order by date of creation; we could equally have used product name, SKU, or similar, to perform the same function.

In this last exercise, we ran a test query to confirm that Shopify returns data to us; as you will see shortly, the developer of our theme has already included some critical queries in code for us, which will save us development time. It's worth taking some time to go through the code in detail, so you can begin to understand what is requested; it will also help with reviewing the code before moving it into production. Let's take a look at these queries in more detail, beginning with the GraphQL statements used in the ProductGrid component.

Reviewing the ProductGrid GraphQL

We use the ProductGrid component from within the gallery page to display the contents of our shop's products on the page. It might indeed seem a cop-out to skip directly to review the code for this component (and others), but this is because the developer of the theme we're using has already included the queries we need in the theme.

Let us start with the query used in the ProductGrid component – here it is in full:

```
const { allShopifyProduct } = useStaticQuery(
  graphql`
  query {
    allShopifyProduct(
```

```
       sort: {
         fields: [createdAt]
         order: DESC
       }
     ) {
       edges {
         node {
           id
           title
           handle
           createdAt
           images {
             id
             originalSrc
             localFile {
               childImageSharp {
                 fluid(maxWidth: 910) {
                   ...GatsbyImageSharpFluid_withWebp_tracedSVG
                 }
               }
             }
           }
           variants {
             price
           }
         }
       }
     }
   }

)
```

Our query starts with using the useStaticQuery function – this performs the same role as query(), but the difference being that query only works on pages, not in components. We then query allShopifyProduct, setting at the same time for it to be sorted by the createdAt field in descending order.

In the bulk of the query, we call in a host of properties – they range from id to title, handle, and childImageSharp, among others! What is of particular note, though, is the childImageSharp property; this allows us to call a responsive version of the image, up to a maximum of 910 px width.

A small point We've used the original queries that came with the theme when we installed it. It's worth checking through it to see if we can optimize the query before moving into production: do we need all of the fields returned?

Exploring the gatsby-node Component and GraphQL

This next query comes from the gatsby-node.js file – it's not a component as such, but acts as the glue/link between the product gallery and individual product pages.

It's wrapped in a promise, so it will only act the next steps once the code returns a successful result. It means that if a product fails, it will not build the page for that product:

```
const { createPage } = actions
return graphql(`
  {
    allShopifyProduct {
      edges {
        node {
          handle
        }
      }
    }
  }
`).then(result => {
```

This time our query uses the standard query function – we query allShopifyProduct as before, but only return the handle for the product. The reason for this is that we only need to return an identifying tag for each product successfully retrieved; the product page template (next) will take care of retrieving a complete dataset for that product.

Breaking Apart the ProductPage GraphQL

The last query forms the basis of the ProductPage template – it's here where we retrieve a complete dataset from GraphQL and use it to render product details to the customer.

The query is significantly longer and returns a host of different values for each product; here is the code in full, reproduced from that component:

```
export const query = graphql`
  query($handle: String!) {
    shopifyProduct(handle: { eq: $handle }) {
      id
      title
      handle
      productType
      description
      descriptionHtml
      shopifyId
      options {
        id
        name
        values
      }
      variants {
        id
        title
        price
        availableForSale
        shopifyId
        selectedOptions {
          name
          value
        }
      }
      priceRange {
        minVariantPrice {
          amount
```

```
        currencyCode
      }
      maxVariantPrice {
        amount
        currencyCode
      }
    }
    images {
      originalSrc
      id
      localFile {
        childImageSharp {
          fluid(maxWidth: 910) {
            ...GatsbyImageSharpFluid_withWebp_tracedSVG
          }
        }
      }
    }
  }
}
`
```

We use the same query() function as before, but this time we query ShopifyProduct, passing in a value to handle that we pass down from the gatsby-node.js file.

In the bulk of the query, we call in a host of properties – they range from id to title, variants, handle, and childImageSharp, among others. It is an excellent query to review at the point of migrating to production, as it is very likely it will contain redundant query fields that we can safely remove from the component.

Adding the Cart and Remaining Pages

We already have our product gallery page in place (which we created in Chapter 2), but we need the means to be able to display more details about each product. We will use the CreatePages action handler that we touched on earlier; fortunately for us, this has already been incorporated into the theme we're using in this project.

It means that although there are other files used to display products, namely

- ProductGrid component, stored in \src\components\ProductGrid

- Page template, stored as \src\templates\ProductPage\index.js

- ProductForm component, stored as \src\templates\ProductForm\index.js

- gatsby-node.js, used to handle the link between the product gallery and page

...none of them requires any changes to help fit in our project: we can use them as they are out of the box! It makes our lives a lot easier in terms of development; that said, they contain some useful code features, so let's take a moment to review the code in more detail from within each page.

Reviewing the Code in Detail

Although the Gatsby theme we're using has done most of the heavy lifting for us, we should take a moment to review the code used in each of the files that make up the product gallery, product page, and connecting code.

In total, we have four files that form this part of the site and which I referenced back toward the start of this chapter – they are as follows:

- ProductGrid component, stored in \src\components\ProductGrid

- Page template, stored as \src\templates\ProductPage\index.js

- ProductForm component, stored as \src\templates\ProductForm\index.js

- gatsby-node.js, used to handle the link between the product gallery and page

Let's take a look at each, in turn, beginning with the ProductGrid component.

You may notice the presence of styles.js files with some of these components; they are the styles created using the emotion library, as part of the original theme.

The ProductGrid Component

This particular component makes use of the React context, which is a great way to pass data around the component tree (aka DOM), without having to propagate through lots of different child components. Typically, we would pass data top-down, but this isn't always possible, so using the React context makes this easier.

In this component, we create something of a lengthy GraphQL query, using the useStaticQuery function; this does the same as the grapql command for pages. Our query calls for a variety of different pieces of information, such as title, handle, image filenames/sources, and price variants; we then map through the allShopifyProducts object to iterate through all of the products and display them on-screen. If allShopifyProducts happens to return zero, then we show a "No Products found!" message in its place.

The ProductPage Template

At first glance, this template might appear somewhat substantial. However, if you look closely at the code, you will find that many of the "components" specified within are just elements that we style using the emotion style library.

If we break this component down, we can see several imports; most of these are for the styles mentioned earlier, but some for the standard Gatsby and React libraries, as well as the SEO component. The bulk of the code lies in the ProductPage constant; this we use to render details of each product on separate pages. The CreatePages action handler (more in a moment) uses the page template to generate static pages at build time. At the end of the component file, we have another lengthy GraphQL query; this one calls in information from Shopify and returns values such as title, price, variants, and product images where applicable.

The ProductForm Component

This file is the most substantial of all four files used to create the product gallery and associated pages; this is the component that renders information on-screen when the customer has requested individual product pages.

We start with several React imports, such as for the useContext and useEffect hooks, before defining our ProductForm component. Inside of this component, we set up several declarations – these are to keep details of information such as price variants and current quantity levels, as well as using a React state to manage them. We then have some functions, the first of which is checkAvailability; it makes use of the Shopify JS SDK to see whether the stock is available for sale. The useEffect hook triggers the call for this at around line 41.

The next two functions take care of updating details when the customer increases or decreases the quantity desired or changes the variant (handleOptionChange). We then have two functions left; the penultimate one adds the product to the Shopify cart, and the last one takes care of disabling a variant if it is not available for sale. The remainder of the component hangs around displaying product details on-screen, such as the product description and available options; these contain the trigger events to update, depending on customer actions.

The gatsby-node.js Connection File

The last file isn't a component as such – it acts more like the glue between the gallery and product page.

This code intercepts any requests from the products.js component (our product gallery) and then requests the handle for each product from GraphQL before iterating through to create each product page. The forEach block specifies three properties, which are the target location of each product page, the location of the template file, and what to use to generate the handle for each page. When we get to the product page template, we use the handle passed in as a property to retrieve the details of each product before rendering its page on-screen to our customer.

Adjusting the Cart

We're getting closer to viewing our shop, but before we do so, there are still some changes we need to make! The next set of changes revolve around the cart and line items displayed within; there are a few improvements we can make to the base theme. Let's dive in and take a look at what we can do to better our code in more detail.

UPDATING THE CART

There are a handful of updates we need to do, so go ahead with these steps:

1. Fire up your text editor, and then crack open the index.js file in the \src\ components\Cart\LineItem folder.

2. Look for the const handleRemove... declaration, then miss a line, and add in these two constants – they will handle the correct formatting of the price and unit total values:

```
const price =  Intl.NumberFormat(undefined, {
  currency: item.variant.priceV2.currencyCode,
  minimumFractionDigits: 2,
  style: 'currency',
}).format(item.variant.priceV2.amount)
```

```
const unitTotal = Intl.NumberFormat(undefined, {
  currency: item.variant.priceV2.currencyCode,
  minimumFractionDigits: 2,
  style: 'currency',
}).format(calculateSubTotal(item.quantity, item.variant.priceV2.
amount))
```

3. Next, go ahead and replace the return() block with this code – it contains a number of tweaks and changes to how details are displayed on the page in the cart:

```
return (
  <>
    <ul>
      <li><button className="remove" onClick={handleRemove}><img
      src={bin} alt="Remove item" className="bin"/></button></li>
      <li><Link to={`/product/${item.variant.product.
      handle}/`}>{variantImage}</Link></li>
      <li>
        <span>{item.title}
        {item.variant.title === !'Default Title' ? item.variant.
        title : ''}
        </span>
```

```
            <span>{selectedOptions} @ {price} each</span>
        </li>
        <li>{item.quantity}</li>
        <li>{unitTotal}</li>
    </ul>
  )
```

4. Save the file – you can close it at this point.

5. Next, crack open the index file under \src\components\Cart, and look for the opening return(entry.

6. Adjust the code so that it includes the check for the number of items in the cart, as highlighted in the following:

```
return (
    <>
      {checkout.lineItems.length !== 0 ? (
        <>
      <div>
...
      </div>
      </>
      ) : (
        <p>Cart is empty!</p>
      )}
    </>
  )
}
```

7. Go ahead and save that file too – you can close it, as the changes to it are now complete.

We're getting ever closer to testing our code changes and viewing the shop in all its glory for the first time! This last demo was very much a refinement exercise; we could easily have skipped it, although the steps we've worked into our demo will add an extra level of quality to our site.

Nevertheless, we should treat any code change we make as important, so let's take a moment to go through the modifications and understand what impact they have on our shop.

Breaking Apart the Code Changes

When we first installed this theme, we could have taken the easy route and kept the cart functionality as is. Nothing wrong in doing so, I hear you say!

However, it's nice to put one's own stamp on it and begin to tweak it for our needs; this gives it a more distinctive look and feel. These formatted the price and total unit cost into local currency format (for me British pound, but it will for whatever country you live in).

We then replaced the `return()` block within this component; the core functionality didn't change, but we replaced the text "Remove" with a bin icon and reformatted how we display some of the prices and options on-screen.

Once done with the `LineItem` component, we switched to the main `Cart` component – this required a single change to implement a "Cart empty" message if the cart didn't contain any products. It's not entirely essential for now, but if we were to push this site into production use, it's something we should add as a matter of course!

Okay, let's change tack; we're almost at a point where we can test the changes made to the site since the last update. However, there is a little sting in the tail – when developing the code for this project, I noticed a couple of warnings appear. Nothing critical, but something we should address...

Implementing Some Fixes

Up until now, we've been sailing through, gradually adding code changes and improvements to our store – so far, so good, right? Well, yes and...maybe not quite.

While I was developing the code for this book, I came across two code warnings in my browser's console log. These appeared during the initial build process and look similar to the ones shown in Figure 5-4.

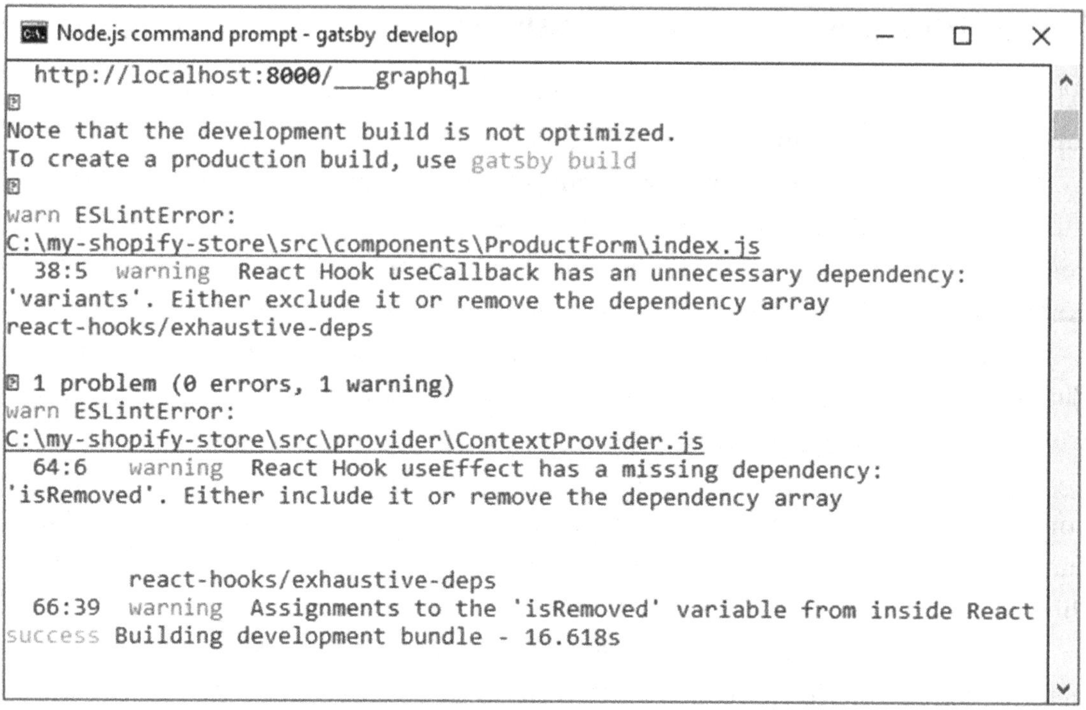

```
Node.js command prompt - gatsby develop                    —    □    ×

  http://localhost:8000/___graphql
 ▣
Note that the development build is not optimized.
To create a production build, use gatsby build
 ▣
warn ESLintError:
C:\my-shopify-store\src\components\ProductForm\index.js
  38:5  warning  React Hook useCallback has an unnecessary dependency:
'variants'. Either exclude it or remove the dependency array
react-hooks/exhaustive-deps

▣ 1 problem (0 errors, 1 warning)
warn ESLintError:
C:\my-shopify-store\src\provider\ContextProvider.js
  64:6   warning  React Hook useEffect has a missing dependency:
'isRemoved'. Either include it or remove the dependency array


         react-hooks/exhaustive-deps
  66:39  warning  Assignments to the 'isRemoved' variable from inside React
success Building development bundle - 16.618s
```

Figure 5-4. *Warnings generated during the Gatsby build process*

These may at first seem somewhat disconcerting, but fortunately, they are easy to fix. To rectify these errors hardly warrants an exercise in its own right, so here are a couple of pointers:

- In ProductForm\index.js, add in `variants`, as indicated:

  ```
  },
  [client.product, productVariant.shopifyId, variants]
  )
  ```

Remove the highlighted text from this line.

- In `\src\provider\ContextProvider.js`, remove the highlighted isRemoved, as indicated:

  ```
  initializeCheckout()
  }, [store.client.checkout, isRemoved])
  ```

Add in the highlighted text to this line.

- In \src\provider\ContextProvider.js, add the highlighted text to this line:

```
useEffect(() => () => { updateIsRemoved(true); }, [])
```

Add in the text as highlighted.

Three easy fixes, which should now mean our Gatsby build process will complete without showing warnings! Okay, so we've finally hit the end of the chapter: it's time, ladies and gentlemen, time to update our demo... Yikes...what will it look like? I wonder.

Updating the Test Version on Netlify

Cast your mind back to the end of Chapter 4, where we took a significant step forward in releasing a version of our site onto Netlify as a test site; I'll bet it felt good to see something in the virtual flesh!

It's time to update what's on our demo site, to reflect the changes we've made in adding the product gallery, template, and linking code – without further ado, let's jump in and get our demo updated to the latest version of our code.

UPDATING THE CONTENT ON NETLIFY

To get our demo site updated with the latest version of the code, follow these steps:

1. Fire up a Node.js terminal session, and then change the working folder to our project area.

2. We need to create a .nvmrc file to help tell Netlify which version of Node.js to use – it can complain if we don't set it explicitly. To do this, enter this command at the prompt, and then press Enter:

```
echo "12.8.0" > .nvmrc
```

I would recommend not doing this in a standard command prompt – the use of quotes will lead to an invalid file! This should be done in a Node.js terminal session.

---

3. You will see this file appear at the root of your project folder; make sure it is there and contains the value "12.8.0" (or higher) in the file.

4. Next, crack open the package.json from the root of your project folder, and look for the "node" entry under the "engines" key.

5. Change it to reflect the same value as used in step 2 – it should look something like this:

```
"engines": {
    "node": "12.8.0"
},
```

6. Save the file, and close it – switch back to the Node.js terminal session.

7. At the prompt, type `gatsby build` – this will create a production build. It will run through a series of tasks, similar to that shown in Figure 5-4.

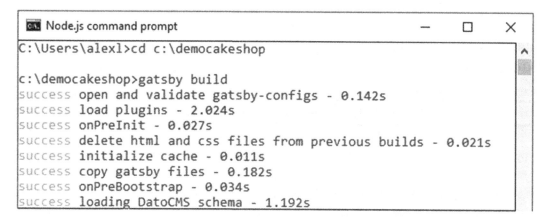

Figure 5-5. *Running through the gatsby build process*

8. Next, log in to Netlify at www.netlify.com, with the credentials you set up back in Chapter 4.

9. Once logged in, switch to the Sites tab. Then click the link to your demo site and then Deploys.

10. Fire up your file manager, and then navigate to the \src\ folder of our project area.

11. Drag and drop the public folder over to the window on the Netlify site, marked "Need to update your site?..."

12. Wait for Netlify to rebuild your site — if all is well, we should see confirmation of this, similar to the screenshot in Figure 5-5, shown overleaf.

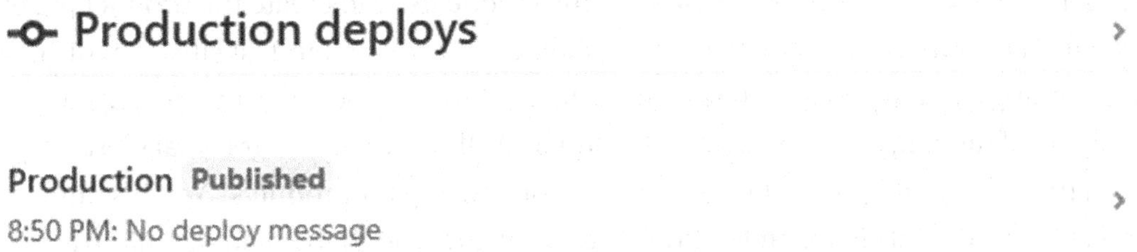

-o- **Production deploys**   >

Production Published   >
8:50 PM: No deploy message

Figure 5-6. *A successful deployment*

13. Assuming Netlify was successful, we can then browse to it via the link at the top of the page, which will be in the format `https:///XXXXX.netlify.app`

And we wait with bated breath... There's our updated site, in all its glory! One of the great things about Netlify is that it makes it so easy to update the website that we could (and perhaps should) do it more often. The only thing to bear in mind, of course, is the cost involved; as we're on a free plan, we need to be mindful that each build will consume minutes from the free allocation in our plan.

That said, updating the Netlify site was very easy. We first logged in using the credentials set up back in Chapter 4; we then uploaded a copy of the `public` folder. Netlify then took over and automatically built our site for us; provided all went well, we could then browse to it using the provided URL from Netlify.

Summary

In the words of a great rock song, "Another chapter bites the dust..."

Okay, perhaps I'm skewing things a little, but we've indeed completed one more step into having a fully working site that we can use as a basis for developing something more involved in future projects. Let's take a moment to review what we've learned thus far in this chapter.

We started by exploring the structure of how our product gallery and pages would fit together; this explored the benefits gained from using a template system, over hard-coding each product page and suffering the pain of updating each one at a later date.

Next up, we then ran through completing the setup for Shopify and testing it with a GraphQL query; we then moved on to reviewing each of the GraphQL queries already set up in our starter theme for this project. We then worked our way through constructing the gallery itself, before examining the remaining code used to create the product pages.

We then rounded out this chapter by updating the code on our test site, to confirm all is still working as expected and that we can move on to the next stage in our project.

Talking of moving on, what is next? I wonder. Well, we've built our initial site and created the gallery and product pages – how about paying for products? Yes, it's time to add in a basket and checkout facilities; we could go through the pain of building something from scratch, but with what's available, this isn't necessary. Stay with me, and I will explain why, with a little research, we can save ourselves a world of pain.

CHAPTER 6

Checkout and Order Processing

In the previous chapter, we worked on building our basket – no e-commerce site is any good, though, without some means to pay for our products! It's time for us to add in a checkout and payment process: the question is, how will it look?

Adding this facility is where things will start to get interesting. Throughout this chapter, we will dig into the process and code required to check out and complete the ordering process for our store via the Shopify checkout process. At the same time, we will explore some of the ways we can customize and tweak the overall experience for our customers.

There is plenty to cover – indeed, we can only scratch the surface of what Shopify can offer! However, before we can get stuck into more practical matters, we first need to deal with the thorny issue of security. This subject will raise a few questions, so let's cover this off first before continuing with configuring our site.

In many of the screenshots and demos, you will see a focus on UK-based examples. This focus is because Shopify settings default to your country of location in the first instance. It's the essence of each demo that is important, plus making sure you allow for regional/market differences in your country.

Dealing with Security

Security is paramount to the success of our store – customers won't touch us with a barge pole if there is the faintest whiff of any security issues! Although there is always a risk when connecting to services over the Internet, there are several factors that will help maintain security and trust for our customers:

© Alex Libby 2021
A. Libby, *Gatsby E-Commerce*, https://doi.org/10.1007/978-1-4842-6692-2_6

- Access has to be made over HTTPS, particularly when it comes to developing our apps within Shopify. We should do this as a matter of course, to help protect sensitive data; Google also places greater preference on sites that are secured when it comes to SEO rankings. If we go further and develop our apps within Shopify, Shopify will reject any requests made over HTTP by default.

- API requests are limited to two requests or fewer per second – this helps prevent Denial-of-Service (DOS) attacks.

- The only link between our site and Shopify is at the point of clicking the checkout button – Shopify content stays within its area, hosted on its servers. It means that we don't deal with anything related to card numbers, customer details, or even CCV numbers – doing so will only lead to a world of pain for us!

- Shopify has systems in place to monitor suspicious activity and allow two-factor authentication – if any is detected, such as hacking, then Shopify will lock access to our account. We can then reconfirm our identity and, if needed, reset our password if someone gains access illegally. If others get to know your password when they shouldn't and you have two-factor authentication enabled, then this will also help limit the damage they may cause if they access the site.

- Although API keys are available for use in Shopify, not all are available for public use; it is up to us as developers to ensure that we use the right key for the right circumstances. We should store any private keys in a password vault, and access to that vault will be limited to ensure security is maintained.

- GDPR is a legal standard that has to be followed by all developers, particularly those who develop custom apps within Shopify that target EU markets. However, Shopify takes this further and enforces the same principles worldwide. It means that we can only hold limited data about customers (enough to satisfy a sale and no more) and that we must take steps to correct that data if it's incorrect or remove it if requested. Our shop does not contain any data stored outside of Shopify, so although we are not keeping details, we still need to be mindful of GDPR requirements and respond promptly to demands for removal or updating when required!

These are just some of the security concerns we need to be mindful of or address when operating our store. Even though much of the hard work we do is within Shopify, we as developers are still ultimately responsible for making sure our site is as secure as it can be for our customers!

Okay, let's move on: now that we've covered off security, let's move on to more practical matters. Although much of the payment process is handled automatically for us by Shopify, we should have at least a high-level understanding of the process. With that in mind, let's dive in and take a look at how it works in more detail, so we can help identify the root cause if we have issues later when the shop is fully live.

Breaking Apart the Process

When it comes to accepting payments by credit cards, the process can seem like a real minefield – there is a lot to consider and potentially a lot that could go wrong! As a developer, it's crucial to have a sense of how the process should work, so that you can advise your customer (store owner) where the problems are and potentially if they need to speak to their bank or financial institution.

Each time a customer pays, we know payments have to be processed first – after all, who wants to be sending out goods when we haven't received funds? This processing will appear to the customer to only last a few seconds, but it hides a complex four-stage process:

- Authorizing the card – The customer pays with their card; your chosen payment provider then requests authorization from the card issuer. As long as the card is valid and has funds, then the issuer authorizes the card for use; we do not transfer funds at this point.

- Capturing the card details – Once the provider or card issuer authorizes payment, we need to capture card details and send them to the acquirer (payment provider).

- Clearing – The acquirer checks the payment details and, assuming they are valid, then requests the necessary funds from the company that processes the customer's credit card. The credit card processor sends the transaction information to the issuer, which subtracts a transaction fee and passes this back to the credit card company, who does the same as well before returning the amount to the acquirer.

- Funding – The acquirer subtracts a small fee from the amount and then transfers the final amount to the merchant account.

Now that we understand the process at a high level, there are a few things we need to bear in mind when using Shopify – let's take a look at them in more detail.

Some Points to Consider

So far, we've covered a high-level version of how the checkout and payment process works – let's bring it into the context of using Shopify, with a few essential pointers we should consider:

- It's important to note that the store may have a delay of a few days to allow payment to be processed, before being paid – we won't receive funds until the bank receives them from the customer. It means we need to make sure our process is smooth and fault-free, to avoid adding any unnecessary delay!

- Shopify doesn't charge fees in the same way as other card issuers, acquirers, or credit companies – instead, it sets a rate plus a fixed fee per transaction (using Shopify Payments). This rate is typically around 2.5–2.9% plus a 30-cent charge; the exact amount depends on the type of subscription used. It's worth considering using this as a start point, so you only have one company to deal with when it comes to fees, so we keep costs under control. (For specific details of expenses, take a look at `www.shopify.com/pricing`).

- All credit cards have authorization periods – these typically last seven days, but can be as long as 30 (in the case of Visa). Shopify Payments' period is seven days – if we're not capturing payment details until later, we could run the risk of incurring extra costs if we go outside of this authorization process.

- If you capture payment in foreign currency, then note that conversion is done at the time of sale **and not** at the time of authorization. Depending on how you capture the payment details, you could end up losing money, if currency values fluctuate too much!

- If you decide to use Shopify Payments, at least to start with, then it's worth noting how your customer will get paid. The payment point depends on whether they use Shopify or a third-party payment gateway; you may not see the transaction in your admin area and that the length of time it takes to get paid will differ, depending on which provider we use.

For more details on this, take a look at `https://help.shopify.com/en/manual/payments/getting-paid#how-you-get-paid`.

There is plenty more to consider when it comes to how we implement payments within Shopify, and that's in addition to the technical coding requirements! I would recommend reading the extensive documentation from `https://help.shopify.com/en/manual/payments/`, to get a feel for some of the more advanced topics, such as dealing with disputes and the like – there is plenty to consider when it comes to using Shopify!

Okay, we can now move on to something more practical. The first stage in this process is the shopping cart itself, so let's dive in and take a look at what is involved in more detail.

You will see `https://XXXXXXX.myshopify.com/admin/` (or a variant) appear as a URL; please replace XXXXXX with the name of your shop when shown.

Constructing the Cart

Okay. It's time, ladies and gentlemen...

Yes, it is indeed time for us to take a look at the cart – I must admit, though, that the title of this section is something of a misnomer, as we've already built/adapted it back in Chapter 5!

That said, it's an integral part of the site – we focused on adding tweaks to the code in the previous chapter and have not spent any time reviewing the code in more detail. Let's put that right in our next two "exercises," where we're going to walk through the code that makes up the cart in more detail, so we can understand how it fits into the bigger picture of our site. As a start, here's a reminder of how it looks when running in a browser (Figure 6-1).

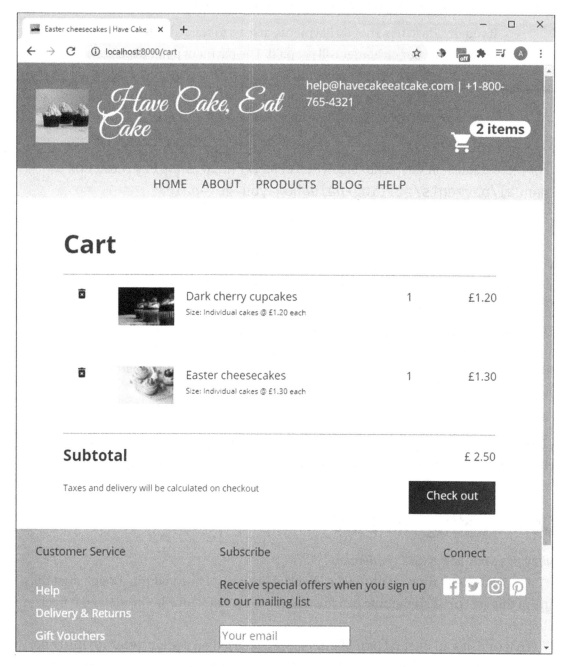

Figure 6-1.   *The cart for our site, developed back in Chapter 5*

I know it won't win any style awards anytime soon, but that doesn't matter for now – it has all of the essential elements, though, which is what counts at this point! Let's move on and dive into that code, starting with the main Cart component.

REVIEWING THE CART CODE

This next exercise will be something of a departure from the norm – as we already have our cart in place, I'm going to walk us through each block, so we can get a better understanding of how it works:

1. The first block contains the obligatory imports – also, we use React's useContext feature to store details of actions taken so that we can pass details across multiple components throughout the site:

```
import React, { useContext } from 'react'

import StoreContext from '~/context/StoreContext'
import LineItem from './LineItem'
```

2. Here we start the main Cart component – we start by initializing the store object to use the useContext function, into which we assign the results from the StoreContext component defined in our site. We also create an onClick handler for firing up Shopify when we click the checkout button and iterate through all of the items in the basket, using the LineItem component (more on this shortly):

```
const Cart = () => {
  const {
    store: { checkout },
  } = useContext(StoreContext)

  const handleCheckout = () => {
    window.open(checkout.webUrl)
  }

  const lineItems = checkout.lineItems.map(item => (
    <LineItem key={item.id.toString()} item={item} />
  ))
```

3. We now begin to render content on the screen – it's wrapped in a ternary operator, so that basket contents are only displayed if we have one or more items in the basket. If not, it displays a suitable message to indicate that the basket is empty:

```
return (
  <>
    {checkout.lineItems.length !== 0 ? (
      <>
        <div>
          {lineItems}
        </div>
        <div className="totals">
          <h3>Subtotal</h3>
          <p>£ {checkout.subtotalPrice}</p>
        </div>
        <div className="taxes">
          <p>Taxes and delivery will be calculated on checkout</p>
          <button
            className="checkout"
            onClick={handleCheckout}
            disabled={checkout.lineItems.length === 0}
          >
            Check out
          </button>
        </div>
      </>
    ) : (
      <p>Cart is empty!</p>
    )}
  </>
  )
}
```

4. We then finish with the obligatory export statement, to make the component available for use elsewhere in the site:

```
export default Cart
```

Adding in the main cart is only part of the story, though – we must not forget the reference to `LineItem`, which we use to display the items within the cart! It is something of a lengthier component; it looks more complicated than it is in reality. Let's dive in and take a closer look at this code to see how it fits into the Cart component.

REVIEWING LINEITEM CODE

As before, we're going to review the code in more detail, given we've already added in the necessary changes back in Chapter 5:

1. We start with the obligatory imports – this time, we're importing React and the `useContext` function, along with `StoreContext` and an image of a bin (which we use to remove items in the cart):

```
import React, { useContext } from 'react'
import { Link } from 'gatsby'

import StoreContext from '~/context/StoreContext'
import bin from "../../../images/bin.png"
```

2. Next up, we define the main `LineItem` object; this has a number of properties and events, including setting the image, selected options, formatting prices, and dealing with removing an instance of the item from the cart:

```
const LineItem = props => {
  const { item } = props
  const {
    removeLineItem,
    store: { client, checkout },
  } = useContext(StoreContext)

  const variantImage = item.variant.image ? (
    <img
      src={item.variant.image.src}
      alt={`${item.title} product shot`}
      height="60px"
    />
  ) : null
```

```
const selectedOptions = item.variant.selectedOptions
  ? item.variant.selectedOptions.map(
      option => `${option.name}: ${option.value} `
    )
  : null

const handleRemove = () => {
  removeLineItem(client, checkout.id, item.id)
}

function calculateSubTotal(a, b) {
 return (a * b).toFixed(2)
}

const price =  Intl.NumberFormat(undefined, {
  currency: item.variant.priceV2.currencyCode,
  minimumFractionDigits: 2,
  style: 'currency',
}).format(item.variant.priceV2.amount)

const unitTotal = Intl.NumberFormat(undefined, {
  currency: item.variant.priceV2.currencyCode,
  minimumFractionDigits: 2,
  style: 'currency',
}).format(calculateSubTotal(item.quantity, item.variant.priceV2.
amount))
```

3. Here we render content for each LineItem – the bulk of the code is used
    to display each cart item, along with an onClick handler to take care of
    removing the item if it is no longer meant to be in the basket:

```
return (
  <>
    <ul>
      <li><button className="remove" onClick={handleRemove}><img
      src={bin} alt="Remove item" className="bin"/></button></li>
      <li><Link to={`/product/${item.variant.product.
      handle}/`}>{variantImage}</Link></li>
      <li>
        <span>{item.title}
```

```
      {item.variant.title === !'Default Title' ? item.variant.
      title : ''}
      </span>
      <span>{selectedOptions} @ {price} each</span>
    </li>
    <li>{item.quantity}</li>
    <li>{unitTotal}</li>
  </ul>
 </>
 )
}

export default LineItem
```

Phew, it might seem a fair chunk of code, but as we've seen, we use most of it to render content on-screen. At this point, though, it means we now have a working cart that we can use to add and remove products from the shop, ready to check out and purchase as the next stage.

Talking of the next stage, how do we go about checking out and purchasing the products we've selected? It is where we introduce the next part of the process: Shopify! We'll be using it to run through the checkout process and (for now) handle payment; there are a few things we need to take note of around the latter, but we'll cover this in more detail later in this chapter. For now, let's take a look at how we manage payments and what options are available for us to use in our store.

Exploring the Options

Now that we've explored the code used to create our cart, it's time to start configuring the payment provider we will use for our shop.

If you were to take a look at Settings ➤ Payments and Settings ➤ Payments ➤ Alternative payment providers from within your store's dashboard, you might be forgiven for thinking that there is a pretty bewildering list of choices to choose! While this is indeed true, there are a couple of pointers we should consider which will help narrow down the list of options – at least for testing purposes:

- Do you have an existing merchant account with a provider, or are you setting up from scratch?

- What type of cards do you want to accept?

- What payment methods do you want to accept, such as bank transfer or cash on delivery?

- Is it possible that one or more of your target markets may not support the payment methods you want to use, or which might be prohibitively expensive?

- What costs will you incur when using a payment provider?

It might not seem immediately apparent as to why these questions could affect which provider you choose, but a large part of it comes down to costs, risk, and business history with your current provider.

In short, each provider will charge fees for every transaction they process; these can be reduced if you already have existing transaction history with a provider or shop around to help keep costs to a minimum. Bearing these in mind, Shopify offers several options we can choose from – these include

- Bogus Gateway – Designed for testing purposes

- Shopify Payments – `https://XXXXX.myshopify.com/admin/shopify-payments`, where XXXXX will be the name of your shop

- PayPal – `https://help.shopify.com/en/manual/payments/paypal`

- Amazon Pay – `https://pay.amazon.com/`

- Manual payments, such as bank deposit, money order, or cash on delivery

A full list of alternative payment providers plus the cards they accept is available at `https://XXXXX.myshopify.com/admin/settings/payments/alternative-providers`, where XXXXX is the name of your shop.

For this book, we will focus primarily on using Bogus Gateway – it removes any risk of trying to process real cards in a test environment, which is something we should not do! We will, however, try out Shopify Payments in a test capacity, so you can see what it looks like with more realistic (but fake) credit card numbers.

I should point out, though, that as this book is more about how to link in with Gatsby than configuring Shopify, we will only touch on the basics. I would recommend reading the extensive documentation at `https://XXXXXXX.myshopify.com/admin/settings/payments`, to get a feel for how to develop and refine the overall experience for our customers. I would also recommend researching providers to get a feel for which would suit your needs best when moving a site in production use.

Integrating Our Payment Processor

Okay, so we'll be working with Bogus Gateway (definitely scope for a better name there, methinks!); how do we configure it? This configuration is something we can do from within Shopify; it gives us three test "numbers" we can use to simulate accepting cards or to fail them if there is a fault or problem with the card.

SETTING UP BOGUS GATEWAY

To get the (bogus) payment gateway set up, work through these steps:

1. First, go ahead and browse to `https://XXXXX.myshopify.com/admin/settings/payments`, where XXXXX is the name of your shop – if prompted, please log in with your credentials for Shopify.

2. Scroll down until you see (for testing) Bogus Gateway – click Activate Bogus Gateway.

3. On the next page, click Add currency: click those you want to accept for your store, and click Add currencies. You can see an example of how this should look in Figure 6-2.

Enabled currencies

Add currency

 British Pound (GBP)

Default

US Dollar (USD)

∨

Figure 6-2. *Adding in currencies to our store*

4.   Once done, click Save to return to the main dashboard.

Adding in the payment part is a significant step forward – we now have something that gives us a starting point to test the cart from start to finish. The setting-up process is straightforward; we activated it from within the Payments part of our admin dashboard and simply added in the currencies we wanted to support in our store.

There is one small catch, though, which we should bear in mind: the method we've used isn't entirely representative of what customers would need to do! Entering 1, 2, or 3 as credit card numbers will allow us to test the experience. Still, I would recommend factoring in a process to try one of the real processors in a test environment. All good processors should have an option available to do this; failing that, you can activate and use Shopify Payments through the same settings screen, to test the process.

If you activate this new processor, then Bogus Gateway will be deactivated; Shopify only allows one processor to be active at any one time. You will need to also bear in mind the European PSD2 directive; this needs to be tested via a real processor, as Bogus Gateway does not support this feature.

Performing a Run-Through of the Cart

So far, we've focused on configuring our cart and checkout process – while this is great, it's always sensible to check that the basics at least work before we start "fine-tuning" the experience! I say fine-tuning as that usually means we break something somewhere and begin to undo our good work, but hey, I digress...

Anyway, back to reality: it's time we updated what is on our Netlify site and checked to make sure it works as expected. This updating is something we've done before, so without further ado, let's revisit the steps needed to get Netlify updated with our latest code.

UPDATING THE CONTENT ON NETLIFY

To get our demo site updated with the latest version of the code, follow these steps:

1. Fire up a Node.js terminal session, and then change the working folder to our project area.

2. At the prompt, type gatsby build – this will create a production build. It will run through a series of tasks, similar to that shown in Figure 6-3.

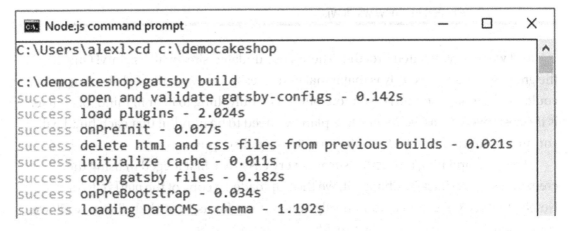

Figure 6-3. Running through the gatsby build process

3. Next, log in to Netlify at www.netlify.com, with the credentials you set up back in Chapter 4.

4. Once logged in, switch to the Sites tab. Then click the link to your demo site and then Deploys.

5. Fire up your file manager, and then navigate to the \src\ folder of our project area.

6. Drag and drop the public folder over to the window on the Netlify site, marked "Need to update your site?…"

7. Wait for Netlify to rebuild your site – if all is well, we should see confirmation of this, similar to this screenshot (Figure 6-4).

–o– Production deploys   >

Production Published   >
8:50 PM: No deploy message

Figure 6-4. *A successful deployment*

8. Assuming Netlify was successful, we can then browse to it via the link at the top of the page, which will be in the format `https:///XXXXX.netlify.app` (this will open in a new window).

And we wait with bated breath… There's our updated site, in all its glory! One of the great things about Netlify is that it makes it so easy to update the website that we could (and perhaps should) do it more often. The only thing to bear in mind, of course, is the cost involved; as we're on a free plan, we need to be mindful that each build will consume minutes from the free allocation in our subscription.

That said, updating the Netlify site was very easy – we first logged in using the credentials set up back in Chapter 4; we then uploaded a copy of the `public` folder. Netlify then took over and automatically built our site for us; provided all went well, we could then browse to it using the provided URL from Netlify.

Adding Shipping Options

Delivery. This is something that can make or break the shopping process. I know from experience: I've lost count of the number of times deliveries have been "lost in transit" or promises of free (or low-cost) deliveries turn out to be something else.

While we can't always control how third parties we contract to deliver our products perform, there is one thing we can do – make it super clear and easy to the customer just how much it's going to cost them to get their goods.

Thankfully, Shopify makes it very easy to set up even a basic delivery charge; it's the same principle to set up something simple through to an elaborate affair that prioritizes delivery based on set conditions such as weight and size.

Although we're only selling small boxes of cakes, we still need to factor in costs for delivery – it's unlikely we're going to be able to provide free delivery! We need to set up appropriate delivery profiles for our customers. There are a few steps required to achieve this, so let's dive in and take a look at what we need to do in more detail.

SETTING UP SHIPPING

To get shipping set up, go ahead with these steps:

1. Log into your Shopify dashboard, if you have not already logged in – once done, click Shipping and delivery.

2. Under Shipping, click Manage rates – we need to review and amend the shipping rates for our shop.

3. Scroll down until you see the Shipping from section – this will, by default, contain the address you used to set up your store.

4. A little further down, you will see a Shipping to section, which will look similar to that shown in Figure 6-5.

Figure 6-5. *The initial Shipping display in Shopify*

5. Click Add rate; then in the dialog box that appears, enter the name of a new rate. For this demo, I will assume we use the name Express, but feel free to use a different name if you prefer. You can see an example of how this will appear in Figure 6-6.

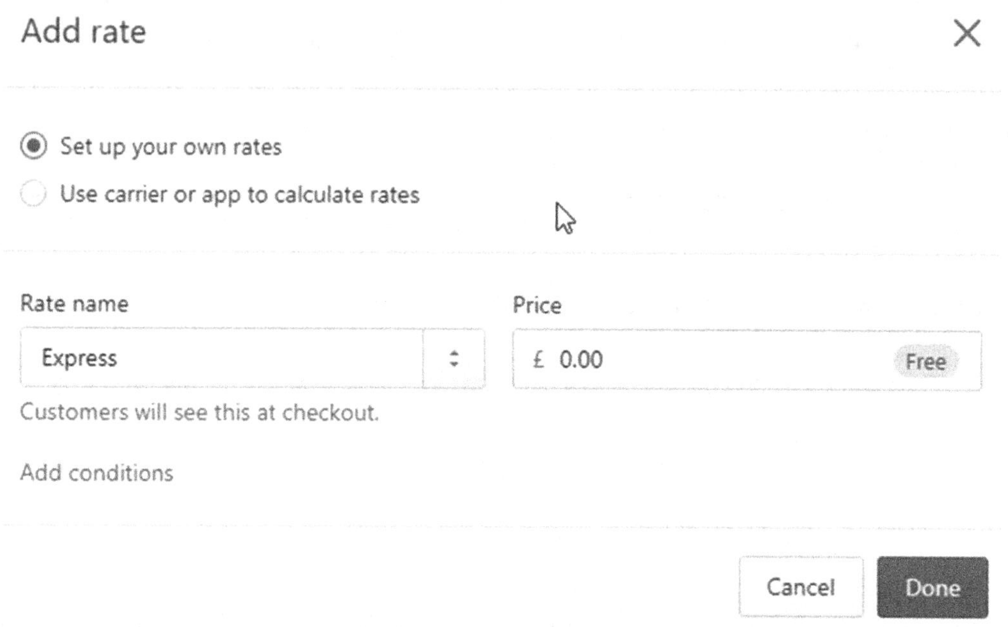

Figure 6-6. *Adding a shipping rate*

6. Once done, click Done – you can see an example of how it should look in Figure 6-7.

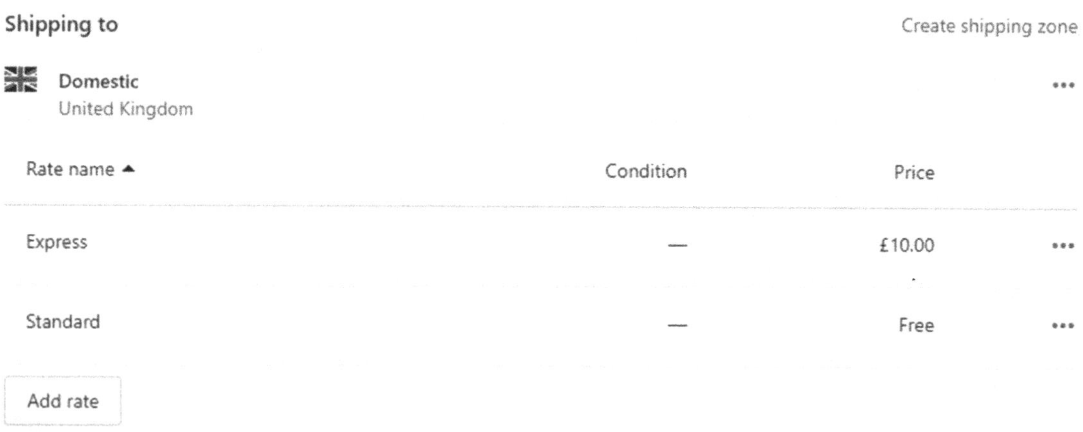

Figure 6-7. *Adding in shipping rates for the United Kingdom*

7. We can use the same steps to add in something similar for Rest of World, as shown in Figure 6-8.

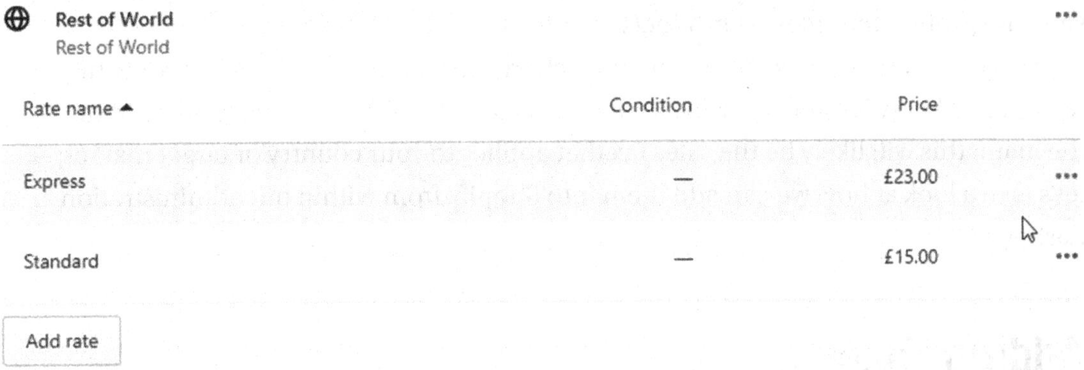

⊕ Rest of World Rest of World			•••
Rate name ▲	Condition	Price	
Express	—	£23.00	•••
Standard	—	£15.00	•••

Add rate

Figure 6-8. *A completed set of shipping rates for Rest of World*

For this exercise, I've kept the setup very simple – this was more about how to add in a shipping rate and not necessarily what the exact figures should be! That said, it's an essential part of the site, so let's take a moment to review both the changes we've made and cover off some important points we should consider if we move our project into production.

Understanding the Impact of Our Changes

It's a well-known fact that customers will gravitate more to those sites that offer free shipping – after all, who wants to pay for a product particularly if they find the costs of shipping it far outweigh the price of the product? There may indeed be occasions where this is necessary if the product is delicate, but the point here is: this is one area we have to get right!

Thankfully, Shopify makes it very easy to add in shipping rates – in this last exercise, we've manually entered our prices, but we could easily choose to use carrier rates if we so desired. We began with locating the Shipping from address (which is added by default), before starting to add in new tariffs, depending on where we wanted to ship our products.

In each case, we gave each rate a proper name and entered an arbitrary price for now; these will need to be updated as part of the production, to ensure we have accurate rates available for our customers. At the same time, we left the conditions as default for now, but we should consider using these if we need to vary costs based on factors such as weights. Once done, we click Save to update Shopify with these rates; they will apply to all products purchased in the current shipping profile unless we decide to add in separate profiles for different products.

Okay, let's crack on: we have one more charge to worry about, which is collecting taxes. Yes, I know it's not everyone's cup of tea (so to speak), but we have to do it! In the main, this will likely be the sales tax that applies to your country or target market; let's take a look at how we can add them into Shopify from within our administration dashboard.

Adding Taxes

With shipping set up, there is one more important charge we must consider – are we obligated to add in any sales taxes?

Adding taxes is something that will be unique to each shop – it depends on factors such as the amount of revenue you make annually, what industry your shop serves, and your geographical location. I know few people will get excited by the prospect of dealing with taxes, but it's still something we have to consider!

To help facilitate things, we can set up the appropriate tax breaks within Shopify, so it does legwork in figuring out just how much to charge, not us. The great thing about Shopify is that it works out most of the tax requirements for us, based on shipping profiles we've set up in Shopify. It does mean that we need to make sure these accurately reflect where we ship our products so that we can collect the correct taxes at the point of checkout. Let's take a look at what's involved in getting charges set up for collection at the point of sale.

ADDING TAXES

To get taxes set up for our store, work through these steps:

1. Log into your store; then once at the main dashboard, click Settings ➤ Taxes.

2. You should find it has already added one or more tax regions; it will look similar to the screenshot in Figure 6-9.

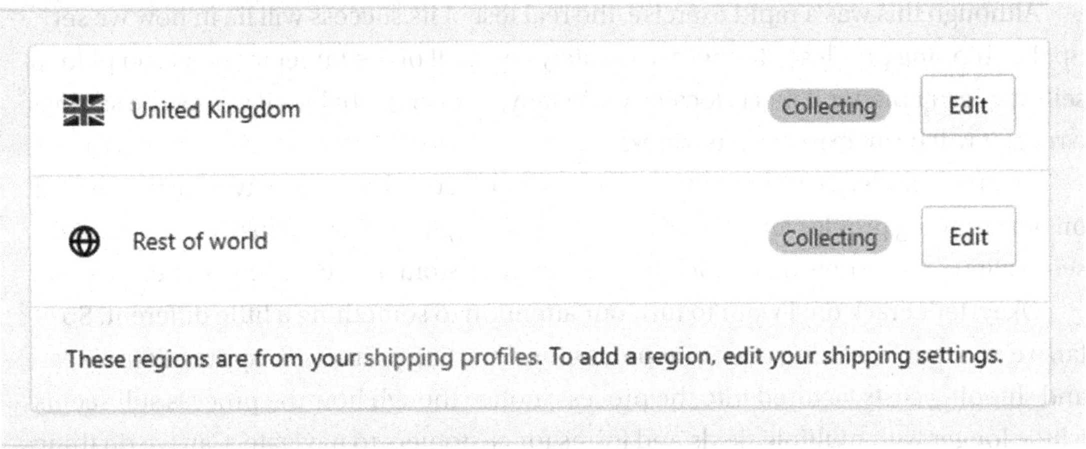
United Kingdom
Collecting
Edit
Rest of world
Collecting
Edit
These regions are from your shipping profiles. To add a region, edit your shipping settings.

***Figure 6-9.** Tax regions set up in the store*

3. Scroll down to the Tax calculations section – we can adjust how the tax calculations are displayed and whether we display prices with tax included. For this demo, I will leave them set as they are, as shown in Figure 6-10.

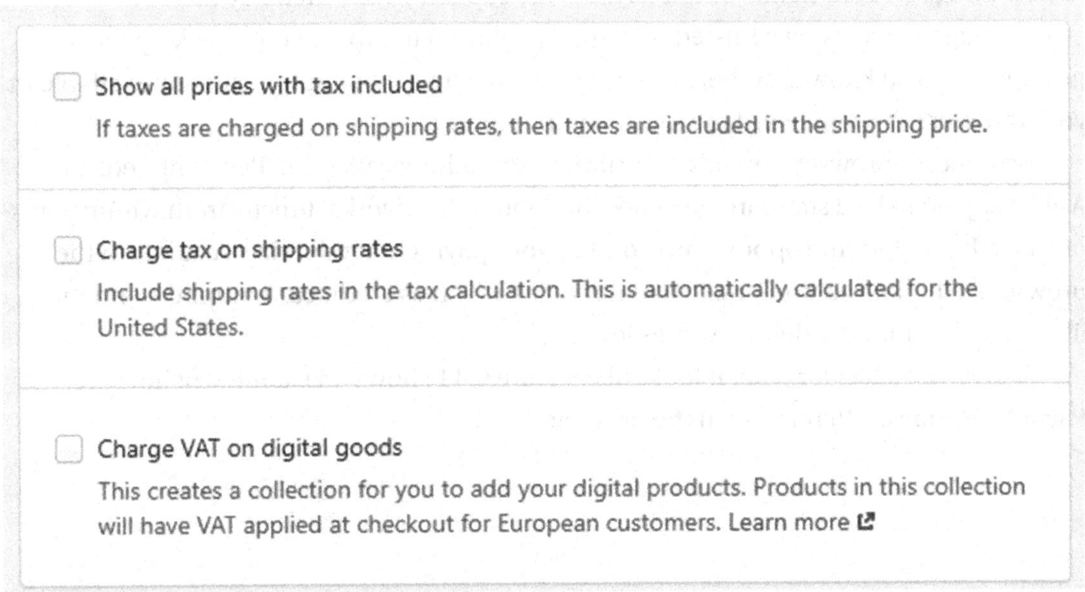
Show all prices with tax included
If taxes are charged on shipping rates, then taxes are included in the shipping price.
Charge tax on shipping rates
Include shipping rates in the tax calculation. This is automatically calculated for the United States.
Charge VAT on digital goods
This creates a collection for you to add your digital products. Products in this collection will have VAT applied at checkout for European customers. Learn more

***Figure 6-10.** Optional settings for controlling tax calculations*

4. Shopify automatically saves any changes you make on this screen – once done, click the back arrow by Settings (top left), to revert to the main dashboard.

Although this was a rapid exercise, the real test of its success will lie in how we set up the shipping profiles – do these accurately cover all of the target markets you plan to sell? It doesn't matter if this is locally, nationally, or even globally – if we get the settings wrong, it will be an expensive business!

In our example, we've kept things mostly as per default; we have two regions based on our shipping profiles and have set the shop to display prices exclusive of taxes. This setup allows us to show how much tax we charge customers, according to their region.

Okay, let's crack on: I want to turn our attention to something a little different. So far, we've set up a starting checkout process as a starting point, with appropriate taxes and shipping costs factored into the process; notice though how the process still seems a little longer with multiple fields and forms for customers to navigate. Can we do things differently? I wonder...

Using the Payment Request API

Well, we can always do things differently. That is true – however, there may be an option to turn things on their head completely! Let me explain what I mean by this.

Although we're using a hosted third-party solution to provide the checkout facility, how many of you know that there is a perfectly good checkout option already available in your browser? Yes, you heard me right – your browser!

Most recent browsers already incorporate something called the Payment Request API, designed to be a standardized checkout option that works directly from within your browser. It provides the opportunity to store your payment credentials securely in the browser such that you don't need to enter details such as credit card numbers and the like – it will display the default values for you.

To give you a feel for what it looks like, Figure 6-11 shows an example of how the Payment Request API renders in the browser.

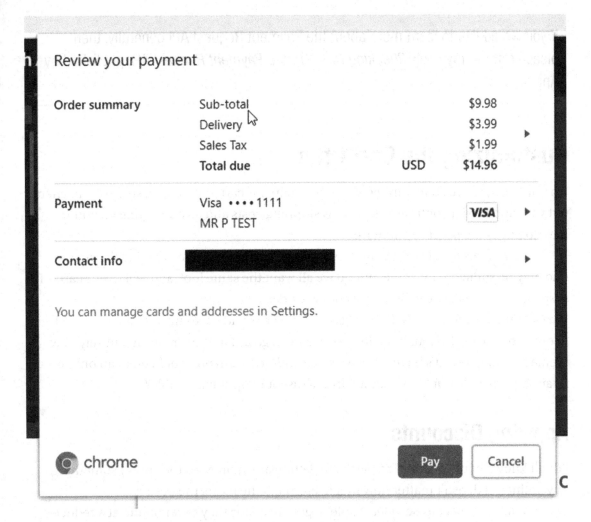

Figure 6-11. *An example of the Payment Request API in operation*

The API is still technically at W3C's Candidate Recommendation status, but it's sufficiently stable enough to be used in production, provided we add in the right safeguards into our site.

If we implement this option, it would mean making a few changes in terms of how we process payments. This addition is something I will explore in Chapter 13, where we will see if we can get this working within our Gatsby site – if we do, then I will also take you through some of the pitfalls we need to be mindful of when using this option!

If you would like to learn more about the Payment Request API generally, then please refer to my book *Checking Out with the Payment Request API*, published by Apress.

Customizing the Cart Offer

Up until now, we've concentrated on building up our cart and making sure we can check out with appropriate options set, such as shipping costs and any taxes that customers have to pay at the point of purchase.

However, this is only touching the surface of what is possible. Keeping the status quo may be sufficient for some, but do we all want the same look and feel to our carts? I suspect not; we can tweak how the process works.

Over the next few pages, I've picked a few tweaks and customizations we can add to our cart – I will also touch on how we can even go as far as to create an entirely new theme for our cart! Let's begin with a simple addition – anyone not been to an online retail site which **doesn't** have some form of discount option available?

Applying Discounts

I don't know about you, but I'm partial to getting any money off the cost of something I buy online – it doesn't matter how much, although the more, the better!

Customers expect to be at least able to get the goods they order online at a reduced price, compared to those sold through brick-and-mortar outlets – it, therefore, makes absolute sense to offer something as part of our checkout process. Thankfully, Shopify provides the facility to do so – it makes adding discounts a snap, leaving us to work out precisely what deals we can offer. Let's dive in and take a look at how we can add in a discount as part of the next exercise.

ADDING IN A DISCOUNT

For this exercise, we'll add a 10% discount to be applied across the entire order – to do so, follow these steps:

1. First, we need to log into our Shopify account if we haven't already done so – once done, go to the main dashboard.

2. Next, click Discounts in the left menu and then Create discount.

3. Go ahead and choose Discount code from the options that appear.

4. For this discount, use the values shown in Table 6-1.

Table 6-1. *Properties to use when setting a discount*

Property	Value to Use
Discount code	10PERCENT
Types	Percentage
Value	10
Applies to	Entire order
Minimum requirements	Minimum purchase amount – £20
Customer eligibility	Everyone
Usage limits	No usage limits
Active dates	Pick a start date of your choosing; you can choose whether to provide an end date by selecting the Send end date checkbox.

5. Once amended, click Save discount code to update the shop with this new discount; click Discount codes top left to return to the dashboard. You should then have a discount present, similar to that shown in Figure 6-12.

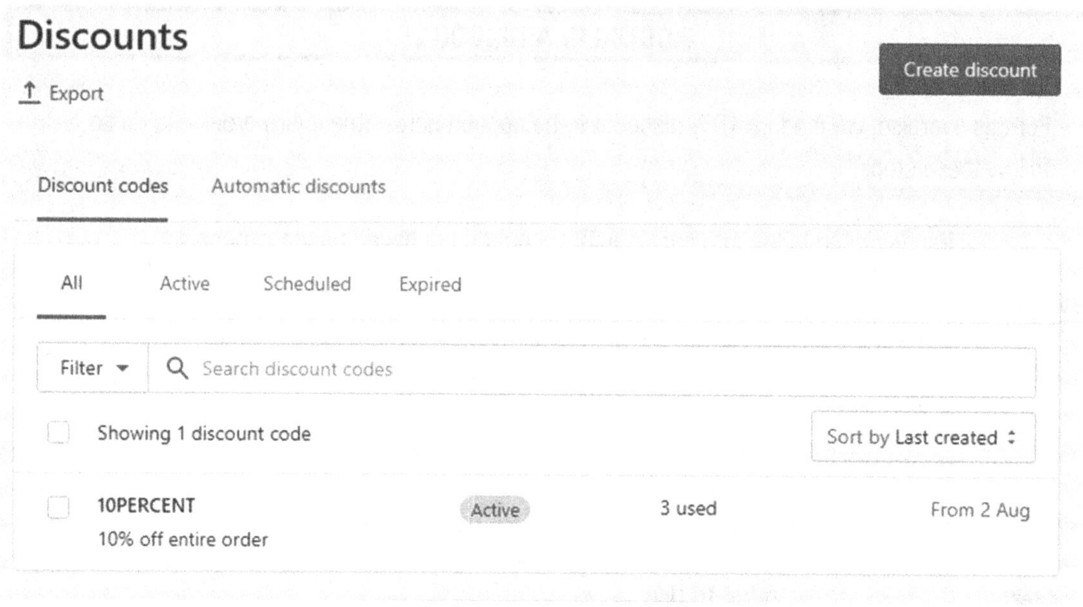

Discounts

⬆ Export

Create discount

Discount codes   Automatic discounts

| All | Active | Scheduled | Expired |

| Filter ▾ | 🔍 Search discount codes |

☐ Showing 1 discount code   Sort by Last created ↕

☐ **10PERCENT**   Active   3 used   From 2 Aug
10% off entire order

Figure 6-12. *The main discounts window, with a 10% discount offer listed*

Although adding discounts is very easy, it can be a double-edged sword. Not only do we have to consider what deals we want to make available but we also need to make sure customers can't abuse them and get goods at substantially reduced prices!

In our case, we kept it to a simple 10% off, but we could have chosen options such as limiting the usage or customer base. The key here is not determining what discounts we offer, but planning how and when we offer these discounts to customers. We could use them to promote new cakes or encourage multi-buys (although in some countries I fear this practice may now be banned). There are plenty of opportunities; it all comes down to planning!

Okay, let's crack on: we've added in shipping, taxes, and discounts, so what's left? What about customizing how our cart works so that we can refine the experience for our customers? There are so many options that could almost fill a book in their own right; instead, I've picked a few to help get you started and give you a feel for what is possible when it comes to working with Shopify. Let's start with a simple change, which is to add in our site's logo to the Shopify cart.

Tweaking the Cart's Appearance

One of the great things about Shopify is that we don't always need to add code to customize a feature – we can implement many of the customizations from within the Shopify GUI. A perfect example of this will form the basis for the next exercise – let's take a look at how easy it is to add in a header image into our shop's cart.

TWEAKING THE CART: IMAGES AND OTHERS

To add in a header image into your store, follow these steps:

1. First, log in to your dashboard, and then click Settings ➤ Checkout.

2. Click Customize checkout under Style – the theme editor for your basket will display in a new tab.

3. On the left, look for the LOGO box, then click Select image, and choose to upload a new image. A suitable image is available as `\src\images\checkoutheader.png`; feel free to use something else if you prefer, although I would recommend keeping it to the same dimensions.

4. Once selected, click Open, and then let it process; click Select at the bottom.

5. Once back in the main theme window, change the logo size to large in the LOGO box.

6. At the same time, click Edit to add in the name of the store (for SEO purposes). The Position entry should remain unchanged as Left.

7. Click Save – if all is well, you should see something akin to Figure 6-13.

Cart > **Information** > Shipping > Payment

Contact information

Email or mobile phone number

Figure 6-13. *The updated header for our shop*

Although this exercise might seem relatively straightforward, it does open up a level of risk – this is something we will touch on shortly. Before that, though, let's take a moment to review how we set this up, so you can get a feel for what needs to change, depending on your requirements.

Understanding the Changes Made

For this last exercise, we've used the theme editor available within Shopify to add in an image above the breadcrumb trail shown at the top of our Shopify checkout page. This addition we did by browsing to the Settings page and then visiting the Checkout section; we uploaded an image and told Shopify to add it as a header image for our store.

There is one crucial point to note at this stage – we need to ensure that the image displayed has both the visual logo *and* the text of the store name. Both are critical for customers to recognize your store; unless your brand is as well-known as the likes of Apple or Nike, people won't acknowledge your store! It's worth trying out a few sizes, to make sure your chosen image best fits on the page without pushing content down too much – I used one sized at 525 px by 95 px, as a guideline.

Okay, let's crack on: we've seen how a simple change to our store's checkout page can begin to provide better visual identity. There is one area I want to cover next, which is around delivery: are you set up to deliver to every country in the world, or do you have areas where delivery isn't yet possible or not available?

Limiting Delivery

It might sound odd to ask that question around delivery (as clearly, we want to sell to as many people as possible). There is a practical reason for asking this question though: there may be legal requirements that mean you can't ship goods to certain countries, where, for example, people use those products to incite war or terrorism.

Shopify has a feature within which allows us to specify countries that are no-go for shipping; let's take a look at how we might instigate such a restriction for our shop.

LIMIT DELIVERY

For this exercise, I've picked Afghanistan as our no-go country; I've chosen this entirely at random, so I could easily have selected any country so desired! Assuming we're using Afghanistan, work through these steps to add the exclusion into Shopify:

1. The first step is to log in into our dashboard – once done, click Settings ➤ Shipping and delivery.

2. Next, scroll down to CUSTOM SHIPPING RATES and then click Create new profile.

3. In the name box, enter Excluded markets as the text. The customer does not see this; it's purely an internal label to help classify the type of exclusion.

4. Next, click Products ➤ Add products.

5. Click Select all products and then click Done (it's at this point you could choose to select individual ones if you preferred).

6. In the Shipping to box, click Create Zone.

7. When prompted, enter Afghanistan in the Zone name field, and then click Done. If all is good, we should see something akin to Figure 6-14.

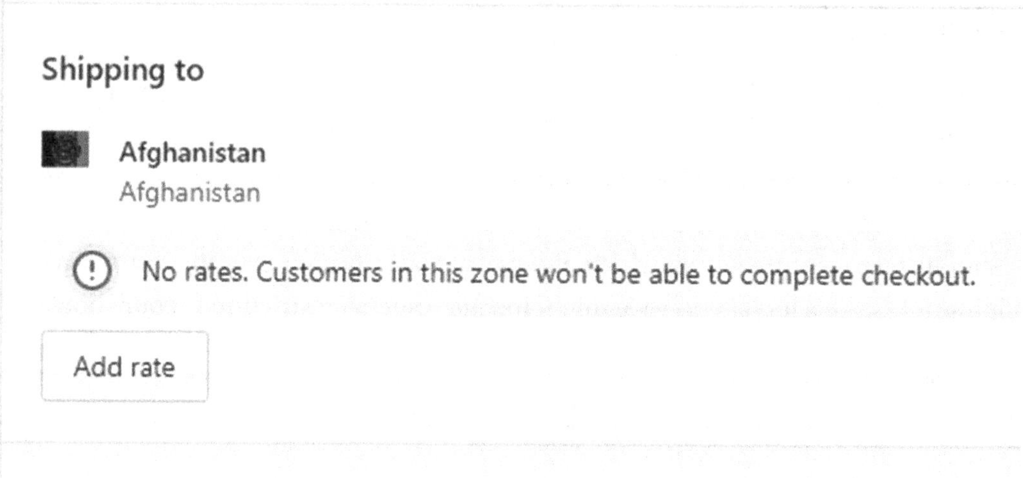
Shipping to
Afghanistan
Afghanistan
No rates. Customers in this zone won't be able to complete checkout.
Add rate

Figure 6-14. *Adding an exclusion zone*

8. Click Save to update Shopify and return to the main dashboard.

   Adding in the exclusion is only part of the story – we need to test any exclusion, to ensure it works! To do this, follow these steps:

9. First, browse to our site on the Netlify test URL; then choose a product and add to basket.
10. Next, click the basket to view; then click Checkout.
11. Enter details as appropriate in fields, but make sure Afghanistan is in the Country/Region field. Click Continue to shipping.
12. You should see a warning similar to that shown in Figure 6-16.

Shipping method

 This order can't be shipped to your location. Contact the store for more information.

We don't offer shipping to Afghanistan.

Figure 6-15. *A warning that shipping to Afghanistan is not available from our shop*

This message confirms that we have successfully excluded Afghanistan as a delivery destination from our shop.

Although this exercise might seem relatively straightforward, it does open up a level of risk – this is something we will touch on shortly. Before that, though, let's take a moment to review how we set this up, so you can get a feel for what needs to change, depending on your requirements.

Exploring the Code in Detail

We started by creating a new shipping zone – Shopify works using zones, either for shipping to or exclusion, the latter controlled by whether we set rates for that country. We then selected all of the products; once saved, we then did not specify a tariff for delivery. This step is vital, as this tells Shopify to treat this as an exclusion. If we had set a rate, this would override any we set previously, such as the Rest of World rate we set earlier in this chapter.

However, that all aside, it does raise that critical question we touched on earlier: why are we excluding a country? In some cases, there might be a practical reason, such as not having suitable means to ship, being too expensive, or the risk being also significant. Alternatively, the reason might be more politically based, such as war or terrorism in that country, making the risk of delivering goods safely and securely impossible. Ultimately it's up to us to make sure that we include the relevant zones in the shipping section of our site so that we only have those countries or regions where we can safely deliver goods to our customers.

Okay, let's move on: we have one more change I want to run through. Anyone who visits a site may well see something to indicate how much stock is available for a particular item. It's not entirely related to the cart, but it nevertheless uses a method that shows how we can get access to the core data available in Shopify. Stay with me, and I will explain all, as part of our next exercise.

Displaying Inventory Levels

At this point, I can take a pretty good guess at a question that will be on all of your lips: why are we talking about displaying an inventory level on the product page, when we're on the cart and in the checkout process?

There is a good reason for this: Shopify provides a theme build option that allows you to add in custom elements to the cart – one of these is inventory! Therefore, it (kind of) makes sense to include it on the product page; I would even go as far as having it on a category page too. I will go into more detail a little later on, but in the meantime, let's take a look at how we might set up a suitable option to display inventory levels in our store.

DISPLAYING INVENTORY LEVELS

For this demo, we're going to focus on one product for now – this is very much a proof-of-concept that focuses on getting the information and not necessarily how we get it! Let's take a look at the steps involved:

1. First, we need to create a new data folder in the src folder of our project area.

2. Next, browse to `https://XXXXX.myshopify.com/admin/api/2020-07/inventory_levels.json?location_ids=YYYYY`, where

   XXXXX – The name of your Shopify store.

   YYYYY – The location ID for your store; you can get this by logging into your Shopify store's dashboard and then clicking Settings ➤ General. Hover over the name of your store in the Locations list – the ID you need is the 11-digit number shown in the URL behind that list entry.

3. Once there, right-click and save the file into the data folder created in step 1, as inventory.json.

4. We now need to create a new stock level component – go ahead and add the following into a new file, saving it as stocks.js in the \src\components folder:

```
import React from 'react'
import { stockData } from './stockdata'

export const Stocks = () => {
  return (
    <>
      {stockData.map((data, key) => {
        return (
          <span key={data} className="stocklevel">
{data.inventory_levels[2].available} available</span>
        )
      })}
    </>
  );
};
```

5. To complete the code, we need to transform the JSON file saved in step 3 into a component – open that file in your text editor, then add in the code at the start and end, and save it as stockdata.js. It should look something akin to this – the additions are in bold:

```
export const stockData = [{
  "inventory_levels": [

  (rest of code from JSON file)

  ]
}]
```

6. Last, but by no means least, let's add a style rule to give the inventory level some color. Add this at the bottom of the global.scss file within the \src\ styles folder:

```
.stocklevel { color: #006400;  font-weight: bold; }
```

7. We now need to call in our code – crack open `ProductForm.js` from within \ `src\components\ProductForm`, and then add in the `<stocks />` element reference as indicated in Figure 6-16.

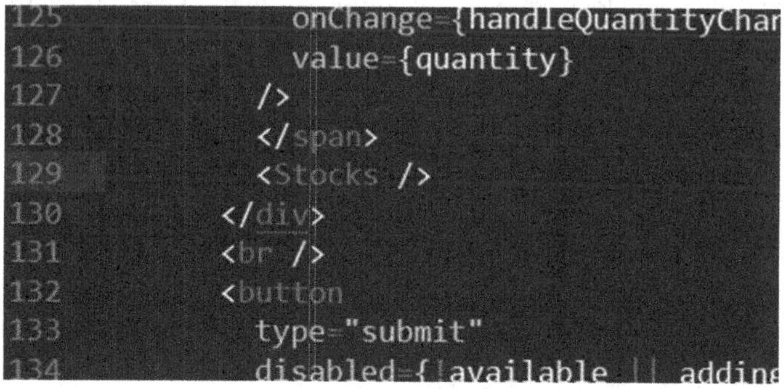

```
125                    onChange={handleQuantityChan
126                    value={quantity}
127                />
128             </span>
129             <Stocks />
130          </div>
131          <br />
132          <button
133             type="submit"
134             disabled={!available || adding
```

Figure 6-16. *Insertion point for the <stocks /> component*

8. At this point, we have finished with editing code – if we compile a production version of our code and upload to Netlify, we would see something akin to Figure 6-17.

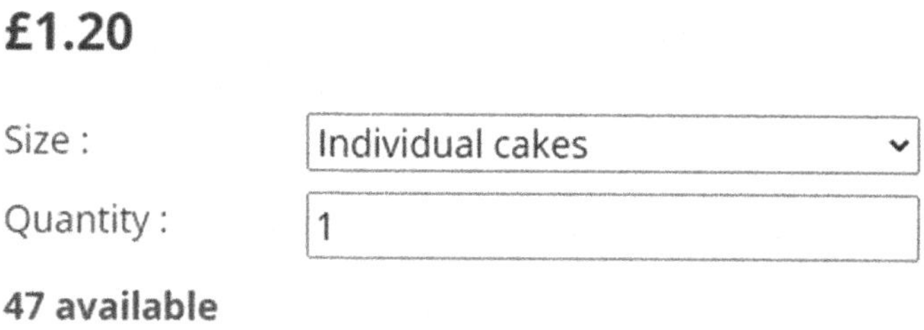

£1.20

Size :   Individual cakes   ∨

Quantity :   1

47 available

Figure 6-17. *An updated product page, with inventory levels shown*

Although this is a relatively straightforward change to make, it's not the end of the story, though; if you were to click any product, you would find it shows the same value! That's because I've hard-coded it to show what is possible – we would need to develop this further so that the amount is unique to each product. Leaving that aside, it offers a useful technique to source extra data from Shopify using its API, so let's pause for a moment to review this change in more detail.

Analyzing the Code in Detail

So how exactly did we make this change? Well, it all centers around the extensive APIs that come with Shopify – you can query all manner of different values, such as orders, customers, sales, and, of course, inventory levels! We can access the APIs in one of two ways – either by using a REST-based query or working with GraphQL.

For this exercise, we used the REST route. In an ideal world, I would prefer to use GraphQL; this is for reasons of performance, as well as not wanting to introduce too many different sources into our site! There is also another consideration: we used the gatsby-source-shopify plugin, which doesn't support all of the fields available using GraphQL, hence using REST.

We started by navigating to one of the API endpoints that displays the current inventory levels in JSON format; this we saved as a file, before converting the JSON into a JavaScript-based plugin within our site. We then created a second component (stocks. js) to return a hard-coded value (for now) that represents an inventory level – this was then added to the `ProductForm` component so that we could call and get that data back. We then rounded out the demo by adding some rudimentary styling to the text returned from the stocks.js component.

Sounds relatively straightforward, right? Well, there is a bit more to this story.

Although Shopify does maintain extensive documentation around the various APIs it operates (such as `https://shopify.dev/tutorials/manage-product-inventory-with-admin-api`, for our inventory example), it's not as easy as it might seem to get that data back. A part of this is due to how those APIs are architected. For example, the Admin API (that sources the inventory levels) only contains a few fields – you have first to query Shopify using a different API to get the location ID, before using that to get your inventory levels! It's worth reading through the documentation thoroughly if you want to develop this feature further; it will help you to work out exactly how to get the data you need, most concisely.

Thinking further afield though, displaying the inventory does raise a question – should we? Okay, I know it might sound a little odd given that we've just done that, but you may feel wary of advertising to rivals just how much stock you hold and whether higher numbers can give an idea of the popularity of a product.

The risk around displaying the inventory value is less of an issue for a larger enterprise, as you will likely go through that stock a lot more quickly than a smaller outfit so that numbers will change dramatically. For smaller traders, it may be more sensible to display a rough indication such as "more than 10 in stock" or "low stock" to reflect what you have – it's an excellent way to hide details from your competitors, without disrupting the customer experience too much!

The one thing to bear in mind – and why I've included this example here – is that we can display a similar inventory level within the cart if so desired; for that it's worth taking a look at the Themes option, available from within your dashboard (Online Store ➤ Themes).

Summary

Adding in an option to check out and pay for goods is momentous for us – we've reached a point where the customer can perform an end-to-end transaction through our site and that from here on in, it's very much about supplementing the experience with additional features! It was something of a meaty chapter, but with good reason – there is a lot to cover when it comes to checkout and payment, but it's all critical to the site. Let's, therefore, take a moment to review what we've covered in this chapter.

We kicked off with a quick look at some of the security concerns we may have with introducing third-party providers; it's not the most enticing of subjects to start with, but it was necessary to ease concerns at the outset. We then explored how we would add the process of checking out and paying into our cart, before constructing the cart and associated components used in the cart.

Next up came the all-important payment processing; we took a look at how to integrate Shopify, before moving on to adding some additional features, such as shipping and taxes. We split off to the side for a moment to quickly cover off a potential change coming later in the book, before swiftly moving on to customizing the cart with three relatively simple changes that we can make to any cart.

Phew, yet another monster chapter! I think I'm getting a reputation for them, although they should give you, my dear reader, plenty to consider! But I wouldn't rest on your laurels for too long – there's plenty more to come. When operating an online retail outlet, it's become almost obligatory to have some form of social media presence; it might be Instagram, Facebook, or Pinterest. There is no reason not to change this, but I'm going to take a slightly more old-school approach: what about adding a blog to our shop? It's a perfect way for readers to get an insight on baking ideas and the like – stay with me, as I cook up (if you pardon the pun) the means to get social on our site...

PART III

CHAPTER 7

Adding a Blog

So far, we've constructed the beginnings of our online store – we still have a way to go before we can release it to the paying public, but that will come with time! However, there is one key element that is missing for us.

Although many e-commerce sites focus on selling products, many will include some form of social contact – a great example is a blog. It adds a personal touch to the whole shopping experience and potentially gives shoppers ideas on what to buy that they may otherwise have not considered.

For this next project, we will look at adding such a blog, focusing on how we can fit it into the shop so that it becomes an integral part of the experience and link to products that customers can buy directly from the site.

Setting the Scene

Okay, so where shall we start?

That's a good question. Let me answer that by setting the scene: we're going to create a simple blog using tools already at our disposal, plus a couple of new ones.

This blog certainly won't break any awards in terms of styling or functionality but will focus on providing a solid ground on which we can build and develop a more fully fleshed-out affair. For this tool, we will, of course, use Gatsby, but this time around, use Markdown as our data source.

At this point, I can hear you ask: why use yet another data source when we already use GraphQL? It's a great point: we could easily use GraphQL, which would be a perfectly acceptable option. However, I would say this: why not use another data source? The creators of Gatsby designed it to consume data from multiple sources, so this should be a walk in the park for the tool. It also gives you a flavor of how we can mix in new functionality to an existing site.

A. Libby, *Gatsby E-Commerce*, https://doi.org/10.1007/978-1-4842-6692-2_7

Okay, enough chitchat. Let's crack on with coding! To give you a flavor for how our site will start to look, take a look at Figure 7-1, which shows a screenshot of the completed blog, with some styling applied.

Figure 7-1. *A screenshot of the finished article*

We have a few steps to work through before we see that for real – the first one is to download and install a couple of plugins that are required to transform Markdown files into content suitable for hosting in the blog.

Installing the Required Plugins

As with any project, we need to start somewhere, so there is no better place than to get and install any plugins we need to construct the blog. Fortunately, there is only one additional plugin we need to install; we will use a second, but this we set up as part of setting up the original site theme (`gatsby-source-filesystem`).

The plugin in question is `gatsby-transformer-remark`; we use it to transform Markdown pages into something we can display as valid pages in our blog. It only takes a handful of steps to get it installed and configured, so let's dive in and take a look at the steps required in more detail.

ADDING THE PLUGINS FOR OUR BLOG

The first step to getting our blog set up is to get the plugins installed – to do this, work through these steps:

1. First, we need to create two new folders to store content – go ahead and create the `assets` and `blog` folders at the root of the `\src` folder in our project area.

2. We have two plugins to install, so crack open a Node.js terminal session, and change the working folder to our project area.

3. Next, enter this command at the prompt, and press Enter:

   ```
   npm install gatsby-transformer-remark gatsby-remark-images
   ```

4. Once we finish installing these two plugins, you can minimize or close the Node.js terminal session – we don't need it for the remainder of this exercise.

5. The next task is to tell Gatsby about the new plugin, plus tweak the configuration for an existing plugin. For this, crack open the `gatsby-config.js` file, and look for this line of code:

   ```
   `gatsby-plugin-react-helmet`,
   ```

6. Immediately below it, add in this block:

```
{
  resolve: `gatsby-source-filesystem`,
  options: {
    path: `${__dirname}/src/assets`,
  },
},
```

7. We have another, similar, block to add in – add this immediately below the code from step 5:

```
{
  resolve: `gatsby-source-filesystem`,
  options: {
    path: `${__dirname}/src/blog`,
  },
},
```

8. With that in place, there is one more block to add in – this configures the newly added gatsby-transformer-remark plugin. Look for this line of code:

```
`gatsby-plugin-sharp`,
```

9. Add in the following code, immediately below the code from step 7:

```
{
  resolve: `gatsby-transformer-remark`,
  options: {
    plugins: [
      {
        resolve: `gatsby-remark-images`,
        options: {
          maxWidth: 800,
        },
      },
    ],
  },
},
```

10. Go ahead and save the file and then close it – we're now ready to add in the source files required to create our blog.

Completing this exercise is a significant step forward – we now have the requisite plugins in place and configured, so we can go ahead with constructing our blog! We've made a few changes in this demo that are key to the success of the blog working, so it's worth us pausing for a moment to review these changes in more detail.

Understanding the Changes

Although we've worked through a few steps in this last exercise, the reality is that much of what we've done is standard fare when it comes to installing NPM-based plugins.

We started by installing two plugins, `gatsby-transformer-remark` and `gatsby-remark-images`. The former we will use to convert Markdown files into a format suitable for our blog, and the latter processes images referenced in those files so that Gatsby can insert them during the build process.

We then ran through several steps to add in resolve references for each plugin, plus two for the (already installed).

This latter plugin needs to take files from several locations (one for posts, another for images); the configuration entries tell it where to look for source files.

Okay, let's crack on: we have the plugins installed, so let's turn our attention to writing the first of our code files – the main blog page.

Creating the Main Blog Page

Okay, so what's next? Well, now that we have the plugins installed and configured, we can crack on with adding in the blog code!

The first step is to update the existing blog.js page we already have on the site; we'll use this to display a summary list of all of the posts created in the blog. In a nutshell, we will replace the existing `blog.js` file in its entirety; let's dive in and make a start on updating this file.

CREATING THE MAIN BLOG PAGE

To create the main blog page, follow these steps:

1. First, crack open a copy of the `blog.js` file in your text editor – the file is in the `\src\components` folder.

2. Highlight and remove all of the code within – the result will look very different from what it is now!

3. Go ahead and add in the following code, which we will do block by block, starting with the necessary component or function imports:

```
import React from "react"
import Sidebar from "./sidebar"
import { Link } from "gatsby"
import { graphql } from 'gatsby'
```

4. We then add in the main default function for this component – leave a line blank after the import statements, and then add in this:

```
export default function Index({ data }) {
  return (

<...INSERT CODE HERE...>

  );
}
```

5. Go ahead and replace `<...INSERT CODE HERE...>` with this constant, to reference all of the Markdown files we will be compiling into the blog:

```
const { edges: posts } = data.allMarkdownRemark;
```

6. This next block takes care of rendering what customers see on-screen; the first part adds in a title and sidebar to the blog summary page:

```
<h1>Blog</h1>
<div style={{ display: 'flex', flexDirection: 'column',
width: '300px' }}>
  <Sidebar
    title="About Author"
```

```
      description="Phasellus a ex scelerisque, cursus mi eu,
      vehicula risus. Ut ac pharetra ipsum. Ut tortor sem,
      laoreet non cursus vel, imperdiet at nisi."
   />
 </div>
```

7. Immediately below this, we need to add in this <div> which iterates through all of the posts to provide the summary list on the page:

```
<div className="blog-posts">
  {posts
    .filter(post => post.node.frontmatter.title.length > 0)
    .map(({ node: post }) => {
      return (
        <div className="blog-post-preview" key={post.id}>
          <h2>
            <Link to={post.frontmatter.path}>{post.frontmatter.
            title}</Link>
          </h2>
          <span className="published">{post.frontmatter.date} by
          {post.frontmatter.author}</span>
          <p>{post.excerpt}</p>
        </div>
      );
    })}
</div>
```

8. There is one more block to add, which is the GraphQL statement that requests the data from our Markdown files – leave a line blank at the end of the Index function, and then add this code:

```
export const pageQuery = graphql`
  query IndexQuery {
    allMarkdownRemark(sort: { order: DESC, fields: [frontmatter___
    date] }) {
      edges {
        node {
          excerpt(pruneLength: 250)
          id
          frontmatter {
```

```
              title
              date(formatString: "MMMM DD, YYYY")
              path
              author
          }
        }
      }
    }
  }
`;
```

9. We need to add in another component, which is the Sidebar; for this, crack open a new file, and add in the following code:

```
import React from "react";

const Sidebar = (props) => (
  <div style={{
    border: '2px solid #e6e6e6',
    width: '200px',
    padding: '0.5rem',
    marginBottom: '25px',
      marginLeft: '50px',
      fontSize: '14px'
  }}>
      <strong style={{ display: 'flex' }}>
        {props.title}.
      </strong>
        {props.description}
    </div>
  );

export default Sidebar
```

10. Go ahead and save this as `sidebar.js` in the `\src\components` folder.

11. Go ahead and extract copies of the `\src\assets` and `\src\blog` folders from the code download that accompanies this book; save them to the root of the `src` folder in our project area.

12. You can close any files still open – the changes are now complete for the main blog page.

We are one step closer to a working blog! Okay, if we run up `gatsby develop` to view the site, you may well find it doesn't show any blog posts.

This lack of posts is to be expected, as we need to make changes to the `gatsby-node.js` file for it to trigger the compilation process for Markdown files. That will come a little later in this chapter, but for now, let's pause for a moment to review the code we've added in as part of this last exercise.

Breaking Apart the Code

This last exercise was a lengthy affair, but necessary – the changes that we've made to the original `blog.js` page are so substantial it's become a new page in its own right!

We started with the usual requisite imports before setting up the placeholder for the Index function that we will export from this component. We then began to add in the code for the blog page – the first addition was to display a Sidebar component to show details about the author of this mini-blog.

We then moved on to adding a container for the blog posts (in the form of blog-posts) before iterating through each Markdown file and mapping the content of them into the relevant fields on-screen. This content took the form of displaying the `post.frontmatter.path` (where the file was stored), the `post.frontmatter.date` (the date of writing the post), the `post.frontmatter.author` value (for the author of the post), and `post.excerpt`, before finishing with a GraphQL query used to return the values from the Markdown files.

We then finished the demo by adding in the code for a new Sidebar component, which we referenced in the `blog.js` page; this we use to render the content about the author on-screen.

Creating the Blog Template

With the main summary page set up and ready for us to use, the next step is to create a template that we can use to display the content for each blog post.

The blog template is a new component; we will use it when we update the gatsby-node.js file to generate the blog post pages automatically a little later in this chapter. Before we do that, let's first take a look at the steps required to set up the template in more detail.

CREATING THE BLOG TEMPLATE

To get the template set up ready for use, follow these steps:

1. Crack open your text editor, and then add the following code to a new file, saving it as blog-template.js in the \src\templates folder. We'll go through it block by block, starting with the requisite declarations:

```
import React from "react";
import Helmet from "react-helmet";
import { graphql } from 'gatsby'

export default function Template({  data }) {
  const post = data.markdownRemark;
```

2. This next block is the main return statement – this is where each blog post will be rendered on-screen to the customer:

```
return (

    <div className="blog-post-container">
     <Helmet title={`HaveCakeEatCake - ${post.frontmatter.title}`} />
     <div className="blog-post">
     <h3>{post.frontmatter.title}</h3>
     <p>published {post.frontmatter.date} by {post.frontmatter.
     author}</p>
     <div className="blog-post-content" dangerouslySetInnerHTML={{
     __html: post.html }} /></div>
    </div>

    );
}
```

3. The final part of this component is the GraphQL query we need to return data
   back from the source Markdown files used to create the posts for this blog:

```
export const pageQuery = graphql`
  query BlogPostByPath($path: String!) {
    markdownRemark(frontmatter: { path: { eq: $path } }) {
      html
        frontmatter {
          date(formatString: "MMMM DD, YYYY")
          path
          title
          author
        }
      }
    }
  `;
```

4. Go ahead and save the file and then close it. The main source files are now in
   place; we will bring it all together in the next exercise.

The exercise we have just completed may have been more straightforward, but it
still plays a critical role in displaying blog content – its part will become apparent very
shortly. It exposes a few key points that are worth understanding in more detail, so let's
break apart the code we've just added and explore it in greater detail.

Understanding the Changes Made

In comparison to other exercises we've completed thus far, this was probably one of
the shortest, yet that doesn't belie the usefulness of this demo! For this demo we've just
worked through, we created a template component to help render the content generated
from the Markdown source files into something we can view on-screen.

We started by importing the usual suspects, such as React and react-helmet (the
latter used to change the title shown in the browser window). We then created a variable
post to store the data retrieved from data.markdownRemark, using the GraphQL query at
the foot of the component. Once retrieved, we iterate through it to display the content in
the relevant field on-screen.

Tying It All Together

With all of the code files in place, we now have one last step, which is to bring it all together. For this, we will use a similar process to one we've already implemented for the product pages, where we used `createPages()` to generate the pages dynamically during compilation.

It is at this point where things will get a little trickier, as we have to combine two GraphQL queries into one but make sure we only call the right one at the right time! We should also bear in mind that this method does have a few drawbacks – we covered many of these earlier in the book. For now, though, let's go ahead and modify the `gatsby-node.js` file to create the blog posts when we compile our site.

UPDATING THE GATSBY-NODE.JS FILE

We have a few steps to implement to update the `gatsby-node.js` file, so let's make a start:

1. First, go ahead and open the file in your text editor – it's at the root of the project folder.

2. Look for this line, `const { createPage } = actions`, then leave a line blank under it, and then add in this const value:

    ```
    const blogPostTemplate = path.resolve(`src/templates/blog-
    template.js`);
    ```

3. A little further down, you will see this line of code: `allShopifyProduct {`. Modify this line as indicated:

    ```
    {
      shopify: allShopifyProduct {
        edges {
    ```

4. Immediately below this block

    ```
        node {
          handle
        }
      }
    }
    ```

    …add in this GraphQL query:

```
blog: allMarkdownRemark( sort: { order: DESC, fields: [frontmatter___
date] }
      limit: 1000
    ) {
      edges {
        node {
          excerpt(pruneLength: 250)
          html
          id
          frontmatter {
            date
            path
            title
            author
          }
        }
      }
    }
```

The following code extract shows how the GraphQL query should slot into our code:

```
return graphql(`
  {
    shopify: allShopifyProduct {
      edges {
        node {
          handle {
          }
        }
      }
    }
  blog: allMarkdownRemark(
    sort: { order: DESC, fields: [frontmatter__date]    }
    limit: 1000
) {
    edges {
```

5. Scroll down toward the bottom of the page, and look for the line starting `result.data.allShopifyProduct`. Replace the word `allShopifyProduct` with `shopify`, as indicated:

```
result.data.shopify.edges.forEach(({ node }) => {
```

6. Next, look for the closing brackets of the `result.data...` block. Leave a blank line, and then add in this:

```
result.data.blog.edges.forEach(({ node }) => {
  createPage({
    path: `${node.frontmatter.path}`,
    component: blogPostTemplate,
    context: {}, // additional data can be passed via context
  });
});
```

7. As the last step, add in this `Promise.reject` block, immediately below the line `if (result.errors) {`, which is after the end of the GraphQL query:

```
if (result.errors) {
  return Promise.reject(result.errors);
}
```

8. Go ahead and save the file – you can close it, as changes are now complete for this file.

The gatsby-node.js file can be tricky to work with; if we don't add in the GraphQL query correctly, then we might find some odd errors appearing. Blog posts may be listed, but clicking through to them doesn't operate, for example! We've covered some useful tricks in this last exercise, so let's pause for a moment to review the changes we've made to the gatsby-node.js file for our blog.

Exploring the Changes

This last exercise was the most critical to get right – it is where we dynamically generate each of the blog posts, using a similar process to that which we did for the product pages earlier in this book.

We started by adding in a variable `blogPostTemplate` to store the location of the template file used to create the blog posts, before tweaking the GraphQL queries used by Shopify and what will be our blog. The core queries themselves didn't change; we added a tag to help identify them when Gatsby runs the queries during the processing stage.

Next up came the addition of a new `.forEach` block to iterate through each source Markdown file and send the relevant fields for rendering in the blog template. We then rounded it out by adding a `Promise.reject` block to show any errors should the process fail during compilation.

It's important to note that we built this process into a `promise` block; this prevents Gatsby from trying to create the pages if the initial GraphQL queries return errors or no content.

Okay, let's crack on: we now have the basics of our blog in place, so the next task is to see how it runs! Before we do that, though, we need to add in a handful of additional style rules so that content is at least presentable on-screen! This change is a quick task to complete, so let's dive in and take a look.

Styling the Blog Pages

This next section is one where we could go to town with adding styles – yet, we're only going to add a handful! What gives?

Well, the simple answer is that there is nothing special about adding styles to a Gatsby project; we've already set up a style sheet in the form of `global.scss` that uses Sass to process the rules into valid CSS styles.

Once we've added in enough to give us a good grounding, we can then apply different styles in the same way – that is something I will leave for you to do later as a challenge! Bringing things back to reality, let's quickly dive in and add the necessary styles to reformat the content on our page.

STYLING THE BLOG

We won't go into adding lots of styling in this demo, but enough to complement what is already present in each component and on the `blog.js` page and template:

1. We'll start by cracking open the `global.scss` file in the `\src\styles\` folder – scroll to the bottom of the file, and then add in this code:

    ```
    .published { font-size: 14px; font-style: italic; }
    .blog-post-preview h2, .blog-post h3 { margin-bottom: 0; }
    .blog-post-preview h2 a { text-decoration: none; }

    .blog-post-preview h2 a:hover { text-decoration: underline; }
    .blog-post-preview p, .blog-post p { margin-top: 15px; }
    ```

2. Save the file – that's all. Sorry if you were expecting more code! You can close the file – we no longer need it for this exercise.

3. The last step is to preview the results of our work – for this, revert to or fire up a Node.js terminal session, and change the working folder to our project area.

4. At the prompt, enter `gatsby develop` and press Enter. Gatsby will go away and load the development server – when prompted, you can view the site at `http://localhost:8000`. Try clicking the blog link in the navigation; if all is well, we should have something akin to this screenshot (Figure 7-2).

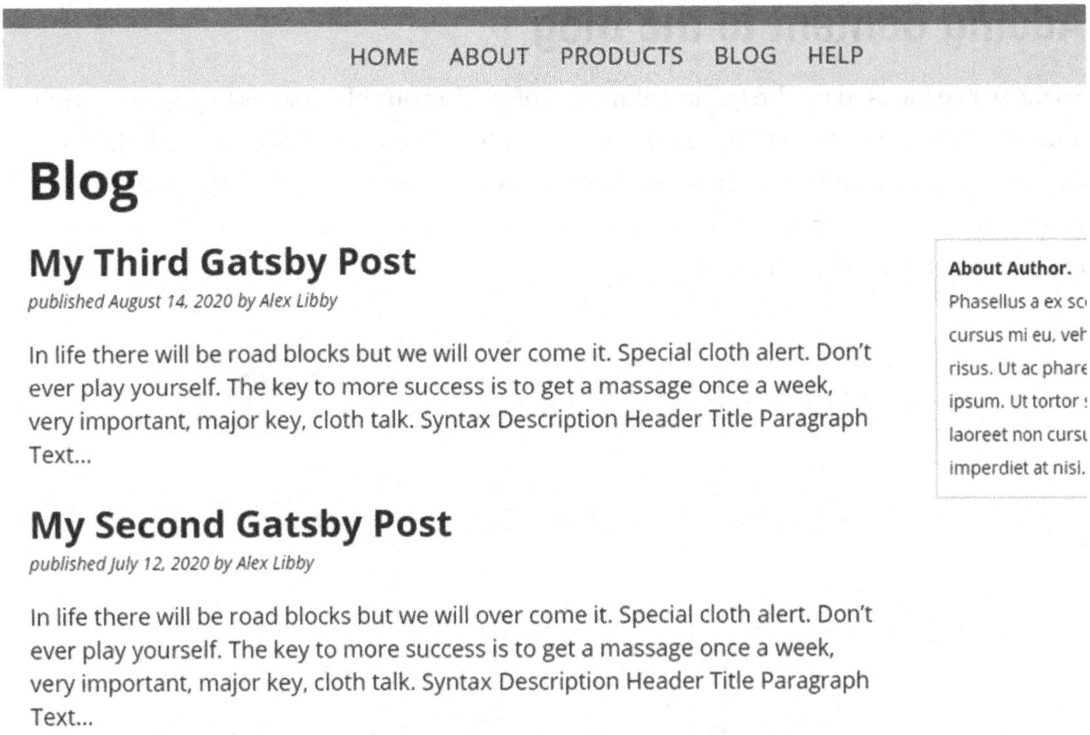

HOME   ABOUT   PRODUCTS   BLOG   HELP

Blog

My Third Gatsby Post
published August 14, 2020 by Alex Libby

In life there will be road blocks but we will over come it. Special cloth alert. Don't ever play yourself. The key to more success is to get a massage once a week, very important, major key, cloth talk. Syntax Description Header Title Paragraph Text...

My Second Gatsby Post
published July 12, 2020 by Alex Libby

In life there will be road blocks but we will over come it. Special cloth alert. Don't ever play yourself. The key to more success is to get a massage once a week, very important, major key, cloth talk. Syntax Description Header Title Paragraph Text...

About Author.

Phasellus a ex sc
cursus mi eu, veh
risus. Ut ac phare
ipsum. Ut tortor :
laoreet non cursu
imperdiet at nisi.

Figure 7-2. *Our (unstyled) blog summary list*

Excellent, we now have all of the basics in place; this last exercise was a quick one, to add in the final styles needed to make our content look at least presentable. At the same time, we did a quick check to see how it looked in a browser; we could have used Netlify, but the command `gatsby develop` is sufficient for us. The styles are local, and there is no need to satisfy conditions such as testing in a secure environment (as we might have otherwise needed with Netlify!)

Let's move on: the next stage is to explore how we can add content to our blog. This is something we've already (in part) done. It's a good point, though, to review how we should do this in a little more detail to help understand the journey from Markdown source files through to valid posts in our blog.

Adding Content to the Blog

So far, we've focused on the technical means of getting our blog pages to appear – what about writing the content? This book isn't about the ins and outs of writing Markdown, but it's still worth spending a few moments to review how the example files were prepared at a very high level. Let's use the second-post as an example, as this has several useful Markdown fields within it.

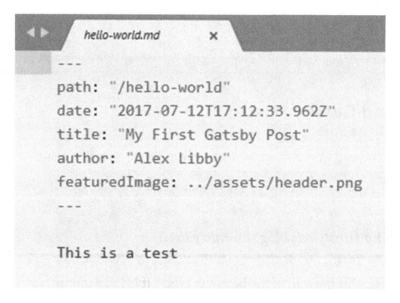

Figure 7-3. *Example headings from a Markdown source file*

Here, we've specified five in total, namely, the source path, date, title, author, and main header (or featured) image. These are all enclosed in two dividing lines made up of three hyphens – as long as we follow this format for each Markdown file, then it stands a chance of being processed into a valid blog post for our site.

In this example, we can reference all of these fields in React using the format `post.frontmatter.XXXXX`, where `frontmatter` is the content in the markdown header and XXXXX represents the field you want to retrieve, such as `post.frontmatter.title` for the title. As soon as we save the Markdown file into the blog folder, it is processed – you will see the summary appear in the blog listing on our site.

The only provision is that if we add in additional fields, we must include these as fields in the queries within blog.js, gatsby-config.js, and blog-template.js. Otherwise, we will see errors where GraphQL tries to query nonexistent fields!

If you would like to learn more about how to format text for Markdown, then I would refer to a site such as the Markdown Cheat Sheet, available at `www.markdownguide.org/cheat-sheet`.

Adding content is just part of the picture, though. As everyone knows, pictures speak a thousand words; we need to add some visual content in too! It is straightforward to do; let's take a look at the steps involved in more detail.

Adding Images to the Blog

Take another look at one of the front matter blocks in our demo Markdown files – noticed the use of `featuredImage` entries there?

You may have also noticed that when we updated the code on Netlify, only some of these images were coming through; in-line ones would be OK, but not the `featuredImage` ones.

Fortunately, this is easy to fix: we need to amend the GraphQL queries in use in three files. Before we work on that, let's quickly cover off how we import images from the body of the text into our blog pages. Deep in the Markdown of `second-post`, we have this in-line image command:

```
![Hopper The Rabbit](../assets/gatsby.png)
```

When adding images, we need to use the format `![name of the image, used as alt tag](physical location of the image, as a relative URL)`. We then use this configuration option to render the images:

```
{
  resolve: `gatsby-transformer-remark`,
  options: {
    plugins: [
      {
        resolve: `gatsby-remark-images`,
```

```
        options: {
          maxWidth: 800,
        },
      },
    ],
  },
},
```

We use the `gatsby-transformer-remark` plugin to render the Markdown, while gatsby-remark (passed in as an option) turns image markdown into real images. This latter plugin does three things:

- Adds an elastic container to hold the image, preventing layout jumping

- Creates multiple versions of images at different sizes – it uses srcset and image sizes to load the correct image, depending on the size of the browser window/platform

- Blurs up the image on the initial load with a small 20 px wide image used as a placeholder until the browser downloads the real image

Okay, theory aside. Let's crack on with updating our code to complete the image support for our blog.

FINISHING SUPPORT FOR FEATURED IMAGES

To complete the image support, work through these steps:

1. First, open up a copy of `blog.js` in your text editor, and then look for the author entry in the GraphQL query toward the bottom of the page:

   ```
   date(formatString: "MMMM DD, YYYY")
   path
   ```
   author

2. Immediately below it, insert this entry:

   ```
   featuredImage {
     childImageSharp {
       fluid(maxWidth: 960) {
   ```

```
        src
        srcSet
        aspectRatio
        sizes
        base64
      }
    }
  }
```

3. It should look something akin to this code extract:

```
author
featuredImage {
  childImageSharp {
    fluid(maxWidth: 960) {
      src
      srcSet
      aspectRatio
      sizes
      base64
    }
  }
}
```

4. Save the file and close it – the change is complete for this file.

5. We also need to update `gatsby-node.js`; go ahead and repeat steps 1–4, remembering to save the file once we complete the changes.

6. We have a couple more changes to make in `blog-template.js`. Crack this open in your text editor, and then add in this line immediately below the one beginning with `<span className=" published"...>`:

```
<Img fluid={featuredImgFluid} />
```

7. We also need to import the Gatsby Image plugin, so go ahead and add this line in, immediately below the last import statement at the top of your file:

```
import Img from "gatsby-image"
```

8. Go ahead and save and close any files open – the changes are now complete.

> At this point, you can either update the code on Netlify (see the previous exercise) or rerun `gatsby develop` at the command line; either will show the updated content. It's essential to rerun `gatsby develop` (or `gatsby build`), as we've edited the `gatsby-node.js` file; any changes made to it do not take effect until either process is rerun.

This particular exercise is something of a double-edged sword; adding several fields to a GraphQL should be easy enough, but it can easily trip us up if we don't get the brackets in the right place!

In this instance, the changes we made were small; it involved merely adding in the featuredImage reference. It is an object reference, so we needed to include `fluid` (to make the image responsive), as well as details such as the `src` location, `aspectRatio,` and `sizes` values. A great way to help make sure your code is correct is to use the GraphiQL editor at `http://localhost:8000/__graphiql`; the Prettify function will soon tell you if the code isn't right!

Refining Our Blog: Taking Things Further

We are almost at the end of this chapter on creating a blog for our site, but I want to leave you with hopefully an answer to at least one question I am sure you will ask at some point: where do we go from here?

It's a great question – to which I could give you a short answer, "The world is your oyster!" For those of you not familiar with that saying, it translates as being you are only limited by your imagination. Yes, it might sound like a cop-out, but that is not what I intended! It is up to you how you want to proceed – to give you a starter, here are a few ideas to whet your appetite:

- We've included some basic styles to make the page look a little more presentable, but what about taking this further? After all, you don't want your blog to look dull, so anything to give it visual impact will be of benefit. You could easily update the individual components to use CSS-in-JS-based styling, but I would start by using classic CSS and tagging it onto the end of the `global.scss` file. Sure, it's not Sass, but that doesn't matter for now: as long as it is syntactically correct, Sass will still compile it into valid CSS.

- What about adding SEO measures? SEO is, of course, essential for the survival of your blog (and site), so adding it is a must. You could make use of the SEO component that comes with most Gatsby starter themes as a starting point and then develop it further once you get it established.

- Any blog worth its salt should have a short bio for the author; I've added in something as a placeholder, but what about adding an image and making the content a little more dynamic? For our example, it would be better to put it in the DatoCMS setup, or potentially the native GraphQL that comes with Gatsby, rather than Markdown – it keeps the content separate.

- A feature we've not added in is next or previous links or a back to homepage link for that matter – check out the article on Medium by Aman Mittal, at `https://medium.com/crowdbotics/how-to-build-your-own-blog-from-scratch-with-gatsbyjs-graphql-react-and-markdown-78352c367bd1` for an example you could adapt for your purposes.

- Although we've created our blog from scratch, there are two or three components available in a Gatsby starter theme at `https://github.com/gatsbyjs/gatsby/tree/master/starters/blog/src/components` – it might be worth trying these out.

- We've focused on just rendering content from our blogs on-screen, but what about really going to town and starting to mix in content from Shopify too? Granted, it's not the easiest to manipulate, but you can at least add in links and images to products, so the pages have content that provides a call to action within the pages.

These are just a few ideas to help get you started and give you something to consider adding to your blog; Gatsby is infinitely versatile, so it is up to you (and your customer's requirements) as to where you want to take your social media presence!

Summary

One of the great things about Gatsby is that it was written using React; this makes it so versatile as it can harness the power of one of the world's most familiar tools. It is no more valid than with creating blogs; although we've only touched the surface of what is possible, we can use this as a basis for developing something more refined for production use. Before we get to that stage, though, let's take a moment to review what we've covered thus far in this chapter.

We began by setting the scene with a quick look at how we would build our blog, as well as previewing how the final article would look. We then moved on to installing the requisite plugins before turning our attention to updating the existing blog.js file to form the basis for our new blog.

Next up, we added in the blog template to display our content on-screen, before tying it all together with changes to the gatsby-node and gatsby-config files. We then rounded out the chapter with a look at how we added in images and content, before exploring some ideas to help you develop the blog into something more suitable for production use.

Phew, we come to the end of another intensive chapter, but certainly not the end of the book! We have the basics all in place. "So what's next?" I hear you ask. Well, now's an excellent time to refine what we have and add in missing features, such as localization, SEO support, and the like. There are plenty of finishing touches we can add to our site as a whole – stay with me, and we work through a few of them in the next chapter.

CHAPTER 8

Finessing the Site

We've gotten everything in place. Our site is running and we have products available for sale, so is there anything missing? At this stage, I am sure there will be: before we can test our site, now is an excellent opportunity to consider finessing the user experience.

I can think of at least four topics to get us started; how about considering SEO, providing language support, and considering any plugins that might enhance the experience? Throughout this chapter, we will explore a handful of mini-projects to fine-tune the experience for customers and work toward adding a little more polish to our site. We've already mentioned three – let's start with arguably the most important, enabling support for SEO on our website.

Before starting on any project, I would recommend taking a backup copy of the site for safekeeping – you can safely exclude `.cache`, `.git`, and the `node_modules` folders. We can reinstate these very quickly using different methods, so backups are not required.

Implementing SEO

If three letters could incite fear in oneself, they could well be S, E, and O. Anyone who spends any time developing sites will, of course, recognize these as referring to SEO, or **Search Engine Optimization.**

SEO is critical to the success of any site – it can be the difference between search engines (and therefore customers) finding your website and you making money and being lost in a sea of websites. Not only is it something of an ongoing battle but we also have to think of that behemoth of a search engine, aka Google! Adding in advanced SEO capabilities falls outside of the scope of this book, but thankfully Gatsby makes it very easy for us to add in a basic level of support.

© Alex Libby 2021
A. Libby, *Gatsby E-Commerce*, https://doi.org/10.1007/978-1-4842-6692-2_8

To do so requires us to create a new component; you may find that if you use an existing starter theme (as we have done), this task isn't necessary. If so, we just need to add a reference to call that component in on every page we create – to see how, let's take a look at the next demo.

ADDING SEO CAPABILITIES

Let's make a start with adding in SEO capabilities to our site – I will assume you have the site running at this point. You also need to run this demo in Chrome to be able to complete the last exercise point:

1. First, stop the Gatsby development server if it is active – for this, press Ctrl+C (for Windows/Linux) or Cmd+C (for Mac).

2. Go ahead and check your project folder – if you do not have a copy of a file called seo.js in \src\components\, then extract a copy of the file from the code download that accompanies this book. If you have one, then you can skip this step.

3. Next, we need to update gatsby-config.js – for this, crack open the file, and modify it as highlighted:

```
module.exports = {
  siteMetadata: {
    title: 'Have Cake, Eat Cake',
    description: 'A demo cake store, built using Gatsby, DatoCMS,
    Netlify and Shopify',
    author: 'Alex Libby',
    url: `https://www.havecakeeatcake.com`,
    twitterUsername: `@havecakeeatcake`
  },
```

4. This next bit gets a little more complicated – we need to update each of the pages to reflect the addition of the SEO component. We'll start with terms.js – go ahead and open it in your text editor.

5. Next, add in this line at the top of the file, before any code:

```
import SEO from "../components/seo"
```

6. Scroll down until you get to the opening bracket at the end of the const declaration – add in the highlighted lines as indicated:

```
const TermsPage = () => (
```

```
<SEO title="Terms and Conditions" keywords={['gatsby', 'application',
'react']} />
```

7. We also need to add a closing React fragment, so do this just before the closing }.

8. We need to repeat this for the remaining pages – use the same steps, but this time swap out the existing text for those shown in the following:

Name of Page	Code Line to Use to Replace Existing Code
products.js	`<SEO title="Products" keywords={['gatsby', 'application', 'react']} />`
help.js	`<SEO title="Help" keywords={['gatsby', 'application', 'react']} />`
gifts.js	`<SEO title="Gifts" keywords={['gatsby', 'application', 'react']} />`
delivery.js	`<SEO title="Delivery" keywords={['gatsby', 'application', 'react']} />`
about.js	`<SEO title="About Us" keywords={['gatsby', 'application', 'react']} />`
blog.js	`<SEO title="Blog" keywords={['gatsby', 'application', 'react']} />`
cart.js	`<SEO title="Cart" keywords={['gatsby', 'application', 'react']} />`
404.js	Replace the existing line with this: `<SEO title="404: Not Found" keywords={['gatsby', 'application', 'react']} />`

Omit `sidebar.js`; this is a component that sits within a page, so we do not need to update it.

9. We've completed the changes, so it's time to restart the Gatsby server. Switch to the Node.js terminal session from earlier or crack open a new one, and make sure the working folder is our project area.

10. At the prompt, enter `gatsby develop` and press Enter – wait for it to prompt that we can view the site, via `http://localhost:8000`.

11. At this stage, we're going to run a Lighthouse audit to confirm that SEO has now been enabled (albeit needing a tweak). Browse to any page of your choice – I will assume the use of `about.js`, but you can choose another if you prefer.

12. Bring up the Developer Console by pressing Ctrl/Cmd+Shift+I, and then switch to the Lighthouse tab. Make sure that Desktop is selected, and then click the Generate report button.

13. When completed, you will see a report appear – we're interested in the SEO part, which will look similar to the screenshot shown in Figure 8-1.

SEO

These checks ensure that your page is optimized for search engine results ranking. There are additional factors Lighthouse does not check that may affect your search ranking. Learn more.

Crawling and Indexing — To appear in search results, crawlers need access to your app.

⚠ robots.txt is not valid — 1 error found ⌄

Figure 8-1. *SEO enabled on our site, ready for customization*

That might have seemed like a longer than normal exercise, but in reality, the change we've implemented is very straightforward – adding in references to a new SEO component. The trouble is it is only scratching the surface of what we can do – to take it further would require the services of someone well-versed in the intricacies of SEO! That said, it does raise some important points, so let's take a look at the changes we've made in closer detail.

Exploring the Code in More Detail

Adding in SEO capabilities to any site is crucial to help with ranking and performance in search engines; adding a basic component or plugin takes minutes, but fine-tuning it is a much longer process! We've focused on the former in this last exercise, on the basis that fine-tuning it would be something we would do post–go live.

We started by adding a copy of the SEO plugin code from the code download that accompanies this book (`seo.js`); this is Gatsby's starter SEO plugin and provides a good base for us to fine-tune the configuration at a later date. Next up, we then updated the `gatsby-config.js` file to add some new metadata properties that our plugin would use before importing it into various pages on the site.

To round out the exercise, we restarted the Gatsby development server (essential when editing `gatsby-config.js`) before running the Lighthouse audit from within Chrome to get a feel for how our page SEO stands with the addition of this component.

We will cover the use of Lighthouse more extensively in Chapter 9 when we start to optimize our site ready for production use.

To see the addition of the metadata (in all its glory), we should check in the console log area of our browser – a quick look at my version shows tags appearing, as indicated in Figure 8-2.

```
<meta name="description" content="A demo cake store, built using Gatsby, DatoCMS, Net]
"true">
<meta property="og:title" content="Home" data-react-helmet="true">
<meta property="og:description" content="A demo cake store, built using Gatsby, DatoCN
helmet="true">
<meta property="og:type" content="website" data-react-helmet="true">
<meta name="twitter:card" content="summary" data-react-helmet="true">
<meta name="twitter:creator" content="Alex Libby" data-react-helmet="true">
<meta name="twitter:title" content="Home" data-react-helmet="true">
```

Figure 8-2. *Verifying that SEO metadata is now displayed*

Looking further afield, this isn't the end of the story though. To take things further, I would recommend checking out the blog posts on the Gatsby website for SEO – you can find them at www.gatsbyjs.com/blog/tags/seo/. The posts provide a wealth of information around how to configure Gatsby for SEO; it shouldn't act as a replacement for standard SEO practice, but complement the basics that any SEO expert would recommend.

> Gatsby also provides an intriguing section on SEO for their framework – the documentation at `www.gatsbyjs.com/docs/seo/` is worth a read too!

Although we will explore using Lighthouse more in Chapter 9, there is one topic I want to cover: adding in metadata tags, using the JSON-LD (JavaScript Object Notation for Linked Data) format.

This format is a useful way to add in data such as contact details to the DOM so that Google can better understand the structure of the page when it comes to crawling its content. Let's take a quick look at how this would work in more detail.

Adding in Metadata

Google uses various methods to crawl and index data, to make it available in search engines – one of these methods is to use snippets of structured data. This method we can do using JSON-LD data; such a code example would look like this:

```
<Helmet>
  <script type="application/ld+json">
    {'
      {
        "@context": "https://schema.org",
        "@type": "Organization",
        "url": "https://www.havecakeeatcake.com",
        "name": "HaveCakeEatCake",
        "contactPoint": {
          "@type": "ContactPoint",
          "telephone": "+1-800-765-4321",
          "contactType": "Customer Support"
        }
      }
    '}
  </script>
</Helmet>
```

In this instance, we're adding it in using the React Helmet plugin; as Gatsby is a server-side rendered framework, the plugin will insert the data into the correct place on the page for us.

This type of change would be ideal for inclusion into a Contact Us–type page, such as the one we have on our site. It will help search engines better understand your content and ultimately improve the page's ranking in search results. Just something to consider, particularly if you have to battle Google and the intricacies of SEO!

Okay, let's crack on: we have plenty more to cover! For our next project, there is one topic we absolutely should cover in this age of global e-commerce: adding comments.

If I had a dollar for every time someone said content (and feedback) is king, I would be a rich man by now! In all seriousness, though, feedback is essential to the survival of any site. It's an opportunity for our customers to give their thoughts on various topics, such as service, their experience of ordering, and the like. Whether they give feedback constructively or negatively, that is a different matter…

Adding Comments

But I digress. For our next project, we will add the Disqus commenting system to our site. Gatsby won't allow for comments to be added manually on a server-side rendered site, so we need to use a third-party system such as Disqus. Disqus is hosted externally, so won't cause a problem in this respect – it only requires a handful of changes, so let's dive in and take a look at how to set up Disqus in more detail.

PART 1: ADDING COMMENTS

To add a comment system to our site, follow these steps:

1. The first task is to sign up for an account at `www.disqus.com`. As part of this process, you will need to choose a site name – keep this name safe, as you will need it later in this exercise.

2. Click Sign Up, and then enter your name, email address, and password – go ahead and tick checkboxes as directed/preferred (the last one is not compulsory!)

3. On the next page, click I want to install Disqus on my site.

4. When prompted, enter your name in the Site owner field.

5. Next, enter your website name, and then select business as the Category.

6. We will use the free Basic plan for now – click Basic and then click Subscribe now.

7. When prompted, click Create Site.

The account is now created; we don't need to get the code for the comment form from the site, as this we will handle in the next part of this exercise, by use of a Gatsby plugin. There are a fair few steps involved in this next part, so have a breather and get a drink, and when you're ready, let's continue with the next part of this demo.

PART 2: ADDING COMMENTS IN THE BLOG

Now that we have a Disqus account set up, we need to configure our blog to use it – for that, follow these steps:

1. First, crack open a Node.js terminal session, and change the working folder to our project area – at the prompt, enter `npm install disqus-react` and press Enter.

2. NPM will go away and install the Disqus package for React; once done, open your text editor.

3. Next, go ahead and open your `.production.env` file and add this statement to the end of the file, where XXXXX is the name you gave your Disqus site/account back in part 1:

```
GATSBY_DISQUS_NAME=XXXXX
```

4. Repeat step 3, but this time, add the same line to your .development.env file as well – this makes sure Disqus is available to operate in both your development and production environments.

5. Next, open the blog-template file from the `\src\templates\` folder, and add in this line immediately after the last import statement at the top of the file:

```
import { DiscussionEmbed } from "disqus-react"
```

I would recommend leaving a blank line after it and before the initial export statement, for readability.

6. Scroll down a bit, and add in this block of code immediately before the `let featuredImage...` statement – leave a line after this block of code and that `let` statement:

```
const post = data.markdownRemark;

  const disqusConfig = {
    shortname: process.env.GATSBY_DISQUS_NAME,
    config: { identifier: post.id },
  }
```

7. A little further down, go ahead and add in this line before the closing React fragment, as indicated:

```
<DiscussionEmbed {...disqusConfig} />
```

8. Go ahead and save all open files and then close them – we've completed the changes needed for this exercise.

9. At this point, we should be able to view the comment block. For this, switch to your Node.js terminal session, and then at the prompt, enter `gatsby develop` and press Enter.

10. Browse to `http://localhost:8000` in your browser – if all is well, we should see something akin to the screenshot in Figure 8-3.

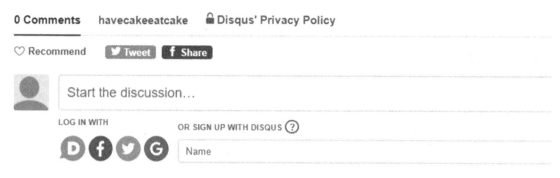

Figure 8-3. *The addition of a Disqus comment block to a post on our site*

Adding comments is an essential step to engaging with our customer base – it allows them to communicate with us, and leaving a comment can be far more powerful than just sending another email! We've worked through several steps to enable this facility, so let's take a moment to explore the changes in more detail.

Understanding the Changes Made

So we've explored the importance of adding comments, but how did we manage it technically? Well, as we saw, it required a few steps – let's work through them.

We started by signing up for an account on the Disqus website – as part of this, we took note of the site/account name that we used when creating the account. Next up, we then ran through the plugin's installation – for the most part, this uses the same process as any other NPM plugin.

The real change comes from configuring our site to use the Disqus plugin; the first change required us to add a value to two .env files before updating the blog-template. js file to insert a call to the Disqus comment system. We then rounded out the demo by rebuilding the content as a production-optimized version; we confirmed it worked by browsing to the site so that we could view it in all its glory.

With our comment system set up, let's move on to our next project: as a change, this one will be simpler, as a break from the last two monster changes we've made! Every site should have a sitemap to help Google find and index our content – let's take a look in more detail at how to configure it for use in our site.

Setting Up a Sitemap

Adding a sitemap in Gatsby is easy to do, as we can use the Gatsby sitemap plugin that takes care of everything; it's hosted at www.gatsbyjs.com/plugins/gatsby-plugin-sitemap/. We need to install it and add a reference to it in our `gatsby-config.js` file. Let's take a look at how, as part of the next exercise.

ADDING A SITEMAP

To get the sitemap plugin set up and configured, follow these steps:

1. First, crack open a Node.js terminal session, and then change the working folder to our project area.

2. At the prompt, enter `npm install gatsby-plugin-sitemap` and press Enter.

3. Next, switch to your text editor, and open your `gatsby-config.js` file.

4. Go ahead and add in the following highlighted lines – your `package.json` should look similar to this:

   ```
   url: 'https://www.havecakeeatcake.com',
   twitterUsername: '@havecakeeatcake',
   siteUrl: 'http://havecakeeatcake.com'
   },
   plugins: [
     'gatsby-plugin-sitemap',
     'gatsby-plugin-react-helmet',
   ```

5. Go ahead and save and then close the file – the change is complete.

6. Switch to your Node.js terminal session, and then at the prompt, enter gatsby build and press Enter.

7. If all is well, we should see a sitemap generated – you can see proof of this in Figure 8-4.

Figure 8-4. *The addition of a sitemap to our site*

A nice simple change, I'm sure you will agree! It may be a simple change, but an important one; it will help Google rank our site better in its search listings. We started by running through the installation, which is standard for any NPM package; we then added a reference to it from the `gatsby-config.js` file to tell Gatsby to use it during the build process.

An important point is that the sitemap plugin works when running in production mode only – you won't see it if you are in development mode.

Okay, let's crack on: the next project is all about communication, specifically from our customers. Yes, it's time to add in that ubiquitous contact form; given we render content server-side, how would we go about adding in such a form? I wonder.

Adding a Contact Form

Before we delve into the intricacies of how we will architect our form, I want to ask a question: hands up anyone who has come across a site that does not have some way for customers to contact them?

Providing a contact mechanism is essential for all sites, as customers will want to get hold of you at some point. It doesn't matter why; every question or request should be treated with the same importance, no matter how stupid it might be! I know companies do provide such a contact form but make it so hard to get to it that it's almost as bad as not providing one....but I digress!

Anyway, bringing things back to reality. We need something, but as Gatsby is rendered server-side, how can we add it? Well, Gatsby lists three options on its site to get us started – they are

- **Getform** – `https://getform.io/`

- **Netlify Forms** – `www.netlify.com/docs/form-handling/`

- **Formspree** – `https://formspree.io/`

For this book, I've elected to use Formspree, as it is free and can run independently of any architecture we use. If we needed to move the code, it would be easier, as it is architecturally platform-agnostic. With this in mind, let's look at how we can add a simple form as a starting point for our website.

ADDING A CONTACT US FORM

To set up a form using Formspree, follow these steps:

1. The first step is to register a new account at `https://formspree.io/` – you will need to verify your email address as part of the registration.

2. Once registered, click New Form.

3. In the Name field, enter Contact Us, and then click Create.

4. For the Send emails to field, add your email address.

5. Copy the value in the Your form's endpoint is… field – this is your form on Formspree, and we will use the value in our site.

6. Next, go ahead and extract a copy of `ContactForm.js` from the code download and save it to the `\src\components` folder.

7. Crack that file open in your editor, and then look for this line: `action=https://formspree.io/XXXXX`. Replace the XXXXX with the value from step 5.

8. Next, we need to create a contact us page – there is a copy on the code download that accompanies this book. Extract `contactus.js`, and save it to the \src\pages folder.

9. We need to add a link to our navigation. For this, crack open sitenavigation.js in your editor and add this link in immediately before the closing `</div>`, thus:

```
<Link to="/contactus/">Contact Us</Link>
</div>
```

It doesn't follow the same format, but this is just a temporary measure to prove it works – we will update this shortly.

---

10. Save and close the file.

11. The contact form by itself won't look great, so to fix that, let's add in some basic formatting – add in these styles to the bottom of `styles.scss`:

```
/***** CONTACT FORM ******/
.contactform { display: flex; flex-direction: column;  width: 50%; }

.contactform label:nth-child(2) {
   margin-bottom: 10px; }

.contactform input:nth-child(4) { height: 150px;  margin-bottom: 10px; }

.contactform p { background-color: #00ff00; color: #ffffff; padding:
10px; }
```

12. Go ahead and save this file. Revert to a Node.js terminal session (or open a new one), and change the working folder to our project area.

13. At the prompt, enter gatsby develop and press Enter; if all is well, we should see our new form appear once we've restarted the server and content rebuilt (Figure 8-5).

Contact Us

Lorem ipsum dolor sit amet, consectetur adipiscing elit. Pelle
sapien massa imperdiet dolor, non sodales sapien augue ac

Email:

Message:

Submit

Figure 8-5. *The newly created form*

14.   Make sure all files still open are closed – this completes the exercise.

Phew, that exercise might have seemed a little on the long side, but at least we now have the option available for our customers to get hold of us! Adding the form is a straightforward affair when using a service such as Formspree.

It takes care of most of the hard work for us, leaving us to create a suitable page to host it (`contactus.js`) and add a preconfigured form (`contactform.js`) as a component to our site. Let's pause to review the code in more detail before we crack on with the next part of this mini-project.

Reviewing the Code in Detail

This last demo was a simple exercise, for which Formspree had done a lot of the work for us already; we simply had to drop in the prepared code, update the form action, and link it into our site. So what did we do?

We began by registering a new account with Formspree; we used the default settings for now, but we could expand this at a later date. We then added a copy of the preprepared contactform.js component from the code download before updating the form action with the URL generated from the Formspree account.

Next up, we then added a copy of the contactus.js page from the code download; this follows a similar format to the other pages on our site. For the last task, we tweaked the styling of the form to make it look more presentable, before rebuilding the content and viewing the results on-screen.

Before we move to our next mini-project, there is one update we should do – remember how we hard-coded the Contact Us URL in the navigation? It was purely to test it works; it would look better if we were pulling data from our data source in DatoCMS. Let's fix that now, as part of the next exercise.

Updating the Link

Everything should look okay at this point, right? After all, we have a form in place; it submits to our chosen email address and looks presentable on the page... There is one thing left to do, though.

"What's that?" I hear you ask. Well, if you remember, we took a shortcut to add in the Contact Us link in the navigation; part of the reason for this was that it required quite a few steps to update our data source, which would have made for a lengthy exercise! It wasn't essential in the short term to prove if our page was accessible; now that it is in place, let's rectify this omission by adding in the correctly formatted link.

UPDATING THE CONTACT US MENU LINK

Updating the link requires us to add in two data fields into the DatoCMS source from earlier, plus update `sitenavigation.js` – to do so, follow these steps:

1. First, log into our DatoCMS project at `https://XXXXX.admin.datocms.com/sign_in`.

2. Next, click the Navigation entry on the left and then Home.

3. In the top-left corner, you will see `Edit Navigation navigation`; click the **lowercase** instance of navigation to begin editing the data structure.

4. Click Add new field, then Text, and then Single-line string.

5. In the field displayed, enter Contact Us as the title.

6. Change Field ID to `contact_us_text`, and then click Save field.

7. Repeat steps 4–6, but use Contact Us Link as the ID. Click Save field when done.

8. Click Go to content editing and then click Home.

9. Scroll down to the Contact Us field, and then enter Contact Us as the text.

10. In the Contact Us Link field, add /contactus/.

11. Click Save, and then revert to your text editor.

12. Open sitenavigation.js, and then replace the hard-coded link we added in the previous exercise with this:

```
<Link to={'${data.datoCmsNavigation.ContactUsLink}'}>
{data.datoCmsNavigation.ContactUsText}</Link>
```

13. At the same time, update GraphQL query as highlighted:

```
        productsLink
        helpText
        helpLink
        contactUsText
        contactUsLink
      }
    }
  ')
```

14. Save the file; then restart the Gatsby develop server by entering gatsby develop in the Node.js terminal session and pressing Enter.

15. Ensure you've saved all of the open files and closed them if they are still open – the changes are complete for this demo.

Although we've had to work through a fair few steps, most of these are ones we've been through before; remember when we built the original data structure in DatoCMS back at the start of this book?

This time around, we added data fields for the Contact Us text and link; we then filled out the relevant text that should be displayed, once we reference the fields in code. Next up, we then amended the sitenavigation.js file to replace the hard-coded link with one that pulls in the information from DatoCMS and updated the GraphQL query.

We then rebuilt the content using the by-now-familiar `gatsby develop` command; although we wouldn't see any change in what appears on the page, we can at least be sure that all of the links now use the same format.

Taking It to the Next Level

Taking things to the next level...I wonder where we could go?

To be truthful, there are dozens of different improvements we could make or changes to evolve the site; it depends on what you want to do and what ties in with your clients! That said, there are a few ideas I've come up with as a starting point to give you some inspiration:

- Animation – I'm wary of adding animation, as it can be overdone and spoil the effects we are trying to achieve. However, we could potentially look at adding in something to give a visual identity to the customer when a product has been added to the basket, for example. This is a perfect way to add in a subtle effect that really adds value to the site.

- I think a change of background color could be required – we've not run it yet, but I happen to know that Lighthouse will report that our header and footer do not show sufficient contrast, so will flag it as an accessibility issue.

- Talking of accessibility, what about adding in ARIA labels to our site? This is essential for a good Lighthouse score – we will touch more on this in the next chapter.

- We added in a basic stock level availability, but this wasn't real-time; there is potential to improve on it and also the wording (we may not want to show exactly how many items we have!).

- I think a magnifying glass effect, or potentially a gallery, could prove useful here – cakes are very visual items, so anything to help show off how they look will help the customer.

- How about adding in support for different currencies? We might decide that English is the only language we can support (as we may not have the resources to add in more). However, we should also consider adding in support for other currencies; in this global age, there is nothing to stop us exporting goods, as long as they are packaged correctly!

These are just a few ideas that come to mind – I'm sure that, given time, you will come up with other ideas worthy of consideration. Ultimately we can't do them all at once, so prioritization is key; this is something we will need to agree with our site owner, according to their business requirements and strategy, before launching into providing the world before they are ready!

Summary

We are almost at the point where we can move our site into production. There's always time to tweak and improve the experience; it's just a case of knowing what to include and when to stop! Throughout the last few pages, we've worked on four mini-projects, to give you a flavor of where we could improve the experience – let's review what we have learned in this chapter.

We began by exploring some of the basics around adding in SEO support for our site; we used a plugin from the Gatsby site and learned that although it significantly improved the rating given by Lighthouse, there was still more we could do to improve on the score.

Next up, we then covered the initial process of setting up localization, using French as our example language. We saw how easy it was to add in the support, but learned that we would have to be careful about how we structure the site. Otherwise, we might risk being penalized by Google – not a good move!

We then moved onto adding in both a contact form and comments mechanisms, using third-party services. We understood that as Gatsby is rendered server-side, it means that traditional methods wouldn't work; using external services allows us to tie in something to our site and for customers to get in touch with us.

Phew, we're making significant progress, but here comes the critical part: before we can release our site into the wild, it's time to make sure it is fully optimized and tested! There are dozens of ways to do this, but I will show you in the next chapter how, with some simple tools, we can already make some tangible improvements to our code, ready for release later in this book.

CHAPTER 9

Testing and Optimization

Until now, we've focused on building our site, and it appears to be working satisfactorily – is this *really* the case, though?

Does it function as we expect, or are there any tweaks we need to perform? Over these pages, we will explore how to perform unit testing and begin to optimize our pages. This process will have a particular focus on e-commerce - we will explore some of the steps we should take to test and optimize our site, and ensure it works as expected before release.

At the same time, we will perform an audit, with the Lighthouse tool, to see if there are any areas of the site we can optimize. We may or may not get a 100% score across the board, but we have to start somewhere! There is one thing we have to do before we can begin, which is to fix a problem that will prevent us from performing any testing, and that is making sure we can produce a production build version of our site.

Some Housekeeping

"Produce a production build version of our site?" I hear you ask...

Yes, that is indeed true: it all boils down to an issue with the Markdown content we are using to produce the blog on our site. Before I explain what I mean, let's quickly run through updating the code to work around the issue.

FIXING THE BUILD ISSUE

The fix is a one-line piece of code we need to add – here are the steps to do so:

1. First, make sure the website is not running under `gatsby develop` – if it is, then press `Ctrl+C` (or `Cmd+C`) to stop it in the Node.js terminal session.

2. Next, fire up your text editor, and then crack open a copy of `gatsby-node.js` from the root of your project area.

3. Scroll down until you see this line: limit: 1000. Then immediately below it, add in the line highlighted in the following:

```
limit: 1000
filter: {frontmatter: {path: {ne: ""}, title: {ne: ""}}}
) {
```

4. Save the file and close it – at this point, we can restart the development version of the site by running `gatsby develop` in the Node.js terminal session.

If all is well, we should see no visual change in our content, but can rest assured that we can now progress on with the rest of this chapter!

This simple change was the difference between us compiling a production version of our code and not pushing forward with making our site live. It might seem a quick one-liner at face value, but it hides a real issue when using Markdown content – let's take a moment or two to explore what this change means for us in practice.

Breaking Apart the Issue

So how does fixing this GraphQL query affect us? Well, there is a simple reason, but to explain why, let me give you a little background first.

For most of the demos, we've used `gatsby develop` quite happily – it's created a version of the site we can preview using localhost, which was perfect for our needs. This process only produces an *unoptimized* version of our code; to go into production, we would need to use `gatsby build` to create that optimized version. We should be able to run `gatsby build && gatsby serve` to view the production version offline, right?

I've combined the `gatsby build` and `gatsby serve` commands into one, for ease, but we can run them separately if preferred.

Well, yes – and no. Running these commands would indeed be valid for the demo up until the end of Chapter 6. Since then, we have added a blog in Chapter 7, and that is where our problem lies! If we run `gatsby build` now, we will end up with this error (Figure 9-1).

```
 7 |   const post = data.markdownRemark;
 8 |
>9 |    let featuredImgFluid = post.frontmatter.featuredImage.childIma
geSharp.fluid;
   |
10 |
11 |   return (
12 |      <>


WebpackError: TypeError: Cannot read property 'frontmatter' of null

- blog-template.js:9
  src/templates/blog-template.js:9:31
```

Figure 9-1. *Error appearing when running gatsby build*

Ugh…that's not a pretty error (is there such a thing?) – plus there is a real sting in this tail!

The problem lies in what Gatsby returns from the markdownRemark object in GraphQL. It produced not only the three posts we created but another three posts with empty or null values within. It is these null values that gatsby build is complaining about; the current setup doesn't have any filtering within, so Gatsby expects to include what are nonexistent values, hence the error!

To see what I mean, try previewing the site using gatsby develop and then running this query in the GraphiQL app at http://localhost:8000/__graphiql:

```
query MyQuery {
  allMarkdownRemark {
    edges {
      node {
        frontmatter {
          title
          author
          path
        }
      }
    }
  }
}
```

You will get three instances of node returned with values similar to those shown in Figure 9-2...

```
  "node": {
    "frontmatter": {
      "title": "My Third Gatsby Post",
      "author": "Alex Libby",
      "path": "/third-post"
    }
  }
},
```

Figure 9-2. *Example of a (valid) node returned in GraphQL*

...but you will also get multiple instances of node returned with empty values! Figure 9-3 shows an example of what we see is displayed.

```
{
  "node": {
    "frontmatter": {
      "title": "",
      "author": null,
      "path": null
    }
  }
},
```

Figure 9-3. *Example of an invalid entry returned from GraphQL*

To fix the problem, we have to make a one-line change in our code; the source of the problem though is not blog-template as indicated, but gatsby-node.js. We need to add in this highlighted line:

```
blog: allMarkdownRemark(
  sort: { order: DESC, fields: [frontmatter___date] }
  limit: 1000
  filter: {frontmatter: {path: {ne: ""}, title: {ne: ""}}}
) {
  edges {
```

This change will prevent Gatsby from trying to pull in nonexistent Markdown content; if you modify this line in the GraphQL query (as indicated), you will see it only return entries that do not show null values:

```
query MyQuery {
  allMarkdownRemark(filter: {frontmatter: {path: {ne: ""}, title: {ne: ""}}}) {
    edges {
```

With that change, we're now good to go – we can start testing our site, so the first task is to get our testing suite installed and ready for use.

Testing the Site

Testing a site is critical to its success – after all, we must ensure it works as we expected it to and does not produce odd or weird effects for our customers! There are dozens of different testing tools available that cater for anything from unit right through to end-to-end or even acceptance testing – it's very much a case of taking your pick!

We could use one of the heavyweights such as Mocha, QUnit, or Selenium WebDriver, but instead, I want to try something different: Cypress.

Available from `www.cypress.io`, it bundles well-known tools such as Mocha and Chai into a single, easy-to-use framework. Cypress makes it easy to perform all of the usual testing tasks, such as run standard tests, spy on network requests, and mock data.

Okay, enough of the sales pitch. Time we got coding! Joking aside, Cypress runs on Node.js, so it will install in much the same way as any package does for this platform. Let's take a look at what we need to do to get it installed and configured, ready for us to write our example test.

There is one thing I do need to point out: Cypress' browser support isn't as extensive as other tools; for this demo, you need to use **recent versions** of browsers, but not Safari (as this one isn't supported). This support isn't too much of an issue for us, as we will focus more on unit testing; it is something to bear in mind if we were to push this site into production at a later date.

PART 1: SETTING UP CYPRESS

Setting up Cypress for testing purposes requires us to run through a few steps – let's work through them now:

1. First, crack open a Node.js terminal session, and then change the working folder to the project area. At the prompt, enter this command and press Enter:

   ```
   npm install --save-dev cypress start-server-and-test
   ```

2. Next, fire up your text editor, and add in the following lines as highlighted to package.json:

   ```
     "node": "12.8.0"
   },
   "scripts": {
     "dev": "gatsby develop",
   "cypress:open": "cypress open",
   "cypress:run": "cypress run",
   "test:e2e:ci": "start-server-and-test dev http://localhost:8000
   cypress:run"
   },
   "dependencies": {
   ```

3. Revert to the Node.js terminal session, and then at the prompt, enter this command and press Enter:

   ```
   npm run cypress:open
   ```

4. As this is the first time, Cypress will run through some setup steps before displaying the main GUI. This welcome screen can take a few moments to appear, so be patient! If all is well, we should see a Getting Started message appear (as shown in Figure 9-4, overleaf).

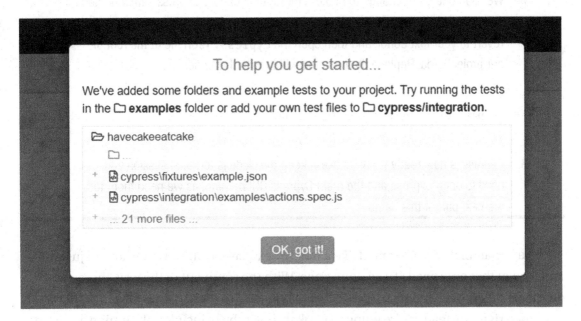

Figure 9-4. *An informational alert seen on the first time of launching Cypress*

5. You can click OK, got it! – this is just an informational alert to say Cypress has set up some example tests, which you can find in the \cypress\ integration\examples folder of our project area.

6. Once we have dismissed the message, we will see the main view of Cypress GUI, as indicated in Figure 9-5.

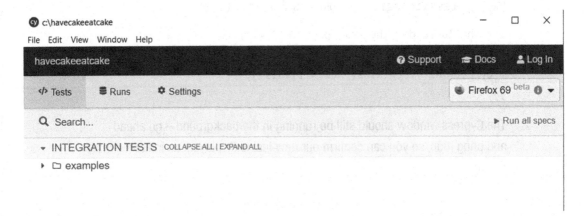

Figure 9-5. *A (partial) view of the main Cypress GUI*

7. We have one more change to make – this is to configure Cypress with a default base URL, to allow us to use relative links when running our tests. For this, revert to your text editor, and then open the cypress.json file at the root of our project area. Replace the contents within with this code:

```
{
    "baseUrl": "http://localhost:8000"
}
```

8. Cypress is now ready for us to use – keep the Node.js terminal session you used to open Cypress and the main Cypress GUI running, as we need them for the next part of this demo.

Okay, that might have seemed like a lengthy exercise! Don't worry, though: just about all of that only needs to be done once. With the setup out of the way, there are dozens of different elements we could test in our site – to do so would fill a mini-book in its own right. Instead, we're going to work through the principles of running a test, so you can then use this as a basis for developing further tests at a later date.

PART 2: WRITING TESTS

To operate Cypress, work through these steps:

1. First, revert to your text editor, and then add this code to a new file, saving it in the \cypress\integration folder as firsttest.js:

```
it('should render the home page', () => {
    cy.visit('/');
    cy.get('h1').contains('New Arrivals');
});
```

2. The Cypress window should still be running in the background – go ahead and bring it up, so you can confirm our new test is displayed, as indicated in Figure 9-6.

▾ INTEGRATION TESTS   COLLAPSE ALL | EXPAND ALL

▸ ▢ examples

▯ firsttest.spec.js

Figure 9-6. *The addition of our test to Cypress*

3. Click `firsttest.spec.js` in the main GUI window to start the test – you may
    get prompted to allow access if running in Windows, so click Allow access if
    prompted.

4. In the background, Cypress will run through the test using its server; you will
    see a message such as those shown in Figure 9-7 appear.

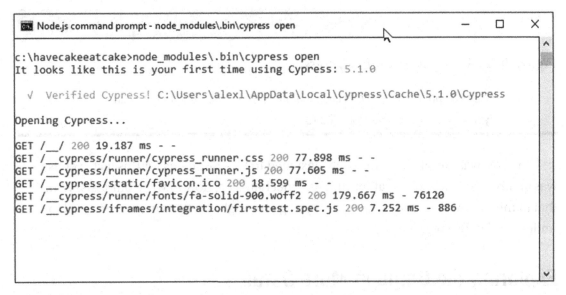

Figure 9-7. *Informational messages from the Cypress server*

5. Another window opens when you run the test, where Cypress runs through
    each of the steps in any test we task it to run; it will look something like that in
    Figure 9-8, where we've completed the run for our test.

Figure 9-8. *A successful test in Cypress*

6.   When you are ready, you can click the Stop button (top right) in the main Cypress GUI to stop and close the runner.

This test was simple but purposely designed to be – our focus for this last exercise was on how Cypress works, rather than the mechanics of how to write our tests. With that in mind, now is a perfect opportunity to go through the steps in greater detail to understand how it works.

Exploring the Demo in More Detail

So what did we achieve in the last two demos? Well, we got Cypress installed and working – we started by creating a production build of our site so that we had something "optimal" to test in Cypress. I use the word "optimal" loosely here, as we have yet to run our site through Google's Lighthouse tool: this will more than likely show up a few issues!

We then added some configuration commands for Cypress into our package.json file before running through the installation process for Cypress. Cypress uses Node.js, so the installation commands will look similar to other tools that use Node.js as their backbone tool. We then made one more change to Cypress' configuration by adding a baseUrl value; this allows us to use relative links in Cypress, which Cypress converts into absolute URLs.

Once opened, we then added a simple test to prove that the H1 tag on the main page shows the words "New Arrival" before running the test and verifying that it passed without issue.

The one thing to note with Cypress – as is the case with many other similar testing tools – is it is URL based. It means that we have to write tests for each page we want to test; not every test will be executable on every page! Thankfully Cypress makes it easy to add in tests, so as long as we are careful with our planning, there is every chance we can reuse at least some of the tests across different pages during the testing process.

We don't even have to run those tests manually either – with the use of a CI (continuous integration) pipeline tool, such as Travis CI, we can automate the entire process. This topic is something we will cover when we move the site into GitHub and get it ready for production use.

Taking It Further

Quality is not an act, it is a habit. —Aristotle

So said one of the world's greatest philosophers. As a saying, it illustrates perfectly the whole ethos around testing and that it should indeed be that: a habit, not an act. We've been through the basics of setting up a testing facility using Cypress; is there more we could do once we've added in more tests?

Absolutely! There is plenty we could set up to help take things further – here are a few ideas to get you started:

- The traditional form of testing is to use statements such as expect() or assert(). Still, this approach is somewhat technical – we're reliant on developers producing the steps to test, who are reliant on their interpretation of business requirements! There is a way around this; we can use feature files. It will allow a more business-oriented individual to write the requirements in natural language steps, which can then be interpreted into valid code steps by a developer. Cypress doesn't include support for feature files by default, but a plugin is available to help – cypress-cucumber-preprocessor. It's available for install via Node.js, from `https://github.com/TheBrainFamily/cypress-cucumber-preprocessor`.

- We've touched on local testing, but that is only part of the story – we should consider adding CI pipeline support. There are a few options we could choose – what about Travis CI (`www.travis-ci.com`), for example?

- We've tested with information available on the site, but this may or may not match production; to help with this, we might consider adding mocked data as part of our testing routine. I suspect many of you might already do this in other projects, but for those of you not familiar with the process, Gatsby has a useful document on this subject, at `www.gatsbyjs.com/docs/testing-components-with-graphql/`, which is worth a read.

These are just a few ideas that come to mind – I am sure there are others you may come across or want to use. The critical point here is that we need to ensure that we test all aspects of our site as thoroughly as possible to be sure it works as expected for our customers.

Okay, let's move on: we've covered the basics of testing, so what's next? Ah, yes, there is one more tool we should take a look at: running a Lighthouse audit. For those of you not familiar with this tool, I'm not referring to some naval-based structure, but a set of tests that can help us fine-tune the architecture of our site even further, to ensure we get the best out of it as possible. Google's Lighthouse audit tool is free to use for simple tests (it comes as part of Chrome); let's dive in and take a look to see what it does for our site.

Performing a Lighthouse Audit

Up until now, we've focused on how to run unit tests with Cypress. This is just part of the story, though – we can do more.

The Gatsby team recommend also running a Lighthouse audit using Google Chrome; we can get a rating of how compliant our site is, as well as pointers to code that needs tweaking or updating, helping improve the score.

The great thing about this feature is that it is entirely free; it may not be perfect, but it will certainly help give us something we can work to improve. With that in mind, let's take a quick look at how we can run the test, before exploring what we can fix to help improve the score.

RUNNING A LIGHTHOUSE AUDIT

There are a few steps to work through to complete a Lighthouse audit, so let's make a start:

1. The first step is to prepare a production build of our site – so far, we've used the gatsby develop route, which produces code that is not optimized. Fire up a Node.js terminal session, and then change the working folder to our project area.

2. Run through each of these commands in turn, pressing Enter after each:

    ```
    gatbsy clean
    gatsby build
    gatsby serve
    ```

3. Next, browse to http://localhost:9000/ in Chrome. For this, use Incognito Mode; this stops any active extensions from interfering with the test. Then, open up the Chrome DevTools – you can do this using Ctrl+Shift+I (Windows/Linux) or Cmd+Shift+I (Mac).

4. At this point, click the Lighthouse tab – you will see the screen presented in Figure 9-9.

Generate report

Identify and fix common problems that affect your site's performance, accessibility, and user experience. <u>Learn more</u>

Categories

☑ Performance
☑ Progressive Web App
☑ Best practices
☑ Accessibility
☑ SEO

Community Plugins(beta)

☐ Publisher Ads

Device

◯ Mobile
◉ Desktop

Figure 9-9. *The initial Lighthouse audit menu*

5. Make sure all of the options **except for Publisher Ads** are checked; then choose Desktop and click Generate report.

6. After a short period, we will see a report appear, looking similar to that shown
    in Figure 9-10.

Figure 9-10. *The initial Lighthouse audit report for Desktop*

7. It's the turn of Mobile, so click the clear all logo (circle with a line through it);
    then select Mobile and click Generate report.

8. If all is well, we should see a new report appear after a couple of minutes
    (Figure 9-11).

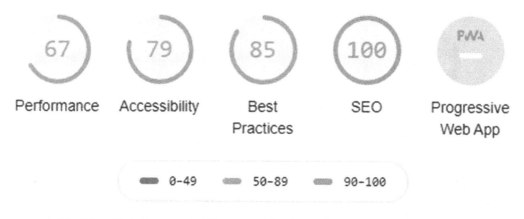

Figure 9-11. *The Lighthouse audit report for Mobile*

We can see there is work to do in both examples! We will explore what is needed to improve
the score for Desktop later in this chapter; Mobile will come in Chapter 12. We will also cover
the PWA score (or lack thereof) as part of moving this site into production in Chapter 10.

Making use of Google's Lighthouse may feel like we're acting as slaves to that behemoth of a company, but in this case, it is definitely worth giving it a try! It's a free tool, and while it may not offer lots of detail, it's still worth using to see where we can improve our code. When I ran it on my version of this demo, it raised a few crucial points that we should explore in more detail.

Exploring the Results in Detail

When it comes to optimizing Gatsby code, there are many different things we could do – all of which require time and resources and potentially come at a cost. However, Google's Lighthouse audit tool is one we can use – it comes free in Chrome and just requires time and resources to run and interpret or fix the results.

Indeed, it may not be great for large sites as we have to run the tool on a per-page basis, but for a small website like ours, it's perfect! In this last exercise, we ran it on the homepage of our site; we first created an "optimized" production build before initiating Lighthouse and setting it to run in Desktop mode.

We repeated the same exercise for Mobile too – it turns out that the Desktop results were solid, whereas the Mobile results weren't quite up to our desired mark! That isn't an issue though: we will be adapting our site to better run on mobile devices in a later exercise, but for now, let's move on to the next part of this demo, which is to understand the results and work out how best to resolve the issues raised by the tool.

Responding to Issues

It's at this point where things will get interesting – I can guarantee four things will happen:

- If you run the audit from the previous exercise, you are unlikely to get the same results as I did (which you will see in the next activity).

- There is a good chance that if you run the audit ten times, you will not get the same results on all ten occasions.

- If you run the audit with browser plugins still enabled, you will likely get different results than with plugins disabled.

- You will want to fix every single issue in sight, yet there are occasions when this might be counterproductive!

"Ouch, what the heck does that all mean?" I hear you ask. Well, let me explain with an example.

While researching this book, I ran the audit on my version of the site. One of the issues that came back related to images that could be optimized.

I duly put the errant image through a compressor to shrink its size, fully expecting it to show issues with the other images. Once I had updated the site with the new image, Lighthouse claimed all of the other images were OK. The score was now 100% – go figure, as they say!

See what I mean? I ran the same audit twice on the same hardware, in the same browser, and (as it so happens) with the same plugins enabled – I ended up with two different sets of results. It's something to keep in mind...

Exploring the Background

But I digress. The issues that Lighthouse reported on my site fell into two camps: Performance and Accessibility. For the former, I had a score of 94%, with the metrics graded, as indicated in Figure 9-12.

Performance

Metrics			
First Contentful Paint	0.3 s	Time to Interactive	0.3 s
Speed Index	0.3 s	Total Blocking Time	0 ms
Largest Contentful Paint	1.5 s	Cumulative Layout Shift	0.002

Figure 9-12. *The results of the Performance audit*

Now, remember how I said things could get interesting? Well, you might at first want to get the score up to 100%, and I wouldn't blame you: anything less than 100% doesn't have quite the same ring to it, does it?

216

To quote an old English saying, hold your horses there, my dear reader – there are a couple of reasons why this may not be a prudent move! Before I explain what I mean, let's cover the Performance issues and opportunities found when I ran the audit tool on my version of the site:

- The principal problem is the Largest Contentful Paint metric – it's reporting as 1.6 seconds, which is too high.

- Text compression could be a benefit if enabled.

- There are elements of JavaScript that we could potentially remove.

- We could serve images in next-generation formats such as JPEG2000 or WebP.

- We are not rendering content under HTTPS.

- Lighthouse discovered three chaining requests in our code.

- Request counts and transfer sizes were a little high in places.

- Several large elements were causing layout shifting.

Yikes, this might seem a little intimidating. In reality, it is easier than it might appear! To see what I mean, let's dive in and look at what is involved in more detail.

Fixing the Performance Issues

Although Lighthouse has identified a few problems and opportunities for us to consider, it doesn't mean that we have to fix them immediately. Indeed, some of them are not fixable, within the current environment; let me explain why:

- Remove unused JavaScript.

- Enabling text compression isn't something we can do in a development environment, so this will have to wait until we move into production.

- Lighthouse tagged a few images which could benefit from being optimized; this is something we can (and should) fix now by running them through a compression tool.

- Save images in next-gen formats. Although this will technically give us smaller media files, not every browser supports formats such as WebP; this will likely require refactoring code to ensure that we use the right format in the right browser.

- Keep request counts low and transfer sizes small – this requires more in-depth work to refactor code into smaller sizes and remove redundant code.

- Avoid chaining requests. This one is coming from the use of Google-hosted font files, which chain by default; there are ways to reduce or remove this issue, which we can investigate.

- Avoid large layout shifts – several elements.

- The main image on the homepage triggers an alert for the Largest Contentful Paint element. However, on subsequent runs, the h1 element generated a similar warning, so both need checking.

- We are not serving any of the links via HTTPS – this would ordinarily be an issue, but as we are working in a development environment, HTTP access is sufficient. We can fix this when we move the site into a production environment, which should have HTTPS access enabled as standard.

If, however, you want to see what the site looks like under a local HTTPS-enabled environment, then the article at `www.gatsbyjs.com/docs/local-https/` would be worth a read.

Now that we know where the issues lie, there are a few things we can do to help improve the score, so let's dive in and take a look at the steps in more detail.

CORRECTING THE PERFORMANCE ISSUES

To help summarize the actions we will take, I will list what we will do in this exercise first:

- Compress images.

- Optimize how the web-based fonts are displayed.

- Save some of the images in a newer format to show the impact of sizes.

- Identify and switch out block-level elements to alternatives.

Let's make a start:

1. The first step is to optimize the images used in our site – browse first to www.compresspng.com.

2. Make sure you have the \src\images folder open in Windows Explorer, then drag and drop each into the CompressPNG page as prompted, and wait for the site to compress each in turn. Save the updated images back into the \src\ images folder.

The new images will have .min.png as the extension; you will need to rename them to remove the .min so that they can work with your existing code.

---

3. Next up, browse to https://convertio.co/image-converter/ – we're going to use this to convert the main header.png image to WebP format. Drag and drop header.png onto the window as directed; then, when it's converted, save a copy back to the original images folder as header.webp.

4. Go ahead and crack open \src\pages\index.js; then change the header.png import to point to the new WebP format image. Save and close the file.

5. The next stage is to swap out the references to typeface-open-sans and typeface-great-vibes fonts with locally hosted versions. Navigate to the node_modules folder and then down to the typeface-open-sans folder.

6. Inside this folder, you will see a files folder; copy the contents of this folder to a new fonts folder, which you will need to create in the \src folder. Repeat these last two steps with the typeface-great-vibes folder.

7. Next, fire up a Node.js terminal session, and then change the working folder to the project folder.

8. At the prompt, enter these commands in turn, pressing Enter after each:

```
Npm uninstall typeface-open-sans
npm uninstall typeface-great-vibes
```

9. Go ahead and crack open the package.json file at the root of the project folder, and then make sure the references to "typeface-open-sans" and "typeface-great-vibes" have been removed. Save and close the file.

10. Delete the package-lock.json file if it is present at the root of your project folder.

11. Next, add in this code at the top of global.scss, before any other code:

```scss
@font-face {
  font-family: 'Open Sans';
  font-style: normal;
  font-display: swap;
  font-weight: 400;
  src:
    local('Open Sans Regular '),
    local('Open Sans-Regular'),
    url('../fonts/open-sans-latin-400.woff2') format('woff2'),
    /* Super Modern Browsers */
    url('../fonts/open-sans-latin-400.woff') format('woff');
    /* Modern Browsers */
}

@font-face {
  font-family: 'Great Vibes';
  font-style: normal;
  font-display: swap;
  font-weight: 400;
  src:
    local('Great Vibes Regular '),
    local('Great Vibes-Regular'),
    url('../fonts/great-vibes-latin-400.woff2') format('woff2'),
    /* Super Modern Browsers */
```

```
    url('../fonts/great-vibes-latin-400.woff') format('woff');
    /* Modern Browsers */
}
```

12. Crack open `layouts\index.js` and remove this line:

    ```
    import "typeface-open-sans"
    ```

13. Save and close the file.

14. In `\src\components\Navigation.js`, remove the highlighted code:

    ```
    <span style="color:#ffffff">
    ```

15. Add it as a new style attribute to the `<header>` element in the same file:

    ```
    <header
      style={{
        background: `#a49696`,
        display: `flex`,
        justifyContent: `space-between`,
        padding: `20px 30px`,
        color: `#ffffff`,
      }}
    >
    ```

16. Save and close any files you have open.

17. Finally, in a Node.js terminal session, change the working folder to our project area.

18. At the prompt, run `gatsby clean && gatsby build && gatsby serve` – you can now view the changes made in the browser window and rerun the audit to confirm the scores reflect the new changes.

Wow, there are a fair few changes there! All of these came from issues reported by Lighthouse, although I will confess I'm not entirely sure if all of them have helped to improve the score. Yes, I know that sounds a little controversial, but there are good reasons for this – let's pause for a moment to review the changes made and see why things may not be as clear-cut as we might expect.

Understanding the Changes

Although it seems like we covered many steps, in reality, the tasks within are very straightforward – indeed, most of them probably should be done as a matter of course!

We kicked off by optimizing the images using the CompressPNG website – admittedly, this was for ease of convenience, but we could equally have done this with any compression tool. We then moved on to replacing the font files hosted from Google with local versions; we moved in the font files from the original NPM installations and added the appropriate CSS styling to the style sheet. We then finished by moving a style attribute from one element to another – this made for cleaner code as the target element already had styling applied to it.

These might not seem to be complex changes, but they reveal some important points – for example, we should (as a matter of course) optimize all images for size, as it saves bandwidth. However, there is a question around format – while WebP may indeed be smaller, not every browser supports the standard (yes, I'm looking at you, IE11!) It's at this point that we have to decide whether we want the extra overhead of managing multiple types or can afford to drop support for IE11. Only your analytics will tell whether this is something even worth considering...!

I should, however, come clean about that confession – while I think compressing the images may have helped, I'm not so sure about changing the fonts. The reason for that was one of chaining – Lighthouse reported at least three chains in use. At the same time, it also flagged an issue around rendering, one that we need to use `font-display: swap`, to swap out system fonts for the web fonts once the browser has downloaded them.

Swapping the font out may have reduced the chaining to two, but as it turns out, the NPM packages we used already have the `font-display: swap` property in place. So, as you can see, perhaps making that change didn't have the impact we expected: as part of several changes, we've still managed to up the numbers to a more respectful level!

This scenario highlights two important points: First, the results we get back will be specific to our project. The second is that we might get issues such as these, but we shouldn't rush to fix them: instead, we should consider whether we make any changes and resolve those that really require our attention.

As an aside   We ran these changes locally: it's worth updating the demo site we created on Netlify and running the same audit there. At the very least, we shouldn't get the issue recorded about not using HTTPS access!

Okay, let's move on. We've sorted out the performance issues raised by Lighthouse. Remember how I said that the main focus was on two areas? The second is accessibility, so let's apply the same principles to this topic and see what we need to fix to improve the overall scores.

Fixing the Accessibility Issues

In the same vein, Lighthouse has identified a few problems and opportunities for us to consider regarding accessibility. The same principles apply when it comes to fixing them; it doesn't mean that we have to do it immediately! Indeed, some of them are not fixable, within the current environment; let me explain why:

- Lighthouse reports an insufficient ratio for contrast, for the h1, p, and five li elements.

- The site jumps from a h1 to h4 element, without any h2 or h3 element in-between.

- There is an input field with no label.

- Some of the links on the page do not have any discernible names present.

- Some of the list elements have extra tags (1x ul), and we have li elements outside of <ul> or <ol> (5x li).

As before, let's take a look at the changes we need to make to fix these issues in our site in more detail.

CORRECTING THE ACCESSIBILITY ISSUES

To get our accessibility count up, follow these steps – I'm assuming for this exercise that the site will still be running and that you may or may not have the results of your Lighthouse audit still visible in the browser window:

1. First, crack open your text editor, and then go ahead and open the newarrival.js file.

2. Look for the <h4>{props.name}</h4>, and change the <h4>...</h4> elements to <p> and </p>, respectively.

3. We need to adjust the styling to reflect this change – crack open global. scss, and look for .newarrival h4. Change it as highlighted:

```scss
.newarrival p {
  color: #302525;
  padding: 15px 0;
  text-align: center;
  font-weight: bold;
}
```

5. Close the newarrival.js file, and now open subscribe.js in your editor.

6. Look for this line of code: <div className="field">. Then add in the aria-label into the line immediately below, as indicated:

```
<input name="email" placeholder="Your email" aria-label="Enter email address"/>
```

7. Save the file and close it. Next, crack open connect.js so that we can fix the no discernable names issue.

8. In this file, look for the first link, which is for Facebook. At the end of the code, add in this aria-label, as indicated:

```
target="_blank" rel="noreferrer" aria-label="Link to Facebook site">
```

9. Repeat for the remaining three links, but substitute Facebook for each of the remaining three social media sites in turn.

10. The final item we will adjust is in the customerservices.js file – open this in your text editor, and change the contents of the <div> block as shown:

```
<div>
  <p>Customer Service</p>
  <ul>
    <li><Link to="/help/">{data.
datoCmsHomepage.helpFooter}</Link></li>
    <li><Link to="/delivery/">{data.
datoCmsHomepage.deliveryFooter}</Link></li>
    <li><Link to="/gifts/">{data.
datoCmsHomepage.giftsFooter}</Link></li>
    <li><Link to ="/about/">{data.
```

```
datoCmsHomepage.aboutUsFooter}</Link></li>
        <li><Link to ="/terms/">{data.
datoCmsHomepage.termsFooter}</Link></li>
      </ul>
    </div>
```

11. Go ahead and save the file and then close any that are still open, as the changes for this exercise are now complete.

12. There is one step left – we need to run three commands to update the production build of the site. Switch to a Node.js terminal session, then run `gatsby clean && gatsby build && gatsby serve` at the prompt. When done, you can refresh the browser window and rerun the audit to see the change reflected in the scores.

Throughout this exercise, I've focused on making changes where we can get some quick wins – as we will see shortly, it has improved the overall score. However, there are a few important points we should work through as a result of making these changes – you may also spot that we've not included one change too… There's a good reason for this, so with that in mind, let's take a closer look at the changes made in more detail.

Breaking Apart the Changes

In the previous exercise, we made several changes that appeared to help the performance, but which raised doubt about how much impact they made to our site. This time around, though, the Accessibility audit highlighted several changes that (as you will see) will have a positive impact.

We started by swapping the h4 tags in `newarrival.js` for `<p>` elements. Although these should be titles, we jumped from h1 to h4; Lighthouse took exception, hence raising the alert. We still need something that stands out, but in this case, `<p>` tags are sufficient – using h2 or h3 tags would have made them too large and require resizing, which isn't ideal.

Moving on, we then added aria-label tags to each of the social media icons. Ideally, this would have been regular label tags, but this would have added extra visual clutter; as we are fixing for ARIA support, aria-label is enough to keep Lighthouse happy. We also added an aria-label tag to the input field within the Subscribe section, for the same reason. We then revamped the Customer Services block; Lighthouse complained of having extra non-list tags present, both in the list items and within the parent <ul> block. A rebuild of the production files rounded out the exercise, allowing us to view the changes and rerun the report to confirm an improvement in our scores.

Before we move on, anyone spotted that we've not touched one of the issues reported by Lighthouse? I'm thinking specifically of the one relating to insufficient contrast – this was for the header title, one of the <p> elements, and the Customer Services block.

Lighthouse is correct in stating that there isn't sufficient contrast in use; changing it will require changing the header and footer color throughout the site. This change may *technically* be easy to do but is likely to go against any UX designs you may have. It's for this reason that making this change is not one we would do immediately – at least not without proper support from your UX design team.

To help provide detail in cases like this, it's worth installing the WCAG color contrast checker plugin for Chrome; search online for "wcag-color-contrast-check" to download and install the plugin.

Let's move on: it's time to see just how much we've managed to improve our scores! I'm pleased to say that (at least for my site) we can see a definite improvement; let's take a look at what the results show, and where we go from here, in more detail.

Viewing the Results

Yes, it is indeed time to see how our scores have improved!

Before I do so (and just to keep you all in suspense a little longer), it's worth noting that these results are solely for the homepage only and were good at the time of running them. It doesn't mean you will automatically get the same level of results for your setups, but the hope is that if you review the results of your tests, you can aspire to get similar figures to the ones I had for my site. Okay...now let's see those results (Figure 9-13).

Figure 9-13. *The updated Lighthouse audit scores*

In comparison to the original set, they look pretty good, huh? While the performance one hasn't changed (despite the changes we made), the accessibility score has shot up from 79% to 97%, which is an 18% increase. Given that we've not covered all of the changes that we should do (vis-à-vis not running in HTTPS mode), this isn't too bad!

Indeed, we have not hit 100% across the board – I've seen examples that do show 100%. However, I take the pragmatic view that as long as the results are at or above a reasonable figure (say 90%?), then it's a good start. The law of diminishing returns does apply though: you could spend hours trying to get it up to 100%, only to find that you make things worse – not something we want to do, right?

Where Next from Here?

We've spent a lot of time running the Lighthouse audit and covering the basics of writing tests using the Cypress testing suite. Is this all we need to do?

There are lots more we can achieve as we develop our site! For space reasons, I've not been able to cover them in detail in this book, but here are a few places to check that tools such as Lighthouse can't check and would need manual intervention:

- ARIA roles – We've covered the basic tests using Lighthouse, but Cypress has a plugin for checking accessibility; it's available at https://github.com/avanslaars/cypress-axe. This plugin will be an excellent tool to help give a more in-depth report on what needs tweaking to comply with ARIA standards.

- Tabbing order – We should consider implementing a proper tabbing order; it's not essential to performance. It will make it easier to navigate for those who use keyboards in preference to mice.

- Interactive elements indicate purpose and state – this relates to how different interactive elements are from noninteractive ones. In essence, it's about checking to see if you can tab to each element and whether there is sufficient difference between each type of element.

A good article on this subject is available on the Web.dev site at `https://web.dev/interactive-element-affordance/`.

- Adding a `budget.json` file will help determine what suitable levels are in terms of performance and whether we exceed them during the normal course of operation.

- Manifest file – We should add this to help with offline support; we will do this in Chapter 10.

- Adding a robots.txt file should be done as a matter of course; this will help restrict which areas of the site search spiders should crawl.

- As a final touch, we should change the starter name shown in gatsby-config – not essential to performance, but as it is just a tag, it looks nicer if we can personalize it to our site!

There is also one more area to check, which is the console log area in our browser – I do not doubt that we will see one or more issues that we can rectify, such as the examples shown in Figure 9-14.

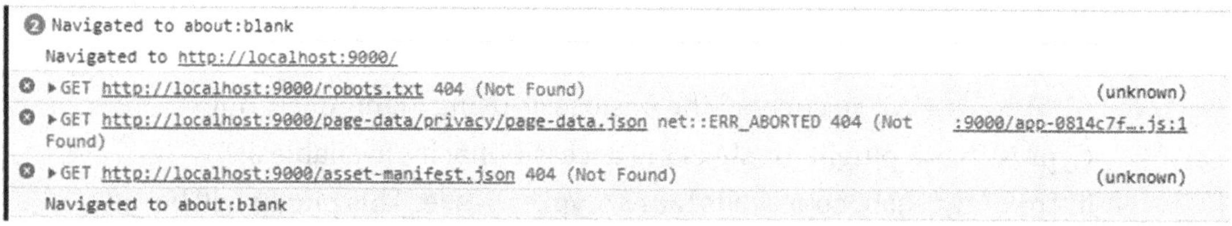

Figure 9-14. *The errors shown in our console log area*

We do have a few issues present, so all of them need fixing – this is something we will tackle as part of the final steps of pushing our site live, in Chapter 10.

Summary

Testing and optimization are two critical parts of developing any software – be it on- or offline. We need to be sure our site works as expected and is running as optimal as possible. We've covered the basics of both and touched on various tips to help with both. Let's take a moment to review what we have learned in this chapter.

We kicked off with some housekeeping, necessary as a result of creating the blog from Chapter 7; without it, this would block us from creating a production version of our site, which is critical for the running of the tests.

We then moved on to exploring how to use Cypress to write some starter tests; we focused on the technical steps for doing so, rather than writing tests, as Cypress is easy to learn.

Next up came a lengthy session on using Lighthouse; we ran it over a production build of our site before exploring why we may not want (or be able) to try to fix every issue raised by Lighthouse. We delved into the two key areas where the results were lower and saw how, with some simple tweaks, we could get the scores up to much more respective levels. We rounded out the chapter with a quick overview of some of the areas that Lighthouse won't touch and that we should investigate further as part of the development process.

Phew, a lot covered, but all very useful! There's still more to come though – we've finally hit the point where we are going to let our content loose into a production environment. Before we do so, there are a few things we need to set up; I will take you through this and more in the next chapter.

CHAPTER 10

Deployment into Production

Yikes, it's time for us to deploy our shop into production and let customers lose it! This step might seem scary, as we're about to show our efforts to customers, but don't worry: Gatsby makes it easy to deploy sites into production use.

Throughout this chapter, we will work through the appropriate steps required to get our site ready for release before deploying it and make it available for others to see via the Web. We'll tidy up our content to make sure it is all presentable before setting up the host and uploading content. There are a fair few tasks to complete, so let's start with finishing off the last few tasks to tidy up our site.

Working Through the Final Steps

We've already made a fair few changes to optimize content in our site, so I'll bet you're asking – what more can we do? There are a few more tasks to perform; we could perhaps call them part of going live! Let's take a look at the remaining jobs we need to complete:

- We ran Google Lighthouse's audit tool back in the previous chapter but didn't cover the Progressive Web Application – or PWA – section (the very last metric in the tool). This omission is something we need to correct, so will do so in this chapter.

- We need to build (compile) a production version of the site, ready for deployment later in the chapter – this we will do once we've made all of the final changes.

- Add in offline support using the gatsby-plugin-offline plugin.

© Alex Libby 2021
A. Libby, *Gatsby E-Commerce*, https://doi.org/10.1007/978-1-4842-6692-2_10

- Remove any signs of using Netlify – we used this to test the domain (and particularly Shopify); we need to ensure everything redirects back to our custom domain.

- Add a Rest of World zone and shipping into our account on Shopify; as it stands, no one will be able to ship without this, as Shopify will block them!

There are a couple of additional changes we should make – as we're using a third-party starter, the author of the starter theme has already completed some of the steps for us:

- Gatsby recommends using the gatsby-plugin-react-helmet plugin to add in site metadata; this is already installed, but it's worth just reviewing what is set up.

- We should also add a manifest file to help search engines such as Google to understand our site's content and help rank it better in the listings. The plugin is available from `https://github.com/gatsbyjs/ gatsby/tree/master/packages/gatsby-plugin-manifest` – it already exists in the theme, but there is a change we can make to update the image used in the manifest, as well as the version of the plugin installed in our site.

These steps will complement the work we did on page metadata back in Chapter 8.

The site is also still technically a demo, so there is a chance that people might try to use it, thinking it was a real site. To prevent problems with incorrect usage, we should put up a banner for this demo. It's not something we would do on a production site, but then again, our site is still a development one, even though I talk about moving it into production!

So, as you can see, we still have a few things to cover off before we can "go live"! Let's take a look at each, in turn, beginning with updating the manifest file. Creating the file should allow us to produce several resized images, among other things; Figure 10-1 shows an example of what this will look like, from within the browser's console log.

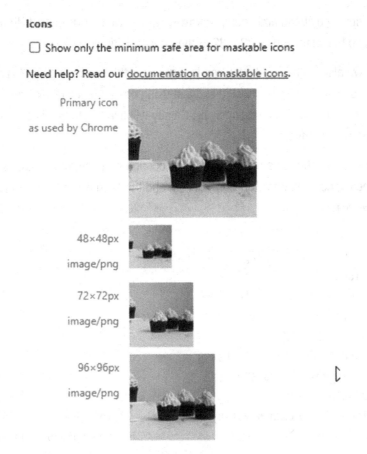

Icons

☐ Show only the minimum safe area for maskable icons

Need help? Read our documentation on maskable icons.

Primary icon
as used by Chrome

48×48px
image/png

72×72px
image/png

96×96px
image/png

Figure 10-1. *A (partial) display of the site's icons in the manifest file*

With this in mind, let's crack on and update the manifest file assigned to our site.

PART 1: ADDING A MANIFEST FILE

To get the manifest fully operational, first, stop the Gatsby develop server if it is running in a Node.js terminal session, and then follow these steps:

1. The first step is to upgrade the plugin – for this, crack open a Node.js terminal session, and change the working folder to our project area.

2. Next, enter this command at the prompt and press Enter:

    ```
    npm update gatsby-plugin-manifest
    ```

3. Once done, go ahead and open `package.json` – we can verify that NPM has installed the latest version (2.4.32 at the time of writing).

4. Next, we also need to add a favicon for our app – this needs to go in `/src/images/favicon.png`. I would suggest using one around 512 px square so that Gatsby can resize it responsively; Gatsby will use this to build each image size for the manifest.

5. The Gatsby starter we are using is already configured to create a manifest file. Go ahead and open `gatsby-config.js`, and then scroll down until you see this section:

```
{
  resolve: `gatsby-plugin-manifest`,
  options: {
    name: `gatsby-starter-default`,
    short_name: `starter`,
    start_url: `/`,
    background_color: `#663399`,
    theme_color: `#663399`,
    display: `minimal-ui`,
    icon: `src/images/gatsby-icon.png`, // This path is relative to
                                        the root of the site.
  },
},
```

Feel free to tweak the `name` and `short_name` fields to something more appropriate if you like; the exact name is not critical for running the manifest, although I would recommend not using spaces.

---

6. The last step is to update the icon path – this needs to point to the new favicon we've created. Change the value in the code to `'src/images/favicon.png'` and save; then close the file.

7. The changes are now complete – go ahead and enter `gatsby develop` in the Node.js terminal session to restart the server.

8. To verify that the change has taken effect, browse to the site in Chrome and then fire up the Developer Console (Shift+Ctrl+I in Windows or Cmd+Ctrl+I for Macs),

9. Change to the Application tab and click Manifest under Application. You will see the manifest displayed, along with screenshots of each image size.

An example of how it will look is in Figure 10-1 before the start of this exercise.

---

10. I would recommend leaving your `gatsby-config.js` file open, as we will use it in the next part of this exercise.

This last exercise may seem like a few steps when we've only updated two items, but I think both are important – if only for visual identity! The theme will likely have had an older version of the plugin installed; it's sensible to update it to a recent version to help keep on top of security and housekeeping.

Okay, let's move on to the next part of this multi-stage exercise; it's time to set up offline support using the gatsby-plugin-offline plugin.

PART 2: SETTING UP OFFLINE SUPPORT

To add offline support, work through these steps:

1. First, make sure your development site is not running – press Ctrl+C (or Cmd+C) to stop the site if it is still active.

2. Next, at the prompt, enter this command to install the offline support plugin for Gatsby, and press Enter:

```
npm install gatsby-plugin-offline
```

3. Once done, revert to your text editor (and into the `gatsby-config.js` file from part 1), and then scroll down to the end of the gatsby-plugin-manifest configuration, which will look like this:

```
        icon: `src/images/favicon.png`, // This path is relative to the
                                        root of the site.
    },
},
`gatsby-plugin-offline`,
```

4. After the closing brackets, add the text as indicated in the preceding code; then save and close your file. Offline support is now installed and configured for use.

We're getting ever closer to releasing our code! We have one more step to complete, which is adding in a demo banner. This step isn't obligatory, but given we're running a demo site, it seems sensible to provide something to warn customers that we are not operating a real website! Adding the banner is an easy change to make, so let's dive in and take a closer look at the code to implement this banner.

PART 3: ADDING A DEMO BANNER

To add in the demo banner, follow these steps – you do not have to stop the Gatsby develop server for this change:

1. First, crack open your text editor, then create a new file, and add this code – save it as demobanner.js in the \src\components folder.

```
import React from "react"
const DemoBanner = () => (

    <div id="demobanner">
        <p>Please note: this is a demo site only - no orders will be
accepted, or fulfilled from this site.</p>
    </div>

);

export default DemoBanner
```

2. Next, open the index.js file located in the \src\layouts folder – we need to add in this new component to our layout. Scroll down until you see the Navigation component being referenced, and then add in the code as highlighted:

```
<Navigation siteTitle = data.site.siteMetadata.title} />
```

```
<DemoBanner />
<SiteNavigation />
<Wrapper>
```

3. We need to add in some rudimentary styling, so it at least looks presentable – for this, add in these styles at the end of the global.scss file in the styles folder:

```
/***** DEMO BANNER *****/
#demobanner {
  display: flex;
  justify-content: center;
  background-color: #000000;
  color: #ffffff;
  padding: 5px;
}
```

4. Save the file, and then give Gatsby a moment to update – if all is well, we should see something akin to that in Figure 10-2.

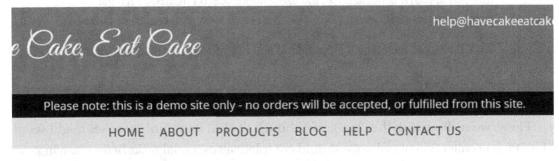

***Figure 10-2.** The addition of the demo banner*

We've almost finished the tidy-up, but there is one more thing we need to do; otherwise, our site may not work as expected once we move it into production!

Remember, back in Chapter 5, where we put a block on Afghanistan as a country and we wouldn't permit shipping? Well, that block has had the effect of blocking everything else so that we can't ship anything! To get around it, we need to add a shipping zone covering the rest of the countries, which we will do in the next exercise.

PART 4: THE FINAL TIDY-UP

To complete the tidy-up, follow these steps:

1. First, browse to `www.shopify.com`, and log into your admin dashboard with your credentials.

2. Click your shop's name to display the dashboard; once in, click Settings ➤ Shipping and delivery.

3. Under the Shipping section, click Manage rates ➤ Create shipping zone.

4. On the dialog box that appears, click Rest of World; enter a proper name to describe the zone. Shopify does not display this name to customers; it's for internal use only.

5. A new section will appear for Rest of World – click the Add rate button below and to the left in this section.

6. For now, we'll put in some example rates. Go ahead and enter Express as the rate name, with a suitable price; the exact figure doesn't matter, as it's the process that counts!

7. Click Done, and then repeat steps 5–7 to add in a new one marked Standard.

8. When completed, click Save to allow the changes to take effect.

Phew, we're done with the changes! Although the last four mini exercises might seem like a ragbag collection of tasks, we should complete all essential tasks before moving code live. We've made some critical changes, so let's take a breather – grab a drink, and when you're ready, let's review the changes made in more detail.

Considering the Steps in Detail

Someone once said to me, "If you stop making changes to your site, then the site is as good as dead" – that might seem a little extreme, but I think he had a point! We should not consider a site as complete unless it no longer serves us; if that time has come, then it's time to retire it…

But back to reality – we've made a fair few changes in the last four exercises, all to get the site ready to launch as our initial version. We began by installing a more up-to-date version of Gatsby's manifest plugin before adding a suitably sized favicon image to our project area's images folder.

Next up, we took a quick look at the existing manifest entry in the `gatsby-config.js` file before tweaking some of the entries and verifying that the changes made reflected in an updated set of icons within the browser console.

In part 2 of this multi-part exercise, we then installed the gatsby-plugin-offline plugin for our site before adding an entry into the `gatsby-config.js` file – no other changes were needed, as this plugin handles everything else automatically.

We then moved on to part 3, which saw us add in a demo banner – this was to tell people that this site is not real and therefore does not accept any purchase requests. Before adding some basic styling, we first created a demobanner component and inserted a call to it from within the `index.js` file that is our layout template. We verified that it appeared correctly below the main header, across the site.

In the fourth and final part of this exercise, we added a new shipping zone within Shopify. We had created a block for Afghanistan in Shopify earlier, but noted this had the effect of blocking all countries – we didn't have anything to deal with the non-excluded countries. This omission we remedied by adding a new shipping zone for the Rest of World region, before applying two shipping rates and saving the changes.

Phew, a lengthy exercise, I know, but all still important! We are now at the stage where things will step up a notch; it's time to upload content. Before we can do that, let's first take a look at preparing our host, ready to receive our site.

Preparing the Host

Cast your mind back to the start of this book: remember how we talked about which provider we would use to host our site?

Well, it's time to put pen to proverbial paper and get our site out into the real world! The hosting provider we will be using is GitHub Pages. We could use others (like Netlify, GitLab), but I wanted to provide a little variety to what we've already used, and as I have GitHub sites, it makes it easier for me to manage!

Where do we start? The first task is to look at how we host on GitHub; we will use a GitHub repository, but we will configure it to display content through GitHub Pages.

The documentation for GitHub Pages is at `https://pages.github.com`.

When using GitHub Pages, there are three ways to host content:

- We can push content to a path such as `https://username.github.io/reponame/`.

- We can host the content via a subdomain based on your username or organization name, such as `https://username.github.io` or `https://orgname.github.io`.

- We can also push to the root subdomain at `https://username.github.io`, and then display content via a custom domain.

For our site, we will push content to the root subdomain and attach a custom domain. The latter isn't obligatory, but it will allow us to see what it will look like in front of customers! With that all in mind, let's take a look at the steps required first to get our GitHub repository set up and ready for use.

PREPARING THE HOST

Before we crack on with code, there are a couple of assumptions you need to bear in mind:

- For this exercise, I will assume we are using the username havecakeeatcake; you will need to think of a suitable name and swap this in as appropriate.

- I'm also assuming that you will create a new account and repository for this exercise; you can use an existing one, but it will make things more complicated!

Let's get started:

1. We'll start by creating a new repository – for this, browse to `https://github.com`, and click Sign Up in the top right.

2. Go ahead and follow the instructions provided on-screen, including adding an email account (it's worth it!) – make sure you take note of the details you use for your account. Once done, sign in with your new account, and make sure it is validated.

3. Next, we need to create our repository – click the + sign in the top right and then New repository.

4. On the next screen, the Owner field will be your account name; enter a repository name in the format username.github.io, where username is your chosen username on GitHub.

5. If you want to fill in a description, then go ahead and do so – it is not compulsory for this exercise.

6. Next, choose Public as the repository type, and click the checkbox to initialize the repository with a readme file.

7. For the Add .gitignore option, choose Node, and set the Add a license to MIT.

8. Click Create repository – if all is working as expected, we should have an empty repository, similar to the screenshot shown in Figure 10-3.

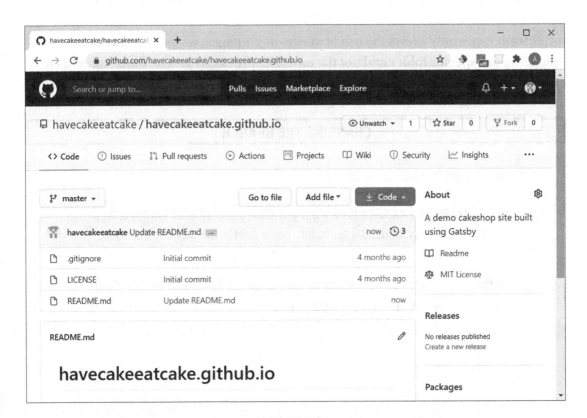

Figure 10-3. Our new repository on GitHub

If you've spent any time developing code, then the chances are that you will be familiar with Git and its GUI-based version GitHub. Many of the steps we covered in the last exercise are not unique to Gatsby; we can use these tools to create sites using any number of different frameworks.

In our case, we started by creating the basic repository; we entered the relevant details before initializing it with the readme and .gitignore files. This step gave us an empty storage facility ready to upload content, which we will cover in the next exercise.

Uploading Content

Now that we have our repository in place, it's time for us to upload content – before we do so, though, there is one more change we need to make.

One of the requirements for using GitHub Pages is that we have chosen a branch to upload content – unfortunately, the choice is minimal! In our case, it's either master...or master!

GitHub Pages only allows the use of master or gh-pages; we use the latter when uploading to a specific folder and not the root. The previous exercise didn't allow us to change this setting, so before we get stuck into uploading content, let's change it now.

CHANGING THE BRANCH

To change the branch, follow these steps:

1. First, navigate to your site's repository, or switch to it if you still have it open in a browser window. Under the repository name (and in the menu to the right), click Settings.

2. In the GitHub Pages section, make sure the value set in the Source drop-down list is `master` – as indicated in Figure 10-4.

GitHub Pages

GitHub Pages is designed to host your personal, organization, or project pages from a GitHub repository.

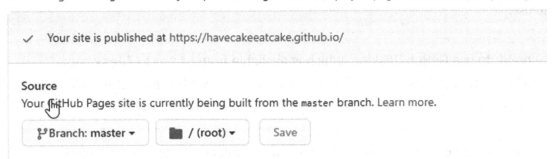

Figure 10-4. *Checking the branch settings in our repository*

3. Click Save – the site is ready to host content.

Excellent, we are now ready to upload content! When done, we should have a site available to view via the Internet; it will look something akin to that shown in Figure 10-5.

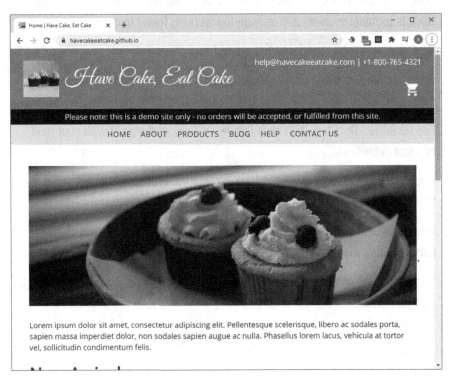

Figure 10-5. *Our newly uploaded site on GitHub Pages*

243

There are two ways we can upload content. The first is manual via a git-based tool (or via the command line). Second, we can also upload by creating and using a script. We will cover both methods in this chapter; feel free to choose whichever route you prefer to use.

I prefer to use GitHub Desktop, which is available from `https://desktop.github.com` in versions for Windows or Mac. I will use this tool for this exercise; please adapt the steps accordingly if you want to use something different.

Assuming we have GitHub Desktop (or your regular GUI client) installed and ready for use, let's crack on with preparing and uploading the content onto GitHub.

DEPLOYING TO HOST

To upload our content, follow these steps.

1. First, we need to create a production version of our site – for this, crack open a Node.js terminal session, and change the working folder to our project area.

2. Next, enter `gatsby build` at the prompt and press Enter.

3. Once complete, browse to our project folder in Windows Explorer (or your file manager) – leave the window open, but minimized.

4. Fire up GitHub Desktop, then click File ➤ Options, and sign in with your new account details.

5. Once signed in, click Show in Explorer to view the files stored locally – it's into this folder that we will store content.

6. Next, go ahead and copy the public folder's contents into the locally cloned folder created in steps 1-3.

7. You should see an `index.md` file in your locally cloned version; open this file in your text editor.

8.   At the top of the file, **before any other content**, add in these lines; then save
     the file and close it:

```
---
permalink: /index.html
---
```

9.   Crack open the `.gitignore` file, which will contain a lot of entries; make sure
     it contains these values:

```
.DS_Store
Thumbs.db
db.json
*.log
node_modules/
public/
.deploy*/
```

10. Save the file and close it. Revert to GitHub Desktop; then enter the initial
     version in the text field above the Description box (bottom left of the application
     window).

11. Click Commit to master and then Push origin to upload your files to your site –
     you now have your content ready for action! Revert to your browser, and then
     browse to `https://XXXXX.github.io` (where XXXXX is your account ID) – if
     all is well, we should see something akin to the screenshot in Figure 10-5 at
     the start of this exercise.

At this point, you can minimize both GitHub Desktop and your text editor – you may
need them again, just in case the build and deployment process doesn't work the first
time! That aside, these last two exercises formed the basis of what is one of the most
critical parts of the whole process – let's take a moment to review the steps we've worked
through to see how the process works in more detail.

Breaking Apart the Changes

The deployment process is a sure sign that we must be reaching the end of the journey!
We can deploy content in one of two ways, either manually or automated; we will cover
the latter shortly, but for now, let's review what we achieved in the last exercise.

We kicked off by creating an optimized, production-ready version of our site, ready to be uploaded – this is critical. While the content we created during the development process will work, it won't be as efficient as possible! We then moved to use GitHub Desktop to copy the contents from our project area into a local version of the GitHub Pages site. At the same time, we checked the .gitignore file to ensure that it contained up-to-date entries (the default usually does, but it's still worth checking.)

Once done, we then pushed up the content as a commit, before viewing the content using the GitHub Pages URL, to be sure it displays correctly in the browser.

Okay, let's crack on: manually updating content using this method will allow us to see how the process works and get familiar with what should happen.

However, I don't know about you, but I'm a big fan of automation: why go through all that rigamarole when we can automate much of the process? I alluded that we can do this just now; it needs a little work to configure it using a plugin, so let's look at how we can save ourselves time when it comes to deploying code.

Deploying Content Automatically

When it comes to automating the deployment process for a Gatsby site, we could potentially write it as a component. However, that can be a more involved process; instead, there is a better alternative:

Instead of writing component code, we can add a custom command to the scripts block in our `package.json` file. It will require us to install an NPM package called gh-pages (available from `https://github.com/tschaub/gh-pages`), but this is to facilitate the upload; once we've done this, then it's just a matter of generating a token and adding a one-line entry to the `package.json` file. Let's take a look at how this would work in practice for our site.

DEMO: DEPLOYING CODE USING A SCRIPT

To switch to a more automated process for uploading content, follow these steps:

1. The first step is to install the gh-pages package – for this, fire up a Node.js terminal session, and then change the working folder to our project area.

2. At the prompt, enter this command and press Enter:

```
npm install gh-pages -D
```

3. Next, we need to tell gh-pages which repository to push to as the origin; for this, enter this command first to verify that we do not have an origin set:

    ```
    git remote -v
    ```

4. This command will display two entries – next, enter this command to set the origin:

    ```
    git remote add origin <URL TO YOUR REPOSITORY>
    ```

    You can see an example of how it should look:

    ```
    origin  https://github.com/havecakeeatcake/havecakeeatcake.github.io
    (fetch)
    origin  https://github.com/havecakeeatcake/havecakeeatcake.github.io
    (push)
    ```

5. We need to create a token to allow the deploy process to work – switch to your browser and browse to `https://github.com/settings/tokens`. Click the avatar logo top right, to make sure you have signed in with your GitHub account.

6. You should be on the Personal access tokens page – click Generate new token. It may prompt you to sign in – use your GitHub password if needed.

7. On the next screen, enter "Building demo Gatsby site" (no quotes!) into the field, and then tick the repo option (which will select all five sub-options).

8. At the bottom of the page, click Generate token. Take a note of it and keep it safe – you will not be able to retrieve it or see it again and will have to create a new one if it is lost or compromised.

9. Once down, switch to your text editor, and then crack open `package.json` – we need to add an entry to the `scripts` block. Look for this line of code, and then add in the code highlighted:

    ```
    "test": "echo \"Write tests! -> https://gatsby.app/
    unit-testing\"",
    "deploy:github": "gatsby build && gh-pages -d public -b master
    https://<YOUR KEY FROM GITHUB>@github.com/havecakeeatcake"
    },
    ```

10. Save the file, and then switch to your Node.js terminal session – at the prompt, enter npm run deploy:github and press Enter. It will be complete when you see Published appear at the end of the process, as shown in Figure 10-6.

```
postid dc26e530-f58d-5736-874b-97a7231674a4
postid 7d4ebee3-0538-5a91-850e-d18667ddf158
success Building static HTML for pages - 1.962s - 25/25 12.74/s
success onPostBuild - 0.002s
     Done building in 28.9172119 sec
Published
```

Figure 10-6. *A completed automatic upload*

11. Once done – and assuming there are no errors – go ahead and browse to https://XXXXX.github.io, where XXXXX is your username; you should see your site in all its glory!

That was relatively painless, right? The initial install is similar to any NPM package we might install in a Gatsby site, but that deploy command... I think now's an excellent opportunity to pause for a moment and explore the code changes we've made in more detail.

Exploring the Steps in More Detail

Although this last exercise may have seemed painless, it contained one crucial step – the code added in as part of step 3. That rather complicated-looking statement is the key to automating the deployment process. We set the command as npm run deploy:github; this executes two tasks.

The first task is to create a full production-optimized version of the site (similar to when we did it manually). The second takes that code and pushes it up using the gh-pages plugin to our site; we created and used a GitHub authorization token so that GitHub recognizes it as a valid commit and grants access. Once the upload completes, we can then view the site in all its glory via our browser.

Excellent, we now have content uploaded, so we should be good to go. Or are we? Until now, we've created a version of our site manually and uploaded it directly to the site – this works fine, but it is a bit cumbersome!

We've partially automated the process via the use of a plugin, but what if we could take it even further? In theory, we can by using a continuous integration (CI) tool such as Travis CI. There are a few things to bear in mind, though:

- The process of setting up CI does require the use of at least one or more secret keys – we need to be careful about how these are implemented, as leaving them exposed will create a security risk!

- Setting up a CI tool such as Travis does require a few steps – we need to be sure it is worth it for the size of the site. Ours isn't that large, so implementing continuous integration is potentially overkill for our needs.

- If we use CI, we need to make sure that we have the right processes to test code before uploading it; we risk creating something which would be overkill for our small site if we are not careful.

The key takeaway is that adding in a CI tool isn't something we should disregard completely. It's better implemented when we have a sufficiently large site and suitable traffic levels to warrant the time and resources needed to implement such a system and maintain its security and associated processes.

Okay, that aside, we have our site running in GitHub Pages: what more do we need? Ah, yes, there is one more task. In some respects, it's a bonus, but as we're creating something that could be developed further for real customers, it's almost a given that we need it. I'm talking about adding a domain name – any ideas for a name, anyone?

Adding a Custom Domain Name

Adding a custom domain is easy when using GitHub Pages, although we do have to factor in a 24-hour delay in the process. There are several benefits, though, in doing this process, irrespective of what tooling or framework we use:

- Using a short domain name is more memorable to customers, rather than what is effectively a custom subdomain – it inspires more confidence and is better for SEO purposes.

- An external domain name can be purchased cheaply, which makes for no excuse when it comes to creating a site.

- Having a subdomain doesn't suit every purpose – after all, why would you have a domain name such as flowers.github.com if you were a florist? GitHub Pages domains may serve technical people such as developers, but not your average Joe in the street!

Let's take a look at the steps we need to run through to get our site set up with a custom domain in more detail.

ADDING A DOMAIN NAME

For this exercise, I will assume you have a registered domain name – it can be an existing one or one registered anew. If it is a new registration, you may want to wait 24–48 hours to allow it to propagate around DNS, before working through these steps:

1. First, browse to your GitHub site using the format `https://github.com/<name of site>`.

2. On the main page, click Settings, and then scroll down to Custom domain.

3. In the Custom domain name field, enter the name of your chosen custom domain (in my case, I used `havecakeeatcake.com`), and then click Save. This action will create a commit that adds a CNAME file in the root of your repository.

4. Next, navigate to your DNS provider and create an A record – use the following IP addresses. You may find you need to create four separate A name records for each of these IP addresses:

   ```
   185.199.108.153
   185.199.109.153
   185.199.110.153
   185.199.111.153
   ```

We're using A records here, as the IP addresses are known and stable; CNAME entries are name aliases that map to other names.

5. To confirm that your DNS record is configured correctly, use the `nslookup` command – enter this in a terminal session:

```
nslookup <your domain name>
```

If you are using Linux (or potentially Mac), then you can use this: `dig EXAMPLE.COM +noall +answer`.

6. It will display something similar to the screenshot shown in Figure 10-7.

```
C:\>nslookup havecakeeatcake.com
Server:
Address:

Non-authoritative answer:
Name:     havecakeeatcake.com
Addresses:  185.199.108.153
            185.199.111.153
            185.199.109.153
            185.199.110.153
```

Figure 10-7. *DNS has been updated to point to our new site*

We have one more change to make, but when you can do it will depend on how quickly GitHub Pages completes a step. This step should be completed relatively quickly, but can take time to update:

7. Revert to the Settings page from earlier, where we added in the custom domain name – if you scroll a little further, you will see an Enforce HTTPS box, similar to Figure 10-8.

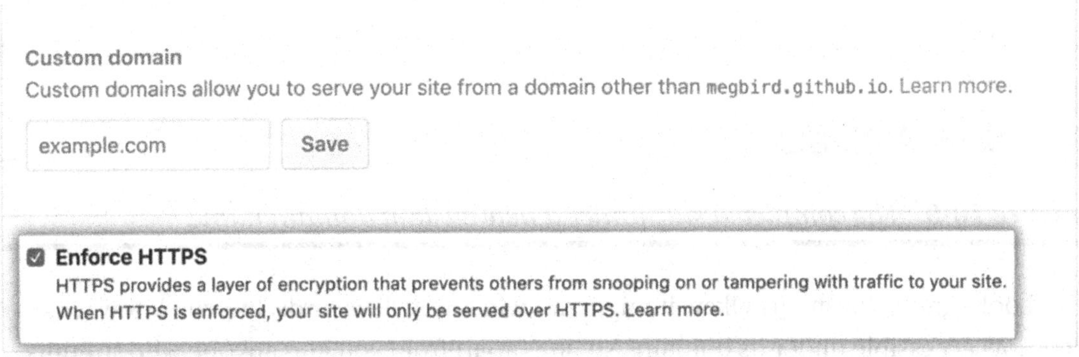

Custom domain
Custom domains allow you to serve your site from a domain other than megbird.github.io. Learn more.

| example.com | Save |

☑ **Enforce HTTPS**
HTTPS provides a layer of encryption that prevents others from snooping on or tampering with traffic to your site. When HTTPS is enforced, your site will only be served over HTTPS. Learn more.

Figure 10-8. *Enabling HTTPS access in our GitHub site*

8. When it lets you, make sure it is ticked (as in the preceding image) – this will force access to your site to be secured. This is now standard practice for all websites!

9. In a separate tab, go ahead and browse to your new site – as an example, Figure 10-9 shows how my version looks, under the new URL of `www.havecakeeatcake.com`.

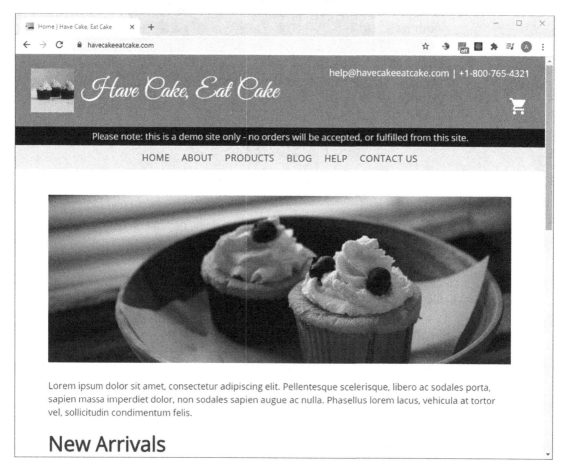

Figure 10-9. *The completed site, under a new custom domain name*

Looks great, doesn't it? Okay, it might not win any style awards, but you know what – it is now accessible under its domain! No one (apart from you and anyone who submits a change) will be any the wiser we are hosting it on GitHub – it's just another site on the Internet…right?

We've added in a CNAME field that tells GitHub what domain name to use; we then pointed it to GitHub's nameservers from our DNS, so that all requests to our new domain will get routed through to the right site. I would advise waiting 24–48 hours to ensure DNS gets updated, but once this has happened, you have a new website set up with a custom domain name, ready for use. It may take a few more hours for visitors further away before they can see the new site, but there's nothing we can do about that – it's just a matter of time!

If you would like more information on working with GitHub Pages and see what features they can offer, please refer to the documentation at `https://help.github.com/categories/github-pages-basics/`.

Summary

Deploying content to our site is an important milestone – we've reached the stage where customers can begin to use the site, purchase goods, and, hopefully, make us some money! Well, okay, perhaps not in our case (as it is a development site), but the principle is still the same. Over the last few pages, we've covered a lot of essential steps while getting our content online – let's take a moment to review what we've learned.

We started with a quick review of some of the last tasks that we needed to perform, such as creating a manifest file, adding offline support, and creating a demo banner. Although we should never consider any site as finished until it no longer serves us a purpose, these steps were essential to getting our initial version ready.

We then moved on to preparing our host on GitHub Pages. Before uploading the content, as part of this, we set several key settings, such as the default branch, ready for uploading using our GUI-based git tool. Next up, we took this a stage further by automating this process – we implemented gh-pages as a tool for uploading content, before adding a script to trigger this process when we are ready to upload content. We rounded out the demo by adding a custom domain name and working through the steps to ensure it points correctly to our GitHub Pages site.

Okay, our site is uploaded and ready for people to view: where next? It's a good question – it's time to have a little fun! Over the next few chapters, we will look at a handful of projects that will help develop the experience for both developers and customers alike. Let's start by asking this question: What if you had an existing CMS-based site with an e-commerce element attached to it? How would you convert it to using Gatsby? Stay with me, and I will reveal the answer in the next chapters.

PART IV

CHAPTER 11

Migrating from WooCommerce

Hands up anyone who uses WooCommerce? It's a highly popular tool, but one still reliant on WordPress. This level of popularity means it will be susceptible to hacking, as WordPress is so popular! Ever thought about whether you could move to a more secure, faster platform that doesn't suffer from the same vulnerabilities as WooCommerce?

The great thing is that we can (with some work) transition from using WooCommerce to Gatsby. It means we can take advantage of the benefits of using a static site generator and reduce our exposure to some of the vulnerabilities and risks of using one of the most well-known blogging platforms, such as accessing databases.

For the next few pages, we'll work on setting up an example WooCommerce installation, and I will show you some of the tricks you need to get started with moving over to using Gatsby as a replacement platform. At the same time, we'll also explore why making that move from WordPress/WooCommerce is beneficial, and we will also cover off some of the next steps we can take once we've completed the initial migration into a Gatsby site. Toward the end of this chapter, we will finish by exploring where we could go from here and what we might want to do to retire WooCommerce eventually.

Okay, plenty to do! Let's start first by answering a simple question.

Why Migrate to Gatsby?

It's an excellent question – after all, WordPress has been around since 2003, so it will be pretty stable by now. It's in use on 60 million-plus websites worldwide, including the likes of CBS News, Walt Disney, Bloomberg, and yes – for the nerds among us – even *the* Star Wars website! WooCommerce is no newcomer either, arriving in 2011.

© Alex Libby 2021
A. Libby, *Gatsby E-Commerce*, https://doi.org/10.1007/978-1-4842-6692-2_11

Both make for a powerful combination, used by millions of websites worldwide; why would we want to migrate away from using WordPress and WooCommerce if it is such a popular combination?

- One of the answers is in that question – its popularity is also one of its Achilles' heels! WordPress' popularity makes it an easy target for people to hack into the application. A hacked WordPress database is harder to restore than simply reinstating a copy of compiled files created during the Gatsby build process.

- WordPress requires us to use a database which is accessed dynamically; this creates a security risk as it exposes vulnerable points that can be hacked. Given WordPress' popularity, it places extra emphasis on us to ensure that the underlying architecture is as secure as possible! Security is absolutely key across all sites, but as content is compiled during build of a Gatsby site, this removes some of the associated risk which makes WordPress less secure.

- Speed – As Gatsby is compiled during build into static content, it makes it significantly faster, which also helps with SEO! WordPress content is dynamically created, which means if there is a slow connection, content will be slower to return and could eventually time out.

- Database-driven systems are also inherently slower than statically generated sites such as Gatsby – while we do use database (or Markdown) content for Gatsby, these are compiled during the build process into static files, which makes them faster and easier to cache.

- As a tool, WordPress has a vast plugin ecosystem; this can make it vulnerable to "bonnet-lifters," or people who like to peer into the internals of WordPress. It might be with good intentions, but there is still the risk that they may decide to do something that can break the site!

- At the same time, WordPress has an enormous plugin ecosystem – while there are plugins to do all manner of different tasks, there is also a temptation to add in lots of additional plugins. Adding in extra plugins will slow the site down and create something of a maintenance headache! If we separate the front-end from the back-end data, we as developers keep control, and the risk of customers completely breaking the site is reduced.

So, as we can see, making a move to Gatsby is beneficial; we gain from having a more secure and performant site and removing some of the risks of what might happen if customers tweak with how the site appears in the browser.

Now that we have that out of the way, let's start setting up our replacement site. We will need to do a few things, but for now, let's crack on with the first exercise, which is to set up the recipient site and install the plugins we need for the move.

Some Basic Housekeeping

Before we get into the guts of coding, there is one necessary evil we must take care of first.

As with any project, it's essential to have the correct software version to get the best out of the exercises. For this chapter, I will assume you are using the latest self-hosted versions of WordPress and WooCommerce. If you are using anything older than version 4.4 of WordPress, then, unfortunately, this chapter won't work for you; it relies on using the WordPress GraphQL engine, which wasn't introduced until version 4.4.

One thing to note is that I will assume that at least three products are with a "New Arrivals" category label; this is essential to allow the New Arrivals component to work as expected. You need to make sure you have something similar to that shown in Figure 11-1, which shows the three tagged products in the All Products view in WordPress:

		Name	SKU	Stock	Price	Categories	Tags
		Mixed Chocolate cupcakes	HCEC0012	In stock (50)	–	New Arrivals	New
		Easter cheesecakes	HCEC0017	In stock (46)	–	New Arrivals	New
		Dark cherry cupcakes	HCEC0010	In stock (38)	–	New Arrivals	New

Figure 11-1. The items tagged as New Arrivals in WordPress

> If you would like to try out this chapter, but don't have a suitable WooCommerce installation available, then feel free to set one up – there are plenty of tutorials available online to help get you started. A good starting point would be the one on the ThemeIsle website at `https://themeisle.com/blog/how-to-set-up-woocommerce/`.

At the same time, I will also be using a local web server – my personal choice is XAMPP, available for Windows, macOS, and Linux from `https://apachefriends.org`, but feel free to use your own if you already have something installed.

Okay, with that out of the way, it's time, my friends – time to start…

Creating the New Site

We won't – shock, horror – be using the site we've been building throughout this book for the first part of this migration. It might seem controversial, but there is a good reason for this: simplicity.

I suspect, if you already use WooCommerce (WC) and want to make a move to using Gatsby, that you won't want to change your existing WC installation, but set up something new that can run side-by-side, right? Taking this approach makes it easier to allow both sites to run, and given that you already store your data in WC, it makes sense to use it if we can and keep some form of continuity until the last possible moment.

So, with that in mind, we won't try to rebuild the site you've worked on thus far but instead focus on what would need to be changed to support sourcing content from WC. The key to making this work is using the `gatsby-source-woocommerce` plugin – more details on this later on. We'll also be using the Gatsby Hello World starter theme as the basis for this first task – let's take a look at the steps involved in more detail.

> A copy of the relevant code for this site is also available in the code download that accompanies this book – feel free to copy from the book or extract the appropriate file from the download as you see fit.

SETTING UP THE NEW SITE

To get our target site operational requires the use of a dedicated plugin:

1. First, fire up a Node.js terminal session, and then change the working folder to the root. I will assume for this chapter that is your C: drive, but please alter if necessary.

2. At the prompt, enter this command and press Enter:

   ```
   gatsby new hcec-demo https://github.com/gatsbyjs/gatsby-starter-
   hello-world
   ```

3. Next, switch to your WordPress admin dashboard, and click WooCommerce ➤ Settings.

4. Click Advanced ➤ Rest API and then Add key.

5. In the Description box, enter a title – this describes what these keys are for, such as "Gatsby WooCommerce theme integration."

6. Next, select your user ID, and make sure the third drop-down shows Read access. At this point, click the Generate API key, and then wait for it to confirm completion.

You will see two keys generated – keep a safe copy of both, as you will need these later in this exercise.

---

7. Switch to a Node.js terminal session, and make sure the working folder is our project area.

8. At the prompt, enter npm install --save @pasdo501/gatsby-source-woocommerce and press Enter.

9. Once completed, crack open the gatsby-config.js file at our project's root into your text editor.

10. Modify the plugins block to look like this:

    ```
    plugins:[
        `gatsby-transformer-sharp`,
        `gatsby-plugin-sharp`,
        {
    ```

```
    resolve: '@pasdo501/gatsby-source-woocommerce',
    options: {
      api: 'localhost/wordpress',
      verbose: true,
      https: false,
      api_keys: {
        consumer_key: '<ENTER ',
        consumer_secret: 'cs_a207410cda4a2ab1211daacc0c4
        bc5661a74f149',
      },
      fields: ['products', 'products/categories',
      'products/attributes']
    }
  }
  ]
}
```

11.   Go ahead and save the gatsby-config.js file, and then close it.

12.   Make sure you have your WordPress and WooCommerce installation active and
      running, then switch to a Node.js terminal session, and make sure the working
      folder is our new project area.

13.   At the prompt, enter `gatsby develop` and press Enter. Gatsby will compile
      the site; if all is well, you will see "Hello World!" appear in a browser window
      when browsing to `http://localhost:8000`.

We now have the basis for our migration site! We might not have seen much visually
in this demo, but this is okay; the magic comes later in this chapter. That said, this
exercise covered some essential steps, so let's take a moment to review the code changes
in more detail.

Understanding What Is Happening

This last exercise was designed to be quick and easy – something to get your teeth into
and warmed up for the next part of the process. We kicked off by setting up a new site
using the classic Gatsby Hello World starter; it doesn't contain much functionality
built-in, but that helps keep things clean and simple for us.

We then moved on to installing the plugin that will make all of this work for us – `gatsby-source-woocommerce`. The original version was by Marc Glasser, available from `https://github.com/marcaaron/gatsby-source-woocommerce`; I'm using a forked version by Dominik Paschke, available from `https://github.com/pasdo501/gatsby-source-woocommerce`. Once installed, we then linked it to an existing WooCommerce installation.

We now reach the most critical part, and I can already hear the questions coming: just how are we going to export content from WooCommerce into Gatsby?

Outlining the Proposed Solution

I suspect that you probably think it's a complicated process that requires many steps and needs us to take a big bang approach, right? Well, I hate to disappoint, but the answer – at least to the second part – is no! Let me explain what I mean.

The key to all of this working is to make sure you have a WordPress version 4.4 or greater, since the GraphQL engine was not introduced until version 4.4. of WordPress. Given Gatsby's ability to consume content from all manner of different sources using GraphQL, we can simply query the WordPress/WooCommerce database content and render it on-screen.

What does this mean for us? In the site we've been building thus far, we use Gatsby's `createPages` action to generate each page for us automatically during build. We can continue to do this, but this time sourcing content directly from WooCommerce. It means we effectively only need to focus on replicating the product gallery (and the trigger mechanism to create product pages).

There are two good reasons for taking this approach, which allows us to keep the existing site running during the development process:

- We need a system to store products and manage inventory, orders, and the like – Shopify already does this for us from the original demo, so it makes sense to continue using it.

- We already have products listed in WooCommerce, so rather than manually exporting them and adding them into Shopify, we can simply consume them directly from WooCommerce using GraphQL; after all, we have the content available, so why not use it?

At the same time, it's essential to understand that we won't cover everything in this chapter – it would be impossible to fit it all in! With that in mind, let's explore what we won't cover as part of this process in more detail.

Understanding the Scope

When using this approach, there are a few points we need to be aware of:

- We will still need a payment/checkout system of some description – constructing our own would be overkill for a small site. We have a perfectly good system in Shopify; as part of this, we will still need to store product details and images to allow it to manage orders and inventory. It means that the existing code for the product page template will remain.

- I would almost consider this approach as being a half-way house; there will come the point where we want to retire WooCommerce completely, so we need to make sure all products are moved across before that happens. Using a plugin to query WooCommerce from Gatsby directly gives us that breathing space to migrate content before turning the old system off.

- We will focus purely on what is needed to get the minimum out of WooCommerce – the rest of the content will be the same as we've covered earlier in the book, so there is no need to go through it twice! (I will point out which chapter to refer to, though, where appropriate).

Okay, let's crack on: now that we have our target site in place and understood something of how we will complete the migration, it's time for us to get technical! We will embark on a five-part exercise that will take us through the essential parts to adapt to source from WooCommerce. There are a fair few changes to make, so we'll start by creating a replacement `index.js` page that references the new arrivals from WooCommerce.

Sourcing Data

Sourcing data from WooCommerce is very straightforward once we have the link-up in place – indeed, one might forgive you for thinking it looks almost identical when you start to read the GraphQL queries we use!

It is indeed true that the GraphQL queries will look similar in places – this helps make it easier to complete the transfer from WooCommerce to Gatsby. To see what

I mean, we're going to work through what's required to source the content from WooCommerce instead of Shopify so that you can use it as a basis for building your replacement store.

As mentioned earlier, we will focus on the core queries; it will mean that the results might look a little spartan, but nothing we can't change using styles we created earlier in the book! Let's begin with setting up the replacement pages for our site – the main index page and New Arrivals component.

MIGRATING CONTENT PART 1: CREATING PAGES

In the first part of the migration process, we will create our main index page and a 404.js component – the former will host our replacement NewArrivals block, and the latter is to stop our browser whining about a missing 404 page! To get these files set up, follow these steps:

1. The first step is to create the index.js page, which will host the replacement NewArrivals block. Crack open a copy of the index.js file from within the \src\pages folder, and remove all that is within it.

2. Next, go ahead and add in this code – it will form the basis for our index.js page and call out to the New Arrivals component we will create shortly:

```
import React from "react"
import { graphql, Link } from "gatsby"
import NewArrival from "../components/NewArrival"

const IndexPage = ({ data }) => {
  return (

        <p><Link to='/gallery' aria-label='product-gallery'>Products
        </Link></p>
        <p>New Arrivals</p>
        <ul id="newarrivals">
          {data.wcProductsCategories.products.map(product => {
            return (
              <NewArrival
                key={product.id}
                name={product.name}
                slug={product.slug}
```

```
                    image={product.images[0].src}
                    alt={product.images[0].alt}
                />
            );
        })}
    </ul>

    );
};
```

3. In a new file, go ahead and add in this code – this will be our NewArrivals component:

```
import React from "react";
import { Link } from "gatsby";

const newArrival = (props) => {
  return (
    <li>
      <Link to={`/product/${props.slug}`} aria-label={props.name}
      className="newarrival">
        <img src={props.image} alt={props.alt} />
        <p>{props.name}</p>
      </Link>
    </li>
  )
}

export default newArrival;
```

4. Switch back to the index.js file, then scroll to the bottom, and leave a blank line.

5. After that blank line, add this constant declaration to source the data from GraphQL:

```
export const newArrivalsQuery = graphql`
  {
    wcProductsCategories(wordpress_id: {eq: 18}) {
      products {
        name
```

```
          price
          slug
          id
          images {
            src
            alt
          }
        }
      }
    }
  `;
```

6. In the previous step, we need to replace the number 18 shown in the query –
    this relates to the New Arrivals category. It's not the category itself, but the
    grouping of all three products we've included as new arrivals.

    To get this number, switch to your WordPress admin dashboard, and then click
    Categories under Products on the left menu. Hover over the name New Arrivals
    in the list on the right – in the URL that appears at the foot of the page, look for
    tag_ID=XX; XX will be the number you need to use.

7. The last change is to extract a copy of the global.css file from the code
    download that accompanies this book – drop it into a new folder called styles,
    under the \src folder. It will contain some basic styling to make our pages look
    at least presentable!

This style sheet will contain styles for this page, plus the remaining pages we
create later in this chapter.

---

8. To link the styles file into our site, crack open a new text file in your editor, and add
    this line; then save it as gatsby-browser.js at the root of our project folder:

    ```
    import "./src/styles/global.css"
    ```

9. The last step is to create a 404 page – this isn't necessary for the site's correct
    operation, but Gatsby will complain if it is not present. Go ahead and copy the
    404.js file from our original site and paste it into the \src\pages folder –
    this will work fine.

10. Save all three files and close them, as we no longer need them open. Fire up a Node.js terminal session, and then change the working folder to our new project area. At the prompt, enter `gatsby develop` and press Enter.

11. Once prompted, browse to `http://localhost:8000/` – if all is well, we should see something akin to the screenshot in Figure 11-2.

Products

New Arrivals

Mixed Chocolate cupcakes

Easter cheesecakes

Dark cherry cupcakes

***Figure 11-2.** Our refactored New Arrivals widget*

If you're not sure that these products are coming from WooCommerce, then right-click each image in Chrome, and select Copy image address. You should have a URL similar to this: `http://localhost/wordpress/wp-content/uploads/2020/10/mixedchocolate.jpg`. This is coming from WooCommerce and not our original Gatsby demo.

Although the site will look very basic, we now have something we can start to develop. The next part of this multi-stage process is to create a replacement product gallery, so let's crack on and work through the steps required to display our products directly from WooCommerce.

MIGRATING CONTENT PART 2: CONSTRUCTING THE PRODUCT GALLERY

This next exercise will use similar principles to create the core code for our replacement product gallery – to do so, follow these steps:

1. First, fire up your text editor, and add in this code – there is a good chunk of code required, so let's go through it block by block, starting with the imports:

```
import React from "react"
import { graphql, Link } from "gatsby"
```

2. Next up comes the main Gallery Page object – this will render our product gallery on-screen:

```
const GalleryPage = ({ data }) => {
  return (

      <div id="gallery-container">
        <p>Products available for sale</p>
            ...INSERT CODE HERE...
      </div>

  );
};

export default GalleryPage;
```

3. Go ahead and replace the ...INSERT CODE HERE... statement with this block – we iterate through each product in turn, to render the products for sale:

```
<ul id="gallery">
{data.allWcProducts.edges.map(edge => {
  return (
    <React.Fragment key={edge.node.id}>
      <li>
        <Link to={`/product/${edge.node.slug}`}
aria-label={edge.node.name}>
          <img src={edge.node.images[0].src} alt={edge.node.images[0].
          alt} />
          <p>Name: {edge.node.name}</p>
```

```
            </Link>
          </li>
        </React.Fragment>
      );
     })}
   </ul>
```

4. The last part we need to add is the GraphQL request – leave a blank line after the export statement, and then add in this block:

```
export const GalleryQuery = graphql`
  {
    allWcProducts {
      edges {
        node {
          images {
            src
            alt
          }
          name
          price
          id
          wordpress_id
          stock_quantity
          slug
        }
      }
    }
  }
`;
```

5. Go ahead and save the file and close it – the changes are complete.

6. Fire up a Node.js terminal session, and then change the working folder to our new project area. At the prompt, enter gatsby develop and press Enter.

7. Once prompted, browse to http://localhost:8000/ – if all is well, we should see something akin to the screenshot in Figure 11-3.

Products available for sale

Figure 11-3. *An extract of the (refactored) product gallery*

Excellent, we now have a product gallery in place! It has the same information as before, although if we were to try to click images to view product details, we would get...a big fat nothing!

There's a good reason for this – we need to add two more things before viewing product details correctly. Cast your mind back – do you remember fiddling around with the gatsby-node.js file? We also created a product page template – it's time to revisit the code and refactor it to work using WPGraphQL, or WordPress' implementation of GraphQL.

MIGRATING CONTENT PART 3: BUILDING THE PRODUCT PAGE TEMPLATE

To create our product page template, follow these steps:

1. First, fire up your text editor, and add in this code – there is a good chunk of
   code required, so let's go through it block by block, starting with the imports:

```
import React from 'react'
import { graphql } from 'gatsby'

const ProductPage = ({ data }) => {
  return (
    <>
      <div id="product-page">
        <div><img src={data.wcProducts.images[0].src} alt=
        {data.wcProducts.images[0].alt} /></div>
        <div>
          <p>{data.wcProducts.name}</p>
          <p dangerouslySetInnerHTML={{__html: `${data.wcProducts.
          description}`}} />
          <p>Price: {data.wcProducts.price}</p>
          <p>{data.wcProducts.stock_quantity > 10 ? 'In stock':
          'Low stock'}</p>
        </div>
      </div>
    </>
  )
}

export default ProductPage
```

2. The last part we need to add is the GraphQL request – leave a blank line after
   the export statement, and then add in this block:

```
export const singleProduct = graphql`
  query SingleProduct($slug: String) {
    wcProducts(slug: { eq: $slug }) {
      name
      price
      description
```

```
        stock_quantity
        slug
        sku
        id
        images {
          src
          alt
        }
      }
    }
  `;
```

3.   Go ahead and save the file and close it – the changes are complete.

You will notice I've deliberately not restarted the Gatsby develop server at this point – it won't display any data and will more likely error! We will fix this in the next exercise – the results may look a little bare in terms of styling, but I'm assuming this would come as a "next steps" task once we know we have the core functionality working.

For us to fix that error, there is one more step we need to complete, which will tie everything we've done thus far together: create the `gatsby-node.js` file.

This file acts as the glue that allows us to create a series of pages dynamically using a single template; it may not suit enormous sites with thousands of pages, but it's perfect for a small website. If you need to work on large sites and need to create pages in a similar manner, then I would suggest checking out the Gatsby plugin library at `www.gatsbyjs.com/plugins/` to see if there are any plugins suitable for transforming your existing content. Alternatively, you may like to consider creating a transformer plugin to convert from an existing format such as Markdown into something that can be consumed by Gatsby. There is a good article on how to do this on the Gatsby website, at `www.gatsbyjs.com/docs/creating-a-transformer-plugin/`.

We're going to refactor our site in the last part of this multi-stage exercise; it will use the same principles as before, but this time source data from WooCommerce, not Shopify.

MIGRATING CONTENT PART 4: HOOKING IT ALL TOGETHER

To tie everything together, we need to update the gatsby-node.js file – for this, follow these steps:

1. First, fire up your text editor, and add in this code – there is a good chunk of code required, so let's go through it in sections, starting with the main createPages action:

```
const path = require('path')

module.exports.createPages = async ({ graphql, actions }) => {
  const { createPage } = actions

  return graphql(`
    query {

      allWcProducts {
        edges {
          node {
            slug
          }
        }
      }
    }
```

2. Immediately below the last bracket of the previous step, add in this block – it uses the data returned from our query to feed into creating each page:

```
  `).then(result => {
    result.data.allWcProducts.edges.forEach(({ node }) => {
      createPage({
        path: `/product/${node.slug}`,
        component: path.resolve(`./src/templates/ProductPage/index.js`),
        context: {
          slug: node.slug
        }
      })
    })
  })
}
```

3. Go ahead and save the file and close it – the changes are complete.

4. Fire up a Node.js terminal session, and then change the working folder to our new project area.

5. At the prompt, enter `gatsby develop` and press Enter.

6. Once prompted, browse to `http://localhost:8000/` – if all is well, we should see something akin to the screenshot in Figure 11-4.

Fairy Cakes

Our traditional fairy cupcake, delicately baked for that light fluffy sponge, and topped with a generous swirl of our house whipped cream and sprinkles. If you fancy a treat, what better way to indulge yourself?

Price: 2.95

In stock

Figure 11-4. *The new product page*

Our site may still look a little spartan, but we've completed the changes required to source data from WooCommerce directly into Gatsby. At this point, we would consider adding in the styling and remaining pages and link up to our existing Shopify installation to complete the transfer.

I bet though you're probably wondering why we've taken this approach through – the smart-eyed among you may have noticed that we're using GraphQL throughout, so why not merely push everything into Shopify and be done with it?

It's an excellent question and one which hides a bit of a dark secret – we will go through this and more in due course. However, for now, we should review the changes we've made in that last set of exercises, so we can understand how this fits in with what we've created elsewhere in this book.

Breaking Apart the Changes

Throughout the last exercise, the focus was primarily on creating the GraphQL requests we would need to replace the existing ones we made earlier in the book. Many will indeed have left each page looking a little spartan, but I'm assuming that once we crack each demo's core, we would then go away and style each page according to the customer's designs!

In the first stage of this multi-part demo, we concentrated on creating the query (and host page) that would surface the products featured in the original "New Arrivals" component we constructed earlier in the book. The query we've created will contain similar details to the one put together earlier in the book; it's important to note that the critical change is referencing the `wcProductsCategories` object within GraphQL as our replacement data source. We then worked out how to get the correct WordPress category ID for these products, tagging them with a New Arrivals category label. It's this category we use to source the three products displayed in the new Arrivals component.

Next up came the product gallery – this time, we reference the `allWcProducts` object in GraphQL and source from it properties such as `price`, `id`, `images.src`, and `images.alt`. The main page calls in the New Arrivals component; inside this, we iterate through each response returned within the `allWcProducts` object before rendering each on-screen.

In parts 3 and 4 of this demo, we focused on creating the product page template – this we use in conjunction with the changes we make to the `gatsby-node.js` file to create pages for each of our products dynamically. Each time someone clicks a product in the gallery, we capture the slug value from that product and use the `createPages` action in Gatsby to dynamically create our page. We pass several properties into this action – the intended path of the final page (i.e., display as `http://localhost:8000/product/XXXXX`), the component to use (in this case, our product page template), and the slug (which we use to source product details.)

Once captured and passed to the page template, we then query GraphQL for this product, using the slug value as the key. Any properties returned are then fed into the `ProductPage` object and rendered into the correct slot on the page.

If you would like other examples of GraphQL queries that we can use with the gatsby-source-woocommerce plugin, then head over to `www.gatsbyjs.com/plugins/@pasdo501/gatsby-source-woocommerce/#some-graphql-query-examples` for more details.

Okay, let's move on: I made mention of the fact that many of you might be asking why we've used the approach we've taken in this chapter. Why not push the products directly into Shopify if we are already using it for the payment and checkout process?

These are good questions – indeed, we could have taken one of several different approaches. It raises some critical points we need to consider, as part of the broader "migration" process, so let's take a moment to explore what this means in greater detail.

Exploring Alternative Options

At the end of the last exercise, I referred to a question I suspect many of you might ask: why have we used the approach outlined in this chapter instead of merely pushing products into Shopify and sourcing them directly from there? It is indeed a good question; there is nothing wrong with this approach. However, there are several reasons for taking the path we've used – let's go through them:

- It buys us time – instead of taking the big bang approach, we can gradually transfer content across, which reduces risk and pressure on us.

- The content is already in the database, so why not make use of it? It's a perfect excuse to show Gatsby's ability to source from multiple locations – as long as your version of WordPress supports GraphQL, then it should be easy to incorporate content from it in our new site.

Hopefully, this will begin to look more like a no-brainer! Looking further afield, though, how would we migrate content from WooCommerce if we didn't go down the route we've chosen to use?

Let's assume that we still want to automate the process and not rely on a manual export/import of the data into a format we know won't be 100% perfect. Well, a quick check of the plugin library on the Gatsby website will show a handful of plugins that, at first glance, would appear to be suitable for use with WooCommerce. However, all is not what it seems. Other authors forked these from the version by Marc Glasser; they are virtually the same, albeit with some minor changes and tweaks to features.

At this point, things get a little more complicated: the plugin we're using is undergoing a significant rewrite, so things are in a state of flux until the new version hits version 1 and the original version is retired from use. The replacement will be the `wp-graphql-woocommerce` plugin, available from `https://github.com/wp-graphql/wp-graphql-woocommerce`. I've avoided using it here, as I wasn't able to get it operational with current versions of Node.js (version 12.5 at the time of writing, although yours may be newer by the time this book comes out in print).

What does this mean for us? We could stay with merely adding more products to Shopify – there's nothing wrong with this approach technically. We already source details for the product pages from it, so it makes sense to expand on it. However, this will put more pressure on us to move the content over – we could export it from WooCommerce as a CSV file and import it, but there is no guarantee of how it will appear in Shopify! WooCommerce already has the correct information available, so why not only change the presentational layer part by rendering it in Gatsby, not WooCommerce?

We can still keep WooCommerce running, and as long as we set the GraphQL queries used in this chapter to be read-only, we can protect the existing data. The officially recommended option will indeed change, but we shouldn't feel obliged to have to use it – it's far more critical (now) to use a stable, tried, and tested solution, even if it will be depreciated over time. Of course, the new plugin will change things, but that's yet to come – we can only work with the here and now, rather than what we don't yet know!

Alright, let's crack on: we're coming to the end of this chapter, and it's time to answer an important question. Yes, I know – it's an absolute killer one, the $64,000 question. Call it what you will... How can we develop things further?

Taking It Further

Okay, perhaps I was hyping things a little too much there, but with good reason! Let me explain what I mean.

Over these last few pages, we've focused on what would be needed to source content from WooCommerce, assuming that we might use this as our data source, not our existing system, DatoCMS. Yes, it has meant that the pages we constructed were somewhat spartan, but this was deliberate – we can add styling afterward, once the core code is operational.

Now that we've done this, "What next?" I hear you ask. Well, there are a few things we can do to get started:

- The top of the list should be to switch to using the gatsby-image plugin to source images; the queries we've used return direct links back for the images, which works fine. However, the gatsby-image plugin offers a host of extra features that we can't get by merely querying GraphQL.

- At the same time, we should also consider taking copies of all of the images from within WordPress related to products we're selling and move them to a new location. Assuming that this location supports GraphQL, we can then create queries to reference these images directly and swap them in – another step closer to dropping WooCommerce!

- We've focused on migrating from WooCommerce, but what if you also happen to use WordPress as a social blog for your retail offer? If it's the current version (and I am assuming it is), we can equally use the same migration approach to source blog posts and WordPress pages into a new blog in Gatsby. It requires a little work to configure it using a different plugin, but the principles are pretty much the same as for WooCommerce.

For reasons of space, I've not included details on how in this chapter, but I've included a bonus PDF with instructions that is available in the code download that accompanies this book.

- An important point to consider is links to our new site – granted, we're nowhere near ready to make our new one live, but we will still need to consider how to move customers away from WooCommerce to Shopify/Gatsby. It is incredibly important for SEO purposes, as well as making the whole experience seamless for customers.

- Let's say for a moment that we use the same styling as before. Nothing wrong with this, except for one small but critical point: it's not optimized. "Aie," I hear you say, "not optimized?" Yes, this is true – I used the old-school method of storing style rules in a style sheet. The existing code works but isn't the most favored approach for Gatsby – instead, styles should be in-lined, ideally using a base component and building them out from there.

- Once we have our interim site operational, we can use this as an opportunity to export content from WooCommerce and transfer it to a new data source. It might be DatoCMS or Gatsby's internal GraphQL offer. It doesn't match which: as Gatsby can source from multiple GraphQL sources, it will all look seamless, and the customer will be none the wiser that we're using various sources.

The ZapERP website has an interesting article on making a move from WooCommerce to Shopify and suggesting how we might manage link redirects. You can read the article at `https://blog.zaperp.com/how-to-migrate-from-woocommerce-to-shopify/`.

There are just a few ideas to whet your appetite – most of what you do will, of course, depend on your circumstances and the requirements of your customers. However, with a little care and forethought, we can see how easy it is to display content from a WooCommerce back-end database as a precursor to moving it into a more secure and performant solution using Gatsby.

Summary

WordPress has become extremely popular as a tool – its constant development and huge ecosystem mean it has come a long way since the heady days of its first release. With the advent of WooCommerce, it became a useful alternative to some big names for online retail – the problem being its popularity has also become its Achilles' heel! Over these last few pages, we've explored some useful techniques to begin the process of migrating to a more secure, faster alternative in the form of Gatsby; let us review what we have learned.

We kicked off by exploring the benefits of moving to use Gatsby before covering some of the basic requirements we needed to get the most out of this chapter's projects.

Next up, we then created the base site for our migration before outlining how we would perform this migration. We then moved on using a Gatsby plugin to source data from WooCommerce, before covering some of the reasons we used this path and what alternatives we might have available. We then rounded out this chapter by covering some of the next-step actions we might want to take – having focused on the core GraphQL queries, the direction we might take is up to us (and our customer's wishes, of course!)

Phew, another project bites the dust: it might not suit all, but for those of you who do use WooCommerce, hopefully, this has shown you that it is possible to migrate to a more secure, faster system and eventually retire WooCommerce from active use.

Okay, let's move on: so far, we've focused on the desktop experience for our site. But - with us being in an age of responsive design (as such), increasing numbers of people browse via mobile devices.

This raises an important question: how *would* our site look on a mobile device? My early tests indicate that the answer would be "not too great", and that we clearly have some work to do! To find out more, stay with me, and I will explain all in the next chapter.

CHAPTER 12

Adapting for Mobile

I'm generally not someone who gambles, but I will lay pretty good odds that some of you will be reading this book on an iPad or some such mobile device.

Okay, so only time will tell if this is true, but here is a fact that is true: there are over 4.54 billion smartphone users in the world today. Yes, you read that right – 4.54 billion. Don't believe me? Try this for size: According to the DataReportal site, mobile web traffic at the end of 2019 outstripped desktop (and laptop) traffic by 20% to the point that over half of all traffic is now via mobile phones.

See a picture here? Yes, it is indeed true: surfing the Web on mobile devices has become big business. It is, therefore, essential to have a website that works on a mobile device! In this age of responsive design, we should take a mobile-first approach, but that isn't always practical or possible. This chapter will look at our site and explore what we might need to change to ensure our site operates in a mobile environment while still using Gatsby.

Why Is Mobile So Important?

Okay, it's clear that we can tap a vast market when designing our site. That is only part of the picture: there is more to it that we need to consider.

As I am sure you are aware, Internet connections have become faster over the years; I can still remember when I had to use a 36.6 K modem! Thankfully that is long since gone, and we are blessed with always-on broadband or cable connectivity. The problem is faster connections have not translated to faster sites – indeed, load times have gone up, not down.

Much of this is from user expectations – we want to do more, so functionality must increase to keep apace. Gone are the days when you might head into a shop when you can do your retail therapy online in the comfort of your own home.

© Alex Libby 2021
A. Libby, *Gatsby E-Commerce*, https://doi.org/10.1007/978-1-4842-6692-2_12

The real problem is that people rely more and more on smartphones, particularly in countries where telecoms infrastructure isn't excellent. Sites may offer more functionality, but this comes at a cost – a small change such as adding scripts to include a new feature could introduce a blocking call when loading the web page and increase the TTI value accordingly.

Therefore, we must work in a mobile mindset where possible.

This includes working toward making existing desktop-based sites more responsive. With that in mind, I want to focus on both the technical changes and some of the mindset behind what we can do to make the mobile experience more performant.

To make this a reality, we're going to work through our original design to see how it performs on a mobile and then work through some of the steps we need to take to improve the experience. Our journey will focus on using the iPhone as the basis for this design, but this could be for any mobile device. Let's start first by assessing how our current design looks on a mobile device.

Testing the Existing Layout

For this first exercise, we will use Chrome Developer Console to emulate our chosen iPhone design – granted, it won't be perfect, but it will at least give a good indication of where we might have issues with our design.

Throughout this chapter, I will use Chrome to emulate the design, as this is the most popular browser; feel free to use any browser to test, as the principles behind adapting our site will be the same for any browser.

TESTING THE EXISTING LAYOUT

To test our site as it stands, follow these steps:

1. First, fire up a Node.js terminal session, and then change the working folder to our project area.

2. At the prompt, enter `gatsby clean && gatsby build && gatsby serve` and press Enter.

3. Go ahead and open Chrome Developer Tools, and click the Responsive Mode button.

4. Browse to `http://localhost:9000` – if all is well, we should see our site in a mobile view, as indicated in Figure 12-1.

Figure 12-1. *Initial view of our site on an iPhone*

Although that last picture only shows the header, the site doesn't look great, does it? Try sliding it to the right – you will see the navigation doesn't fit correctly, and the footer...well, that just looks a mess! True, it could be worse: we need to make quite a few changes to get it looking right, so let's crack on and assess what we can do to improve our customers' experience.

Assessing the Layout

When assessing the layout, we must take an objective view of what should or should not be changed. It's not only about what we want to offer customers, but the practicalities of doing so on mobile devices; you can forget large videos, but YouTube ones would work!

In the last exercise, we saw that our design needs some remedial work. There are quite a few issues that need fixing, which include the following:

- Header – Most elements need repositioning, as it's a mess.

- The main hero banner image looks squashed.

- Our menu needs to be made responsive (we will work on this later in this chapter).

- We need to center the "new arrivals" images on the homepage.

- Items in the footer need completely reorganizing.

- The text and images in the copyright block need reordering.

As you can see, there is a real mix of issues we need to fix! Most of these are in the header and footer, so we'll focus on editing from the homepage; the changes will cascade throughout the site automatically.

I'm sure there is more we can do, but this will give us something we can start with to make our mobile experience more pleasant. Let's make a start by doing something that some of you might find a little…controversial?

Simplifying the Original Design

Yes, as the title of this next section says, we are going to simplify our design! Some of you might ask why we do this – there is a good reason. Let me explain.

As we're using a responsive design, there will be aspects where we have to be a little flexible in our approach; not everything will work on mobile and desktop, so we have to keep this in mind. When it comes to updating existing desktop-based designs, the existing code markup isn't likely conducive to restyling or adapting for use on a mobile device. It's at this point where updating the markup will be a better option than using an ugly CSS hack to style our site.

It might seem controversial because some people think we could be sacrificing visual appearance if we change the markup; it's not about altering what we have agreed with UX designers. It's all about making it easier to code – at the same time, if we have to change the design, then it's likely that your UX team hasn't entirely grasped the concept of mobile design.

Okay, time for our next exercise, methinks! In this next demo, we will update the CSS and markup; we'll focus on adapting for the iPhone, but the same principles apply for other mobile devices. Once we've altered the markup, we'll move on adding in media queries to make the design a little more palatable for mobile devices.

UPDATING THE DESIGN PART 1: THE MARKUP

To update the existing markup, follow these steps:

1. First, crack open a copy of the index.js file that sits under \src\components\ navigation in your text editor.

2. Scroll down to the opening <header> tag, and then delete everything down to **but not including** the closing </header> tag.

3. Go ahead and add in this replacement code between the two header tags – the tags in bold mark the original code's points. There is a fair bit of code to add, so we will do it in sections, starting with the opening header tag:

    ```
    <header
      style={{
        background: `#a49696`,
        display: `flex`,
        justifyContent: `space-evenly`,
        padding: `20px 30px`,
        color: `#ffffff`,
      }}
    >
    ```

4. Next, add in these two div statements and image reference:

    ```
    <div style={{ display: `flex`, alignItems:`end` }}>
      <div style={{ display: `flex`, alignItems: `center` }}>
      <img src={headerImage} alt="site header" style={{ marginBottom:
      `0`, width: `100px`, height: `auto`, paddingRight: `15px` }} />
    </div>
    ```

5. We need to add in a replacement link to the homepage from anywhere in the site, via the main site title:

```
<div>
  <MenuLink to='/'>
    <h1>
      {siteTitle}
    </h1>
  </MenuLink>
  <p>help@havecakeeatcake.com</p>
  <p>+1-800-765-4321</p>
</div>
</div>
```

6. The last section is the shopping cart and item count:

```
<div style={{ display: `flex` }}>
  <MenuLink to='/cart' style={{textAlign: `center`}}>
    <img src={shoppingcart} alt="shoppingcart" style={{width:
    `40px`, height: `auto`, fill: `#ffffff`, marginBottom: `0`,
    marginTop: `0.5rem` }} />
    {hasItems &&
      <CartCounter>
        {quantity} item{quantity > 1 ? "s": ""}
      </CartCounter>
    }
  </MenuLink>
</div>
</header>
```

7. Save the file and close it.

8. Next, download a copy of the `global.scss - tweaked` file from the `\src\ styles` folder in the code download that accompanies this book – and use it to replace the existing one in our project area.

Don't forget to rename it to global.scss!

---

9. First, fire up a Node.js terminal session, and change the working folder to our project area.

10. There is one more change to make — we need to update a defined style that sits in the \src\components\styles.js file. Go ahead and crack open this file in your editor, and then edit the code as shown:

```
export const CartCounter = styled.span`
  background-color: white;
  color: #663399;
  border-radius: 20px;
  padding: 0 10px;
  font-size: 1.2rem;
  // float: right;
  // margin: -10px;
  z-index: 20;
  display: flex;
  flex-direction: column;
```

11. Save the file and close it — we no longer need it open. Revert to a Node.js terminal session if you have one open, or crack open a new one — make sure the working folder is our project area.

12. At the prompt, enter gatsby develop and press Enter — this will restart the development server.

13. Browse to http://localhost:8000 — if all is well, we will see some changes to how the header looks; we will tidy it up even further in the next part of this exercise.

Right, we're a step closer, although we still have plenty to do! Now would be an excellent time to take a breather and get a drink or take a step away from the computer: when you're ready, we can move on to the next part, to restyle our site for iPhones.

As from before, we will focus primarily on the homepage; this is where most changes need to be made (plus any changes in the header or footer will filter throughout the site anyway). Let's make a start with fixing our design as part of our next exercise.

UPDATING THE DESIGN PART 2: ADDING THE FIXES

To update our design for iPhones, follow these steps:

1. First, crack open a copy of `globals.scss` from within the `\src\styles` folder in your text editor.

2. Scroll to the bottom of the file.

3. Next, we need to add in a series of CSS style rules – there are a good few to add, so we will do this block by block, beginning with adjusting the width for our `<header>` tag:

```
/****** MEDIA QUERIES ******/

@media screen and (max-width: 375px) {
  header {
    width: 100%;
    padding-left: 10px !important;
    padding-right: 10px !important;
  }

  ...INSERT REMAINING STYLES HERE...
}
```

4. Next up, we have a set of descendant elements to restyle within the header. Go ahead and add in these rules, replacing the text `...INSERT REMAINING STYLES HERE...` from the previous exercise:

```
header h1 {
  font-size: 40px;
}

header > div:nth-child(2) > p {
  margin-bottom: 0;
  font-size: 14px;
}

header > div:nth-child(3) {
```

```
    display: flex;
    align-items: flex-end;
  }

  header > div:nth-child(3) > a > span {
    font-size: 0.8rem;
  }

  header > div:nth-child(3) > a > img {
    margin-bottom: -10px !important;
  }

  header > div:nth-child(3) > a > span {
    float: unset;
    display: inline-flex;
  }

  #gatsby-focus-wrapper > div.css-1ar37a1 {
    margin-top: 20px;
  }
```

5. Leave a line blank after the last rule, and then add in these styles for the footer:

```
  #gatsby-focus-wrapper footer {
    flex-direction: column;
  }

  footer > div > p:nth-child(1) {
    margin-bottom: 5px;
    border-bottom: 1px solid rgb(0,0,0,0.8);
  }
```

6. We need to adjust the styling for each of the three areas within the footer – leave a line blank after the last style, and then add in these styles to update the Subscribe section:

```
  // Subscribe section
  #gatsby-focus-wrapper > footer > div:nth-child(2) > form { display:
  flex; flex-direction: row; align-items: baseline; }
```

```
#gatsby-focus-wrapper > footer > div:nth-child(2) > p:nth-child(2)
{ margin-bottom: 0px; }

#gatsby-focus-wrapper > footer > div:nth-child(2) > form > div:nth-
child(2) > button { width: unset; padding: 12px 26px; }
```

7. Next, do the same thing for this style, to update the Connect section:

```
// Connect section
#gatsby-focus-wrapper > footer > div:nth-child(3) > p
{ display: none; }
```

8. We have three more styles left to update, which are the Contact Us form, a
   `<div>` element on the blog page, and the copyright block. Leave a line blank
   after the last style, and then add in these rules:

```
// Contact Us
.contactform { width: 100%; }

// Blog page
#gatsby-focus-wrapper > div.css-1ar37a1 > div {
flex-direction: column !important;
}

// Copyright
div.copyright { flex-direction: column; }
div.copyright > div:nth-child(2) > img {
margin-top: 15px; }
}
```

9. Save the file and close it – the changes are complete.

10. Switch to a Node.js terminal session, and then set the working folder to our
    project area.

11. At the prompt, enter `gatsby develop` and press Enter to rebuild the site.

12. Fire up your browser, and then head over to `http://localhost:8000` – if
    all is well, we should see something akin to the extract screenshot shown in
    Figure 12-3, shown overleaf.

Figure 12-2. *The updated view of our site on an iPhone device*

Okay, it's looking better, but still not perfect! The content is better aligned, although we can see the menu needs adjusting. If we were to look at other pages, we would find most look more presentable, although our shopping cart still needs attention. We will tackle both later in this chapter, but for now, let's take a moment to review the changes made in the last exercise in more detail.

Breaking Apart the Code

Over the last few pages, we've completed what might seem like many steps – they were all needed, though, as our site didn't look right when we first looked at it at the start of the chapter.

We've made quite a few changes – we started by replacing the contents of the `<header>` tag in the Navigation component. Making so many changes might have seemed like a controversial move at the time, but we did this to help tweak the markup to make it easier for us to produce a design that works better on both desktop and mobile devices. Granted, it did alter the appearance, but this is the trade-off: there are occasions where we might have to "compromise" a little to get the best effect on both types of devices!

Next up, we then updated the styles within `global.scss` – this we did to fine-tune the original styles as part of updating our design. We then ran a quick preview to confirm that our site still worked, albeit with an updated header.

In part 2, we focused on adding several individual styles to tweak the design for iPhone devices. Most of these targeted the header and footer as it seems this was where things fell most; we made a few changes to other elements to help realign them on the page. It means that we now have a design that is working better, although there will be some more changes made later in this chapter.

I want to focus on one area, though, as part of this work – the header markup changes. Although it may not be immediately apparent, the changes we made include the following, where we've

- Removed the text "accepted, or" from the demo banner – shortening makes it easier to manage on mobile devices while still imparting the essence of the message.

- Moved the shopping cart icon and text out of the `<span>` element that contained the email and phone text.

- Set the main hero image with an `auto` width – this will fit better on the page.

- Moved the email and phone spans into the `<div>` element, which contains the title – this allows us to lay them on the page better.

These are small changes, but they all help make the design more manageable for us to style, as they contain the markup we need to ensure we render content into the correct location in desktop or mobile format. It's important to note that this is not about compromising the intended design but helping to strike a sensible balance between interpreting the desired vision and ensuring we have the right markup to support that vision.

Okay, let's crack on: our design is coming on nicely, so let's turn our attention to fixing two essential parts that need further adjustment. I'm talking about the navigation and basket page: we'll start with updating the navigation to work better on our (emulated) iPhone device.

Making the Menu Responsive

Navigation is key to any website – customers who can't find what they want quickly will frequently vote with their feet! I once read that any website content should be accessible within two clicks or fewer. I'm not sure if it holds today, but it is still a useful tip to aspire to, to help make our site accessible, particularly on mobile devices.

A quick look at the screenshot back in Figure 12-1 shows that our current navigation falls well short of what we need to have in a mobile device; it may not contain many entries, but doesn't fit at all well in the limited space we have!

It isn't a quick fix, though – the best way to approach this is to replace it with a hamburger-style menu that can slide in and out. Simultaneously, we can add code to show or hide either the desktop or mobile version of the menu, depending on the platform in use. Let's take a look at the code required to adapt the menu for mobile use in more detail.

UPDATING THE MENU

To adapt the menu for mobile use, follow these steps:

1. First, crack open a copy of the code download that accompanies this book – from it, extract copies of burger.js and menu.js, and then store them in a new folder called MobileNav, under \src\components in our project area.

2. Next, open the index.js file in \src\navigation, then scroll down to the end of the useQuantity function, and leave a line blank.

3. Add in these declarations – they will show or hide the appropriate menu, based on the available screen width:

```
const MobileNav = styled.div`
  @media screen and (max-width: 375px) {
    display: block;
  }

  @media screen and (min-width: 480px) {
    display: none;
  }
`
```

4. Next, we need to import the new mobile navigation components (plus the styled library we use elsewhere already) into our component – for this, add in these lines immediately below the last import and before the import StoreContext... line:

```
import Burger from "../MobileNav/Burger"
import Menu from "../MobileNav/Menu"
import styled from "@emotion/styled"

import StoreContext from '~/context/StoreContext'
```

5. Scroll down to the main Navigation component declaration – we need to add in our new mobile navigation component to the render() block. Add in the highlighted lines, as indicated:

```
const Navigation = ({ siteTitle }) => {
  const [hasItems, quantity] = useQuantity()

  const [open, setOpen] = useState(false);
  const node = useRef();

  return(
    <>
      <MobileNav ref={node}>
        <Burger open={open} setOpen={setOpen} />
        <Menu open={open} setOpen={setOpen} />
      </MobileNav>
      <header
```

6. Once the mobile navigation is operational, we will have a slight rendering issue in that the main hero banner will appear too high. To fix this, go ahead and add this code to the bottom of the `global.scss` file:

```
/**** RESPONSIVE MENU ****/
#demobanner {
  margin-bottom: 20px;
  }
}
```

7. To ensure that the desktop navigation only appears at the right point in the experience, we need to hide it if the screen width is too small. Add this code to \ src\pages\sitenavighation.js immediately after the last import statement, and before the code `const SiteNavigation = ...` in the component:

```
import styled from "@emotion/styled"

const DesktopNav = styled.div`
  @media screen and (max-width: 375px) {
    display: none;
  }
`
```

8. There are a few more tweaks we need to make to our CSS styling – go ahead and remove the highlighted words/line from this block of code in \src\ styles\global.scss:

```
nav {
  background-color: $nav-background-color;
  display: flex;
  justify-content: center;
  padding: 10.56px 11.2px;
  margin-bottom: 50px;

  div a { color: $nav-text-color; cursor: pointer; padding: 11.2px
  12px; letter-spacing: 0.03rem !important; text-decoration: none;
  text-transform: uppercase; }

  div a:hover { background-color: $nav-hover-color;
  padding: 11.2px 12px; }
}
```

9. The last change is to add in `<DesktopNav>` tags in `sitenavigation.js`, so they encompass the entire desktop version of the menu, as indicated:

```
<DesktopNav>
  <nav>
      <Link to={`${data.datoCmsNavigation.homeLink}`}
      activeClassName="active">{data.datoCmsNavigation.homeText}</Link>
      ...
  </nav>
</DesktopNav>
```

10. Go ahead and save the files, and then close them – the changes are now complete.

11. Switch to a Node.js terminal session, and then make sure the working folder is set to our project area.

12. At the prompt, enter `gatsby develop` and press Enter to recompile the site with the changes.

13. Fire up Chrome and browse to `http://localhost:8000` – if all is well, we should see some changes to our menu layout when switching Chrome to emulate an iPhone 6/7/8 screen (Figure 12-3).

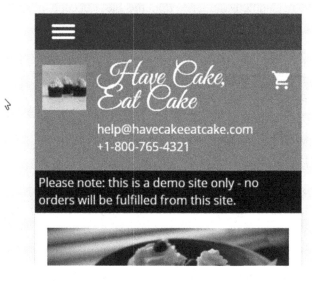

Figure 12-3. *The new hamburger icon for our mobile menu*

14. If we click the hamburger icon, the new menu slides in, as indicated in the extract shown in Figure 12-4.

Figure 12-4. The new mobile menu on display

Wow, if you managed to get to this point, give yourself a pat on the back: adding a mobile menu isn't a five-minute job, but definitely worth the effort!

Try to resize the display window back to full size: you should see the mobile hamburger icon disappear, and the original menu reappears under the header. We've made a fair few changes to achieve this, so let's take a moment to explore the code we've added or changed in more detail.

Breaking Apart the Code Changes

So what changes did we make in that last exercise? There were a fair few changes required to get our new mobile menu installed and more up to par with the existing design, so let's review the changes in more detail.

We first obtained copies of the new menu components from the code download that accompanies this book before adding media query declarations to help control when we render the menu on the screen.

Next up, we added some import declarations into the `navigation.js` file so that Gatsby knew where to locate the new components; we then adjusted the markup returned in the `navigation.js` file to include the new mobile menu. At the same time, we added a similar media query to the `sitenavigation.js` file to only display the desktop menu on resolutions greater than 375 px (the equivalent screen size for an iPhone 6/7/8 in Chrome).

We then rounded out the exercise by adding in some slight styling changes before reordering how the desktop navigation component would be referenced – with the introduction of `<MobileNav>`, it made sense to set the desktop navigation to appear within similar `<DesktopNav>` component tags.

Okay, let's move on: remember how I said there were two areas on which we should focus? Well, it's time we covered the second one, which is the basket page. A glance shows that it renders reasonably well on the main page, but there is still room for improvement! Fortunately, the changes required to fix this are not massive – let's dive in and take a closer look at the details as part of the next exercise.

Making the Basket Responsive

At this point, I'll bet that – after the last mammoth exercise – you're probably thinking: hopefully not another marathon exercise (if indeed there is such a word!).

Don't worry. The changes required for this next demo are substantially smaller than before; all of them sit in the `global.scss` file (at least for now). Let's not waste any time and crack on implementing those changes as part of the next exercise.

TWEAKING THE BASKET

To make our basket better fit the mobile experience, follow these steps – I will assume you still have the site running from the previous exercise:

1. First, crack open a copy of `global.scss` in your editor – it's in the `\src\styles` folder of your project area.

2. Scroll all the way down to the bottom of the file, and in just before the last closing }, add these styles – leave a line blank after the last style already there:

```scss
/**** RESPONSIVE BASKET ****/
#cartpage div.taxes {
  flex-direction: column;
}

#cartpage button.checkout {
 width: 100%;
}

#cartpage > div > ul > li:nth-child(3) > span:nth-child(2)
{ width: 40%; }

#cartpage div ul { padding-top: 20px; display: grid; grid-template-
columns: 100px 80px 345px 90px 100px; }
```

3. Go ahead and save the file and close it – Gatsby will rebuild the styles for the basket page and refresh what is rendered in your browser automatically. If all is well, we should have something akin to Figure 12-5.

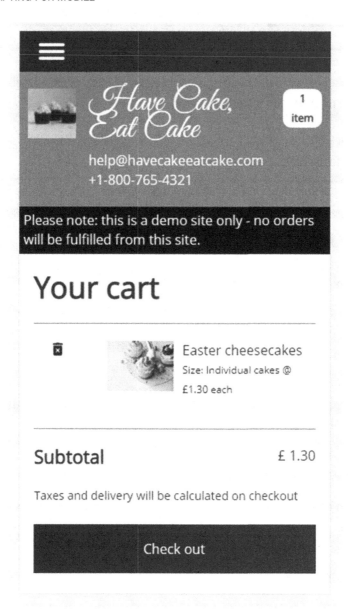

Figure 12-5. *The updated basket page in a mobile view*

That looks better, doesn't it? It fits nicely on the screen – granted, some of the elements could be aligned a little better (such as the vast space around the recycle bin), but what we have is an improvement on the original version.

At this point, I would typically work through the changes we've made, but in reality, these changes are pretty minimal! We've introduced a `flex-direction` to align the items better on the page, plus made the checkout button full width so it sits better across the whole screen. Simultaneously, we've adjusted some of the grid widths too – all simple changes, but ones that help improve how the basket page appears on the screen.

Let's change tack. We've made all of the essential changes; our site now works better on a mobile device, even though we are emulating it using Chrome! I think it's time we checked in and measured the performance of our newly updated mobile design.

Auditing the Site with Lighthouse

Yes, remember when we used Lighthouse back in Chapter 9 for Desktop? It's time we ran it for our Mobile design. Over the next few pages, we will do just that and analyze the results – what we get back is anyone's guess, so let's dive in and find out just what Lighthouse thinks of our site in more detail.

Before we get stuck into that detail, though, I should point out one critical point: **no two sets of Lighthouse audits for the same site will be the same.**

Yes, I know that might seem odd, given that we're using the same code, but other factors can affect how Lighthouse operates. For example, you might be playing a YouTube video in the background while running Lighthouse; this slows the PC down so that audited times will be slower in Lighthouse.

Therefore, it's essential to bear in mind that when running Lighthouse, the results will be different; it's more about how you deal with fixing the issues you see than what Lighthouse renders in the audit results.

RUNNING THE LIGHTHOUSE REPORT

With this in mind, let's crack on and see what the plugin performs:

1. First, fire up a Node.js terminal session, and then make sure the working folder is our project area.

2. At the prompt, enter `gatsby clean && gatsby develop` to clear cache, and then run our site using Gatsby's development server.

3. When prompted, browse to `http://localhost:8000`. Next, press Shift+Ctrl+I (or Cmd+Ctrl+I) to fire up Google's Developer Console, and switch to the Lighthouse tab.

4. On this tab, select Mobile, and then select all five entries under Categories.

5. Click Generate report – after a few minutes, we will see something appear, similar to that shown in Figure 12-6.

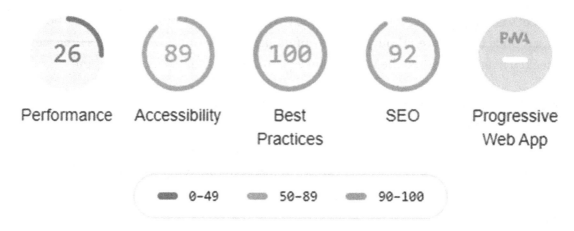

Figure 12-6. *The results of the Mobile report from Lighthouse*

Ouch! That doesn't look great, does it? You know the real kicker, though? I ran this report a dozen times while researching this book – Performance came out anywhere between 9 and 47!

We need to do something about this – if you scroll down, you will see some tips or pointers on what we should fix, which we will look at shortly. However, as you will see momentarily, I discovered a sting in this tail: it seems some of the images we've used aren't rendering as they should be on our site. Before we dive into fixing the report issues, let's first explore what's causing this issue in more detail.

Analyzing the Performance Report

Before we go into the specifics, I want to set you a little quiz:

1. Take a close look at Figure 12-6 – noticed anything missing? I'll give you a hint: make sure you have something added to your basket first!

2. Anyone spotted something intriguing about this phrase, taken from the introduction at the start of "Making the Basket Responsive": "...sit in the `global.scss` file (at least for now)"?

Hopefully, you might work out the answers – in case not, the answer to the first one is that the basket icon is missing, and the second is...well, we'll come to that a little later! (Got to keep you on your toes, *Chuckle!*)

So let's cover a little background first, as to why we seem to have this sting I referred to earlier in the previous section.

When running (or at least trying to run) Lighthouse, I frequently found it wouldn't return any results at all – instead, I would get a blank screen. On occasion, I might see something produced as a report, but in most cases, I got nothing! Eventually, after a bit of digging, I came across several errors in the console log.

You can see examples of these in Figures 12-7 and 12-8.

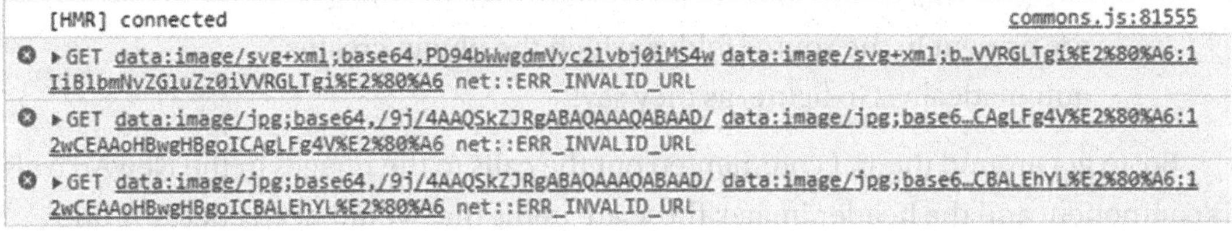

[HMR] connected   commons.js:81555
⊗ ▶ GET data:image/svg+xml;base64,PD94bWwgdmVyc2lvbj0iMS4w data:image/svg+xml;b…VVRGLTgi%E2%80%A6:1
   IiBlbmNvZGluZz0iVVRGLTgi%E2%80%A6 net::ERR_INVALID_URL
⊗ ▶ GET data:image/jpg;base64,/9j/4AAQSkZJRgABAQAAAQABAAD/ data:image/jpg;base6…CAgLFg4V%E2%80%A6:1
   2wCEAAoHBwgHBgoICAgLFg4V%E2%80%A6 net::ERR_INVALID_URL
⊗ ▶ GET data:image/jpg;base64,/9j/4AAQSkZJRgABAQAAAQABAAD/ data:image/jpg;base6…CBALEhYL%E2%80%A6:1
   2wCEAAoHBwgHBgoICBALEhYL%E2%80%A6 net::ERR_INVALID_URL

Figure 12-7. *Examples of the first set of errors*

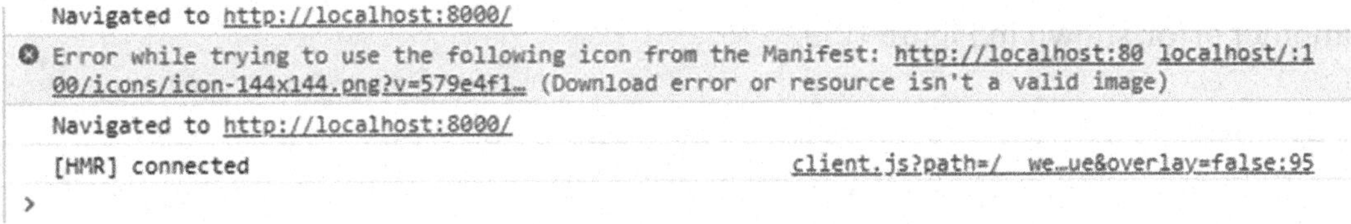

Navigated to http://localhost:8000/
⊗ Error while trying to use the following icon from the Manifest: http://localhost:80 localhost/:1
  00/icons/icon-144x144.png?v=579e4f1… (Download error or resource isn't a valid image)
Navigated to http://localhost:8000/
[HMR] connected   client.js?path=/ we…ue&overlay=false:95

Figure 12-8. *The second type of error returned in mobile view*

Ouch, this was what you might call a little bit of a head-scratcher, to say the least! To cut a long story short, though, it seems we have three problems:

- **Problem 1 – the first ERR_INVALID_URL error**

    Although the images seem to display satisfactorily, the basket icon has some odd characters in there, causing Chrome (and not Lighthouse) to error. We will need to replace the image.

- **Problem 2 – the next six ERR_INVALID_URL errors around a JPG image**

  It was harder to track down as we use some JPEG-formatted images for the products, but it's not them – I tracked it down to the data-image tags used to lazy-load images in the New Arrivals, which are not valid (at least according to Lighthouse).

- **Problem 3 – A specific icon not being referenced correctly from the manifest file for our site**

  I couldn't track this one down, so I haven't made any changes to the gatsby-plugin-manifest plugin that we're using. Research suggests that it can't find an image, but all of the images are present in the source folder, which the plugin creates automatically. Go figure, as they say!

So, to get around them, I commented out the calls to the images in the NewArrivals. js component and the header image; these are items that would need checking and potentially replacing to fix the errors permanently.

At this point, I think that should be all now and that we can get on with what we initially set out to do – unfortunately, this wouldn't be the case. Lighthouse threw up another error, shown in Figure 12-9.

```
⊗  ▶ Error: <path> attribute d: Expected number, "…2c26.5 0 48-21.5\u2026".
   Navigated to about:blank
```

Figure 12-9. *An SVG error shown from Lighthouse*

This odd error might seem a little perplexing, but as it turns out, it's coming from the SVG icons used for the Facebook and Twitter components. Both threw slightly different text (given the icons will be different, of course), but the error itself was identical. I temporarily removed these; while they did throw warnings during the build process, Lighthouse could give me some results to analyze and improve our site.

Fixing the Issues

Now that we have some Lighthouse results come back, it's time to explore what we should do to fix them. At this point, it's worth remembering that if you run the same plugin on your version of the code, you will likely not get identical results; it's all about how we go about analyzing and fixing what we see.

In my case, my reports (and I ran a few!) came back with a real mix of issues – let's list a few examples:

- The `gatsby-icon.png` file is huge for a mobile, so needs resizing.

- We need to add `preconnect` or `dns-fetch` attributes to items to help tell our browser to get them in the background.

- Several images do not have defined width or height attributes – this will help reduce layout shifting.

- Several resource files are creating network payload issues due to their size.

- There is at least one button and link each that do not have discernable name tags present.

- Some of the text is not of a sufficiently contrasting color compared to the background color (notably in the footer).

- The robots.txt file is invalid.

Let's look at how we might fix some of these issues in more detail and achieve some quick wins for our site.

Before going any further, uncomment the code for the images that caused issues earlier – I know these may still cause problems, but without them, we won't get an accurate reading from Lighthouse!

FIXING THE PERFORMANCE ISSUES

There are a handful of quick wins we can make – to do so, follow these steps:

1. The first one is to resize the `gatsby-icon.png` image – its current size is 46 KB, which is enormous for its content! We can easily make it smaller – we can do this using an online app such as PNGCompress, at `www.pngcompress.com/compress-image`. If you have an existing image compression facility already set up, then please feel free to use that – I've used the online site purely for convenience!

2. Meanwhile, rename the existing image in the `\src\images` folder – this is to prevent us from using the wrong image when we update the site.

3. Next, copy the newly compressed image over to the `\src\images` folder.

4. Repeat the same task for the header and manifest images too – you will find the latter in the `\public\icons\` folder, although I'm not 100% sure that their sizes are the cause of the issues reported by Lighthouse.

   Next, we need to add height and width dimensions to a series of images that Lighthouse has flagged as an issue. For each, add in the code indicated to the bottom of the `global.scss` file:

5. The placeholder images in the New Arrivals block:

   ```
   #gatsby-focus-wrapper div ul li, #gatsby-focus-wrapper ul li{
       width: 100%;
       height: auto;
   }
   ```

6. The payment icons image in the footer:

   ```
   #gatsby-focus-wrapper > div.copyright > div:nth-child(2)
   { width: 100%; Height: auto; }
   ```

This is just one of the issues reported – it's worth taking a look at the Web.dev article on this subject, at `https://web.dev/optimize-cls/?utm_source=lighthouse&utm_medium=devtools#images-without-dimensions`.

- On several occasions, Lighthouse also reported large network payloads being present – one example being the header.webp image we use as a hero image. This file weighed in at 207 KB, so shrinking it will remove it from the list of flagged items with heavy payloads.

7. Lighthouse reported an issue with this extension: //fmkadmapgofadopljbjfkapdkoienihi/build/react_devtools_ backend.js. At 437 KB, this would have an impact! It is purely a plugin I have installed, so I should have disabled it when running the audit. It goes to show the danger of auditing any site in a less than clean environment!

8. Two more entries appeared in my results, which both related to font files that we use on the site:

   - /static/great-vibes-latin-400-cd8416a.... woff2(localhost) – weighs in at 38.4 KB

   - /static/open-sans-latin-400-33543c5.... woff2(localhost) – weighs in at 34.1 KiB

   This issue is trickier to solve for several reasons: our code already uses font-display: swap to replace standard text font with the custom font. There are a few things we should consider:

   - Do we use custom fonts at all? We could consider switching out the Open Sans font for a system one, thereby removing the need to download a new font.

   - I think keeping the Great Vibes font in place could still be necessary, though; this is one font we clearly can't replace with a system alternative! As we only use it in the header, we *could* consider making it an image (old school) or turning it into a better brand logo (still an image, but a better one than simply writing text in an image editor).

9. The next step is to update the button and links on the page to have discernable name attributes. There are a few places where we need to do this, but to give you a flavor of how, here are three examples:

   - We only have one button in play – crack open burger.js and add the highlighted code as indicated:

   ```
   <StyledBurger aria-label="mobile menu" open={open}
   ```

- Next, fire up `newarrival.js`, and add in `aria-label={props.name}`, as indicated:

  `....slug}`} **aria-label={props.name}** className = "newarrival">`

- We should do something similar for each link using the menu text in our `aria-label` element. For example, use this format in the `customerservices.js` file:

  `"/help/" aria-label={data.datoCmsHomepage.helpFooter}>{data.dato...`

10. Make sure all files are saved and closed. Revert to a Node.js terminal session, and change the working folder to our project area.

11. At the prompt, enter `gatsby develop` and press Enter – if all is well, we should still see our site running, but safe in the knowledge that we've begun to make inroads into fixing some of the performance hotspots flagged by Google Lighthouse.

Phew, another hefty exercise! But who said fine-tuning a website for performance was anything but an easy five-minute job? There is plenty to consider, particularly as Google Lighthouse doesn't make allowances for us using React/Gatsby. Therefore, it is more important to consider anything flagged by Lighthouse before changing it, as there may be other options that are better suited to our project.

Okay, let's crack on: I want to go through some of the changes we've made in more detail, but before we do so, there is one thing we should cover off. Did you notice anything omitted from that last exercise? This omission was with good reason – let's go through them now, in more detail.

What We Didn't Cover

When running a Lighthouse report, you can guarantee two things – 1) you will get different reports from different machines that are auditing the site webpage, and 2) it will always uncover a host of other things to fix or explore!

It is no different for our site – we've talked about most of the items reported by Lighthouse except for a handful:

- Lighthouse reported an issue with sufficient contrast between some of the colors, particularly in the footer. It isn't something we can change by default, as your designers will have chosen colors with good reason. In this instance, we would need to have a conversation with the designers, show them the metrics recorded, and explore alternatives. Of course, we could simply ignore this, but it comes at risk – some individuals will be put off by text that is hard to read, or others might have a disability that makes it impossible to navigate the site.

- Lighthouse suggested adding in `preconnect` or `dns-prefetch` to manage better resources that we don't need to fetch immediately. It is a wise move in principle, but *it* raises an essential point for Gatsby (and React). React (and therefore, Gatsby) has a new feature in more recent versions, which allows us to lazy-load items and components – it's worth exploring this in more detail, so we can implement something that is more React/Gatsby-friendly.

- We seem to have an issue with the robots.txt file on our site – this appears to be invalid. It's not a surprise, as we have not updated it since we created the website; we would need to address this once the site is fully complete and before moving to production.

For more details, take a look at this article on the Hacker Noon website:
`https://hackernoon.com/lazy-loading-and-preloading-components-in-react-16-6-804de091c82d`.

- Lighthouse also reported an issue with the main `<p>` element on the homepage, which triggered the Largest Contentful Paint alert. There are several ways to fix this, but two of the ones I tried (changing to a non-blocking `<span>` element or using `font-display: swap`) had no effect. This issue is something we should explore in more detail as part of optimizing the mobile experience.

As a starting point, check out this article on the Web.dev site at `https://web.dev/defer-non-critical-css/`, on deferring CSS, and `https://web.dev/largest-contentful-paint/#how-to-improve-largest-contentful-paint-on-your-site`, for fixing the LCP issues reported by Lighthouse.

Phew, we've certainly covered a lot! I know we've not been through things in quite the same way as other exercises, but it's crucial to get a feel for the kind of issues we might get and whether we fix them or look for alternative solutions that might supersede those issues. With that in mind, we've covered a fair few changes in this last exercise, so now's a good time to go through some of them in more detail, so we can understand why we've made them to our site.

Breaking Apart the Code

"Fixing the performance issues" – four words that can open a real can of worms, to quote an old English saying!

For those of you not familiar with that expression, performance optimization can be tricky to get right – with the potential to cause real trouble if not! Today's customers are time-poor and demanding, so sites need to be easy to use and performant. Over the last few pages, we've looked at how we might begin to implement some improvements to make our site faster.

So what did we change? Well, we started by reviewing and shrinking several of the images used on the homepage. Although we focused on the homepage for this chapter, we use some of these images elsewhere; we will see the benefits of shrinking them on those pages too. We then applied width and height values to images on the page, as Lighthouse had flagged the lack of these properties.

For the remaining part of the exercise, we went through some of the other points raised during my audits to understand why they may be causing a problem and suggest the best course of action. For the last part, we updated some of the links and sole button on the homepage to have discernable name tags against each; this is for accessibility reasons. We then ran the usual commands to preview the results in our browser to ensure all was still well with our site.

We should cover one thing at this point – if we rerun the Lighthouse audit, it's very likely we will still get less than 100%, at least for performance. There are several good reasons for this, but one stands out most: our use of a separate CSS style sheet.

312

I've used this route as I have to admit to certain "old-school tendencies" regarding coding; we should consider reviewing all CSS and in-lining it into each component where appropriate. Using an external CSS style sheet may have been good when it lasted, but current preferences are to in-line CSS more, particularly when using React and Gatsby frameworks!

Adding PWA Support: A Postscript

Before we finish our journey through converting the site for mobile use, there is one more topic I want to explore: the subject of PWA or progressive web app support.

It isn't something we've delved into in any detail, as this warrants a chapter (if not a book) in its own right, and we were focusing more on the online site version. However, Lighthouse flagged a few items for attention, which fall into three categories: loading time, installable, and PWA optimized. Let's take a quick look at some examples flagged by Lighthouse:

- **Loading time – how long does it take to load our site/application on a mobile phone?**

  - Page was interactive at 22.0 seconds.

  - The current page does not respond with a 200 when offline.

  - start_url does not respond with a 200 when offline.

  - Timed out waiting for start_url (http://localhost:8000/) to respond.

- **Installable – is our application installable on the front page of a mobile phone?**

  - The site needs to use HTTPS – we are running under HTTP (which is an assumed default when working with Gatsby in development mode).

  - The page does not register a service worker that controls page and start_url.

  - Web app manifest meets the requirements for installation as a PWA.

- **PWA optimized – to optimize the site as a PWA, what are some of the items we need to check?**

    - The site does not redirect HTTP traffic to HTTPS – this would come when moving into production (see the preceding comment about using Gatsby in development mode).

    - The site should have a custom splash screen.

    - The site needs to set a theme color for the address bar.

    - Content is not sized correctly for the viewport – it is showing a size of 374 px, which doesn't match the window size of 360 px.

    - The site has a `<meta name="viewport">` tag with a `width` or `initial-scale` applied – this needs changing.

Ouch, there are a few things there that we would need to check and rectify! It would be dependent on whether we were to go down the route of being a PWA and whether we can justify the time, effort, and resources required to make the changes for our site.

Summary

Adapting content for mobile has become a necessary evil over the last few years – more and more customers are demanding the ability to browse via different platforms. Anyone who doesn't consider mobile as important should have an excellent reason for missing out on a huge market, at least in terms of retail! We've covered various topics throughout this chapter, so let's take a moment to review what we have learned.

We started by asking that all-important question – why is mobile so important? We learned how to tap into huge markets and that this isn't something that will go away anytime soon. We then started to assess our existing site as a mobile device before taking steps to help simplify the design and make it easier to adapt for mobile.

Next up, we then focused on making both the menu and basket pages more responsive, as these needed more than just simple styling changes; we then ran the Lighthouse audit to see what should be fixed.

We then moved on working through some of the quick win–type fixes. We covered those that might require more effort or could potentially benefit from us taking a different approach to our coding. We then finished with a quick look at PWAs and some of Lighthouse's points that we should explore if we went down the route of creating a progressive web application from our site.

We are almost at the end of our journey through creating our e-commerce site! It has been wild, with many ups and downs, but that is all part and parcel of developing e-commerce offerings! We have one more topic we should take a look at - the basket and payment process.

Hold on a moment. Didn't we cover that earlier in this book? "Why now?" I hear you ask. Well, we're going to go out on a limb and look at something that might turn the whole process on its head - it's a little "out there" (so to speak), but definitely something worth exploring. Intrigued? Stay with me, and I will reveal all, in the next chapter...!

CHAPTER 13

Updating the Payment Process

Throughout this book, we've explored the code required to help us start building an e-commerce site using Gatsby and covered some of the more practical concerns we need to consider when using the framework.

However, there is one more project I would like to try, and it relates to the checkout process of our site. "Huh?" I hear you ask. We've got a perfectly good checkout in the form of Shopify – why would we want to replace it? It's a good question, but as always, there is method in the apparent madness!

It might seem odd to cover the payment process again at this late stage in the book. Advances in client-side APIs mean that there is an option we should consider to provide a more streamlined checkout that can be run client-side within a browser, without any third-party tools. I'm talking about the Payment Request API – what if we could use it in a server-side environment, such as Gatsby?

Over the next few pages, we will take a look at how we can use it to help streamline the process, what it means for us going forward, and some of the points we need to consider when using the API (or a variant of it) in our site. I suspect this API may not be familiar to all of you, so let's start with a quick introduction to it and why it can help make the checkout process more effective.

Introducing the API

So, first things first, what is the Payment Request API?

In a nutshell, it's a relatively new API that is native to most modern browsers (I say most, as Firefox and IE don't support it), which allows us to create a basket and checkout within the browser. This feature isn't earth-shattering by itself, but what makes it unique

© Alex Libby 2021
A. Libby, *Gatsby E-Commerce*, https://doi.org/10.1007/978-1-4842-6692-2_13

is that this is **without** the need for extra libraries or costly software tools such as third-party shopping baskets.

Cast your mind back – anyone remembers the likes of Actinic? While great tools in their own right, they are resource-heavy and expensive to run. In 2017, a proposal was introduced to create a lightweight checkout process based entirely on the browser. It would allow customers to store credit card details and check out without the need for heavyweight third-party solutions such as Actinic. Depending on how we set up our site, we can offer something very close to Amazon's famous one-click operation!

While the appearance of this checkout process might differ slightly between browsers, each browser would offer the same features – we can see an example of this in Figure 13-1.

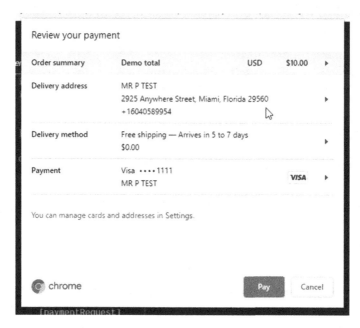

Figure 13-1. *An example of the Payment Request in operation*

The key to making it work is simple – it divorces the presentational layer (what the customer sees) from the underlying payment processing. It means we can switch in and out any payment provider that supports it, such as Google Pay or Samsung Pay, while the user interface will remain the same for the customer!

There is a lot more we could cover, but I think it's better to see it in action – it's easy to set up and requires tools already available in the browser, namely, JavaScript. It's time I stopped talking, methinks – let's crack on and get stuck into setting up a proof-of-concept example using Gatsby.

If you would like to learn more about the Payment Request API, you might refer to my book **Checking Out with the Payment Request API**, published by Apress.

Before Getting Started

For this chapter, I will take the same approach as the previous chapter – we will focus on the core elements needed to implement the API. We're going to use a copy of the WooCommerce site created from Chapter 11 and add in the necessary code to implement the API on our site.

We could easily use the original demo from the end of Chapter 10, but the WooCommerce one keeps things simple to understand better the changes needed to support the API. Before we dive into code, though, there are a few things we need to set up, so here goes:

- Once in production, the API has to work on a site secured with SSL; it won't work on those that are not accessible via HTTPS! There used to be a time when many site owners would not secure their websites in this manner, but with Google favoring secure sites for SEO purposes, it's become a de facto requirement to have this set up.

- The exception to this first point is that we can run it in a localhost environment, although it doesn't quite feel the same! To help get around this, we can create a test site using something like Netlify, in the same way as we did earlier in the book. It's not obligatory, but if you want to experience it in a more realistic environment, you will need a Netlify account.

You will likely have one from earlier – if you do, then you should be able to use this and just set up another site within it. It will use your free minutes from the subscription, so you may want to set up a separate account!

- Last, but by no means least, you may also want to avail yourself of a free Stripe account too. Later in this chapter, I will show you an example of how some payment providers have implemented their version of the API, which you will need an account for it to work if you want to try it out. There are a few things to think about when selecting providers – this is something I will cover in more detail later in this chapter.

Right, let's crack on and work through getting the accounts set up as part of our first exercise. I'm assuming for this chapter that we will deploy to Netlify as suggested at the end; if you don't want to, then feel free to skip this exercise – it will not affect how the demo works later in the chapter.

SETTING UP ACCOUNTS

To get each account set up (as appropriate), follow these steps:

1. We first need to create a repository if we are going to deploy to Netlify – for this exercise, I will assume the use of GitHub, but feel free to use GitLab if you prefer.

You can see my example at `https://github.com/alexlibby/test-payment-api-gatsby`.

---

2. Once on the Netlify site, click Netlify account ➤ Signup, and then select GitHub and Authorize Netlify when prompted. Once authorized, navigate to the main dashboard, and then click Sites ➤ New site from Git.

3. Choose GitHub, then Authorize Netlify, and then Only Select repositories ➤ your chosen repository and click Install. We will complete the remaining part in the next but one exercise.

Excellent, we now have the various accounts in place ready for us to upload our finished demo. The next stage is to add our new site; for this, we will use a copy of the existing one from Chapter 11 and adapt it to display our "one-click" button ready for use.

Setting Up the Project

For our next exercise, we have a few steps to work through; before we can implement the API, we need to set up a base website and update it with content from Chapter 11. Let's take a look at what's involved in more detail.

SETTING UP THE SITE

To get our initial site set up and ready for use, follow these steps:

1. We first need to set up a blank Gatsby site – this will make sure we have the right elements in place, such as the `package.json` file. For this, fire up a Node.js terminal, and change the working folder to the root of your PC's hard disk. Enter this command to create a new Gatsby site:

   `gatsby new prapi https://github.com/gatsbyjs/gatsby-starter-hello-world`

2. Once done, go ahead and copy the files from the code download – if prompted, you should replace the existing ones in the project folder.

3. Switch to your Node.js terminal, and then change the working folder to the `prapi` folder we've just created as part of step 1. At the prompt, enter `npm i` and press Enter – this will make sure we install any dependencies needed for our project.

4. While this is running, go ahead and fire up the local web server you used in Chapter 11 – this is to allow us to surface products from WooCommerce for this demo.

5. When completed, enter `gatsby develop` at the prompt in the Node.js terminal session, and press Enter – this will start the Gatsby develop server.

6. If all is well, we should see our product page appear when browsing to `http://localhost:8000` in your browser. You will first see the main `index.js` page; click one of the products to go to the product page (Figure 13-2).

Mixed Chocolate cupcakes

We're sure you will have heard of the phrase "black and white" - it's an apt description for these cakes! We keep the base simple, but top each cake with a mix of different chocolates - white, hazel, dark, and of varying different strengths. This one is best ordered as a mixed box of six - it's too hard to simply choose one flavor!

Price: 0.80

In stock

One-Click Buy

Figure 13-2. *The base site, ready for us to adapt*

We've deliberately kept this exercise simple, but its simplicity belies its importance – without solid foundations, our site will be of no use to anyone! Although there isn't anything in this exercise that we've not already used before, let's quickly cover off the changes made, so we can understand how this fits into the bigger picture.

Exploring the Changes in Detail

When it comes to starting a project, we have to start somewhere – in this case, we can skip most of the steps we would otherwise have had to do, as we've already done them in a previous chapter!

That said, we still have to perform a few steps to ensure our new site still works – we kicked off by installing a new Gatsby site using the by-now-familiar "Hello World" starter template. We then downloaded and extracted copies of the files from the code download to update the content to a base suitable for adding the Payment Request API. We finished by running up the site into a browser using the Gatsby develop server to ensure all was well.

Moving on, we come now to the essential part of this chapter: adding in the Payment Request API. We will do this in several parts, as there is a fair amount of code to add; let's start by configuring the base properties to run the API.

Setting Up the Payment Request API

Although using the API requires nothing more than pure JavaScript, we still have to work our way through quite a lot of code.

For our next exercise, we will add in the base code required to initiate an instance of the API; at the same time, we will run some basic checks so you can see how it fits in and understand some of what we will need to do to develop it into a complete solution. There are a few stages to work through, so let's start with the necessary code to fire up the API.

CONFIGURE THE PAYMENT REQUEST API

To set up the API (and checkout process), follow these steps:

1. First, crack open a copy of the products template in your text editor from within the `\src\templates\productpages` folder.

2. We have a substantial chunk of code to add in, so we will do this block by block – first, leave a blank line after the second import statement, and add in these constant declarations:

```
let grandtotal = 0

const options = {
  requestPayerName: true,
  requestPayerEmail: true,
  requestPayerPhone: true
};

const deliveryOptions = {
  standard: 0.00,
  express: 12.00
}

const paymentMethods = [
  {
    supportedMethods: "basic-card",
    data: {
      supportedNetworks: ["visa", "mastercard"],
      supportedTypes: ["debit", "credit"]
```

```
            }
        }
    ];
```

3. Next, leave a line, and add in this function – this builds the details required for our shopping cart, such as unit total, taxes (if applicable), and delivery charges:

```
function buildShoppingCart(data) {
    let grandtotal = Number(data.wcProducts.price) + Number(data.
wcProducts.price * 0.1);

    return {
        id: data.wcProducts.id,
        displayItems: [
            {
                label: data.wcProducts.name,
                amount: {
                    currency: "USD",
                    value: data.wcProducts.price
                }
            }, {
                label: 'Sales Tax',
                pending: true,
                amount: {
                    currency: 'USD',
                    value: Number(data.wcProducts.price * 0.1)
                }
            }
        ],
        total: {
            label: "Total",
            amount: {
                currency: "USD",
                value: grandtotal,
            }
        },
    };
}
```

4. We come to the most important part – this initiates an instance of the Payment Request API and displays it on-screen. Leave a blank line, and then add in this code:

```
async function buyItem(data) {
  try {
    const paymentObject = buildShoppingCart(data);
    const payment = new PaymentRequest(paymentMethods, paymentObject,
    options);

    // Show the UI
    const paymentUi = await payment.show();
    await paymentUi.complete("success").then(function() {
      console.log(JSON.stringify(paymentUi));
      // displaySuccess();
    });
  } catch (e) {
    console.log(e.message);
    //displayMessage(e.message);
    return;
  }
}
```

5. There is one more change to make – scroll down to this block of code:

```
className="oneclick"
// onClick={() => buyItem(data)}
type="button"
```

6. Go ahead and remove the comment in the highlighted line.

7. Next, save the file and leave it open – there are no more changes we need to make. We will be using the file throughout this exercise.

8. Gatsby will have recompiled the code in the background – if all is well, we should see the screenshot shown in Figure 12-3 when browsing to http://localhost:8000 in our browser.

Fairy Cakes

Our traditional fairy cupcake, delicately baked for that light fluffy sponge, and topped with a generous swirl of our house whipped cream and sprinkles. If you fancy a treat, what better way to indulge yourself?

Price: 2.95

In stock

One-Click Buy

Figure 12-3. *Our updated site, displaying the new "one-click" button*

9. Hold on – that looks like nothing has changed! That is indeed true, but if we click the button, we can see the API running – Figure 13-4 shows what it looks like from our demo.

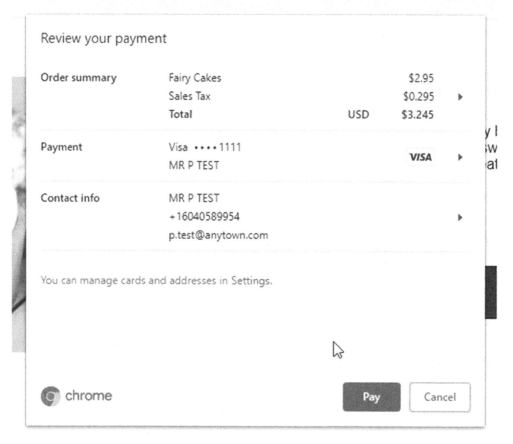

Figure 13-4. *The API triggered by our demo*

See how easy that was to implement? We've not made use of any tools not already available in our browser – for most of it, we've used standard JavaScript, with a smattering of HTML and CSS to support the display of content when needed. We've covered a fair amount of code in this demo, so let's pause for a moment and review what we've added in more detail.

Reviewing the Code Changes: How Does the API Operate?

We began with declaring a set of variables and constants – the first will hold the final total displayed to the customer. In contrast, the others define the various elements required for the API, such as what settings to show, the available delivery options, and the customer's payment methods.

Next, we created the buildShoppingCart() function; this defines what labels to show to the customer for subtotal items, sales taxes (if applicable), and the overall total. In each case, we've specified USD as the currency; this could be any currency, as long as it is determined using the appropriate ISO 4217 standard for currency codes.

A full list of the ISO 4127 codes for currencies is available at www.iso.org/iso-4217-currency-codes.html.

The next block is where things get interesting: when the customer clicks the One-Click Buy button, they trigger the attached event handler, which takes them to the buyItem() function. This function builds up the requisite parts of the Payment Request API instance we're creating.

We then define that new instance as payment before setting an asynchronous call to payment.show() to display our checkout form. Once displayed, we then use paymentUi.complete("success") to indicate a successful transaction – or if things haven't worked, we show the error message generated in the catch(e) block.

Understanding the Wider Picture

It might, at first glance, seem like a lot is happening, right? I appreciate it's been a whistle-stop tour of an API that not everyone will be familiar with; it seems only fair to take time out and understand a little more of the background behind how this API operates.

When we construct an instance of the API, we need to collect together three separate parts – the available payment methods, the details of what we will charge the customer, and miscellaneous options such as requesting email addresses or contact details. In each instance, we create an object or object array to hold the information from the customer. We then build up an instance of the API before using `.show()` to display this to the customer – based on the outcome, we either display a successful transaction message or show an error if the payment has failed for any reason.

Looking further afield, there are a few things to note about the API:

- Although we've created some simple calculations in our code, the API was **not** designed to calculate values; these have to be done by us developers in the appropriate event handler or function. The API is effectively dumb, so make sure your calculations are correct!

- You can't style the checkout form at all, so for all of you budding UX designers, sorry – this is one part you can't change, I'm afraid! The only exception to this is using a custom implementation by one of the few payment providers that support the API; this won't be the actual API, but more likely something that resembles the functionality offered by the API.

- We've covered the basics of using the API with a payment method known as "basic-card"; this is a generic card option that allows us to mimic payment in a development capacity. We should **not** use it in production at all; it is an insecure method, so it opens your site to the risk of hacking. Instead, we can tie in a test account from the likes of Google Pay or PayPal; there is also a development provider called BobPay (yes, you read that right!) at `www.bobpay.xyz`, which we can hook in as well.

- Although most modern browsers support the API (except IE11 – but who uses it anyway?), it's not yet hit wide acceptance in many mainstream payment providers. I suspect a lot of this has something to do with storing sensitive data in a browser, which not everyone will like; we should always consider providing a fallback checkout if we decide to use the API.

- While we can use the API in all sites, I think it works best when used in websites where we might want to offer a one-click buy option. Granted, this is a subjective viewpoint, but you may want to hop in and out of the basket before committing to check out when you are looking to purchase multiple items. This activity isn't ideal for the API; you are initiating an instance of it each time, which means you have to cancel it before you can go back to adding more products. With an ordinary basket, you can dip in and out without issue!

These are just a few of the things to consider using the API. If thought is given to its use during design, it can be a useful tool for those sites that might only want to offer a simple alternative to something more heavyweight and costly.

If you would like to learn more, I would strongly recommend reading my book *Checking Out with the Payment Request API*, published by Apress.

Okay, let's change tack (if you pardon the sailing expression) and move on to something new: we've built the basis for our site, but there is more we can do! Let's turn our attention to see how we can begin to extend the functionality we've set up to offer a better experience for our customers.

Extending Functionality

Some of you may have noticed that when we display the checkout process, we have options to select new addresses, new payment details, and the like – yet if we do, they don't appear to update the entries in our checkout form.

What gives? The options to change selections are present, but **only in part** – we would need to add in events to respond to those changes and ensure the form is updated correctly. To illustrate how we might achieve this, let's update the Payment Request object to add in an event handler to monitor delivery changes and update costs accordingly.

ADDING IN SHIPPING

To set up shipping for the Payment Request API, follow these steps:

1. First, switch to the index.js template file we've had open throughout this exercise; we first need to tell the API to enable shipping, so add in the line highlighted:

    ```
    const options = {
      requestPayerName: true,
      requestPayerEmail: true,
      requestPayerPhone: true,
      requestShipping: true
    };
    ```

2. Next, leave a line blank and then add in this constant declaration – it provides the various delivery options available for the customer:

    ```
    const deliveryOptions = {
      standard: 0.00,
      express: 12.00
    }
    ```

3. Next up, we need to add in the new shipping option to the checkout – scroll down to this block of code:

    ```
          currency: "USD",
          value: grandtotal,
        }
      },
    ```

4. Immediately below the closing } of the previous step, insert this code:

    ```
    shippingOptions: [
        {
          id: 'standard',
          label: 'Standard shipping',
          amount: {
            currency: 'USD',
            value: deliveryOptions.standard
          },
          selected: true,
        },
    ```

```
        {
          id: 'express',
          label: 'Express shipping',
          amount: {
            currency: 'USD',
            value: deliveryOptions.express
          },
        },
      ],
```

5. Now that we have the feature enabled, we need to add in code to respond to
    changes – for this, add in this function:

```
function updateDetails(pr, details, shippingOption, resolve, reject,
stotal, price) {
  if (shippingOption === 'standard') {
    pr.selectedShippingOption = details.shippingOptions[0];
    pr.otherShippingOption = details.shippingOptions[1];
    details.total.amount.value = Number(price) +
    Number(deliveryOptions.standard);
  } else if (shippingOption === 'express') {
    pr.selectedShippingOption = details.shippingOptions[1];
    pr.otherShippingOption = details.shippingOptions[0];
    details.total.amount.value = Number(price) + Number(deliveryOptions.
    express);
  } else {
    reject('Unknown shipping option \'' + shippingOption + '\'');
    return;
  }
  pr.selectedShippingOption.selected = true;
  pr.otherShippingOption.selected = false;

  details.displayItems.splice(2, 1, pr.selectedShippingOption);
  resolve(details);
}
```

6. We need to tie this into our demo – go ahead and scroll down to this line:

```
const payment = new PaymentRequest(paymentMethods, paymentObject,
options);
```

7. Leave a line blank, and then add in this event handler, to respond to changes to the selected delivery method:

```
payment.addEventListener('shippingoptionchange', function(evt) {
  evt.updateWith(new Promise(function(resolve, reject) {
    updateDetails(payment, paymentObject, payment.shippingOption,
    resolve, reject, grandtotal, data.wcProducts.price);
  }));
});
```

8. Go ahead and save the file but leave it open – we will come back to it later in this chapter.

9. Switch to a Node.js terminal session, and then make sure you set the working folder to the `prapi` project folder.

10. At the prompt, enter `gatsby develop`, and then press Enter – if all is well, Gatsby will go away and recompile the code (note: if you didn't stop your server, please skip this step).

If we browse to `http://localhost:8000` in a browser and then click the One-Click Buy button, we should see this in the dialog box that shows (Figure 13-5).

Figure 13-5. *The updated checkout dialog box, with shipping now available*

11. Go ahead and click the arrow shown to the right of Figure 13-6 – we should see that we could choose to select the Express delivery option:

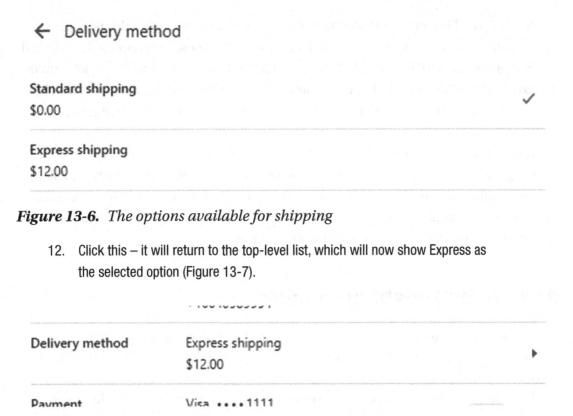

Figure 13-6. *The options available for shipping*

12. Click this – it will return to the top-level list, which will now show Express as the selected option (Figure 13-7).

Figure 13-7. *Our checkout form, with the new shipping method selected*

In this last exercise, we've added a key feature – the ability to select different types of shipping for our customers. Granted, it might only have been two options (and that not specifying it could assume the price includes delivery), but this allows us to tailor the options available to our customer with just a couple of clicks. Let's take a closer look at how we set up the code to enable this feature in more detail.

Understanding the Changes Made

We began by amending the `options` object to enable shipping; this is a required step, no matter what options are set later in the code. We then created a `deliveryOptions` object to specify each shipping method; this we use to work out which price to display on-screen for the customer.

Next up, we then moved on adding in the shipping configuration – this is displayed to the customer and provides a base for the customer to choose different methods based on their preferences. We then added the `updateDetails` function, which we call from the `shippingoptionchange` event handler. This `updateDetails` function works out which delivery mechanism is selected and updates the value on-screen (and changes the final total).

Okay, let's crack on: we've fleshed out our (albeit somewhat spartan) demo with shipping, so we can now offer the core options to customers, should we wish to push this into production. I think, though, there is an excellent opportunity to add in some final touches – they may not seem much, but everything always helps! Let's take a look at what we can add to help lend our demo a little more polish.

Adding the Finishing Touches

I'm a great fan of improving things where one can, although it's important not to do it for the sake of doing it – instead, do it if we can add value and that we can justify the time required!

With this in mind, and as part of the next exercise, we're going to add a few little finishing touches to our demo – some status messages, styling, revamping the address event handler, and reformatting the pricing (although not necessarily in that order). Let's dive in and look at what we need to do to complete our demo's last few steps.

ADDING SOME POLISH

To add the final polish to our demo, work through these steps:

1. First, we will add in some status messages to tell the customer what is going on – for this, we will add a success message and another to render all other messages. For this, crack open the `index.js` file under `\src\templates\ProductPage`, and scroll down until the end of the `buildShoppingCart()` function.

2. Next, leave a line blank, and add in these two functions:

```
async function displaySuccess() {
  document.getElementById("message").classList.add("success");
  document.getElementById("message").innerHTML = "<span>\u2714</span>
Payment received - thanks for your order!";
}
```

```
function displayMessage(mesg) {
  document.getElementById("message").classList.add("info");
  document.getElementById("message").innerHTML = "<span>&#128712;</span>"
+ mesg;
}
```

3. Scroll down until you get to the line starting `await paymentUi.complete…`
    and add this in immediately after the `console.log` statement and before the
    double closing brackets:

```
displaySuccess();
```

4. In the `catch (e)` block just below it, change this function to this:

```
  } catch (e) {
    displayMessage(e.message);
    return;
  }
```

5. The messages are now in, but won't look that great – to fix that, we need to
    add in some styling. Open the `global.css` file in the `\src\styles` folder,
    and add this to the bottom – it won't make it a work of art, but it will at least
    make our status messages look a little more presentable:

```
/* STATUS MESSAGE */
#message {
  margin: 10px 0px;
  padding: 10px 20px;
  display: none;
}
```

```css
#message.info,
#message.success {
  background-color: lightgrey;
  display: block;
}

#message > span {
  font-size: 20px;
  margin-right: 5px;
}
```

6. The next change we're going to make is to reformat the price and sales tax displayed in the checkout – there have been occasions where I've seen it displayed with three decimal places, which isn't ideal! For this, change the middle value: entry in the displayItems block, thus:

```
value: Number(data.wcProducts.price * 0.1).toFixed(2)
```

7. Our next change is a simple one – we're not displaying any currency on the product page, so how about we add something? For this, scroll down to the line starting <p>Price:..., and then add a $ before the opening { in that line.

Okay, take a breather, and get a drink: we still have more to do, but need a break first!

When you're ready to continue, the last change is to alter the shipping event handler we put in earlier to limit what can be selected. It might sound counterproductive, but if we only want to offer free shipping options to specific locations, we need to tell the API how to handle such requests.

We're going to add in one such option, to ship for free in the state of California only, whereas all other US addresses will have standard shipping, and we will not ship outside of the United States.

ADDING SHIPPING RESTRICTIONS

To add in shipping restrictions, follow these steps:

1. To accomplish this, we first need to add an address to our browser – the simplest way is to browse to `chrome://settings/addresses` in Chrome, then click Add, and fill in the details. You need to add in an address based in California, plus make sure you have one for somewhere else in the United States and one for a different country – it doesn't matter which!

2. Once saved, revert to your editor, and then comment out the `shippingOptions` block – we will use a different method to achieve the same effect:

```
shippingOptions: [
  {
    id: 'standard',
    label: 'Standard shipping',
    amount: {currency: 'USD', value: deliveryOptions.standard},
    selected: true,
  },
  {
    id: 'express',
    label: 'Express shipping',
    amount: {currency: 'USD', value: deliveryOptions.express},
  },
],
```

3. At the same time, go ahead and comment out this block too:

```
const deliveryOptions = {
  standard: 0.00,
  express: 12.00
}
```

4. Next, comment out the entire updateDetails() function, and replace it with this – there is a good block of code, so we will go through it section by section, starting with defining the initial shippingOption object:

```
function updateDetails(details, shippingAddress, callback, stotal) {
  let shippingOption = {
    id: '',
    label: '',
    amount: {currency: 'USD', value: '0.00'},
    selected: true,
    pending: false,
  };
```

5. Immediately afterward, add in this set of checks – the first one looks to see if we are in the United States/California and can offer free shipping:

```
if (shippingAddress.country === 'US') {
  if (shippingAddress.region === 'CA') {
    shippingOption.id = 'californiaFreeShipping';
    shippingOption.label = 'Free shipping in California';
    details.total.amount.value = (Number(stotal)).toFixed(2);
  } else {
```

6. If in the United States, but not California, we offer standard shipping – that is taken care of by this block:

```
    shippingOption.id = 'unitedStatesStandardShipping';
    shippingOption.label = 'Standard shipping in US';
    shippingOption.amount.value = '3.99';
    details.total.amount.value = (Number(stotal) + Number(3.99)).
    toFixed(2);
  }
  details.shippingOptions = [shippingOption];
  delete details.error;
} else {
```

7. Anything else is excluded (for the purposes of this demo) – the code for that is
    in this block:

    ```
        // Don't ship outside of the US for the purposes of this example.
        shippingOption.label = 'Shipping';
        shippingOption.pending = true;
        details.total.amount.value = (Number(stotal)).toFixed(2);
        details.error = 'Sorry - cannot ship outside of USA.';
        delete details.shippingOptions;
      }
      details.displayItems.splice(1, 1, shippingOption);
      callback(details);
    }
    ```

8. We have one more change to make – comment out the existing
    shippingoptionchange event handler, and replace it with this:

    ```
    payment.addEventListener('shippingaddresschange', function(evt) {
      evt.updateWith(new Promise(function(resolve) {
        updateDetails(paymentObject, payment.shippingAddress, resolve,
        grandtotal);
      }));
    });
    ```

9. Save and close the file. Gatsby will recompile the code; if all is well, we should
    now have an updated address option when clicking the One-Click Buy button in
    the demo.

10. Try changing the address to the one that is outside of the United States – it
    should gray out the address and show the message in Figure 13-8.

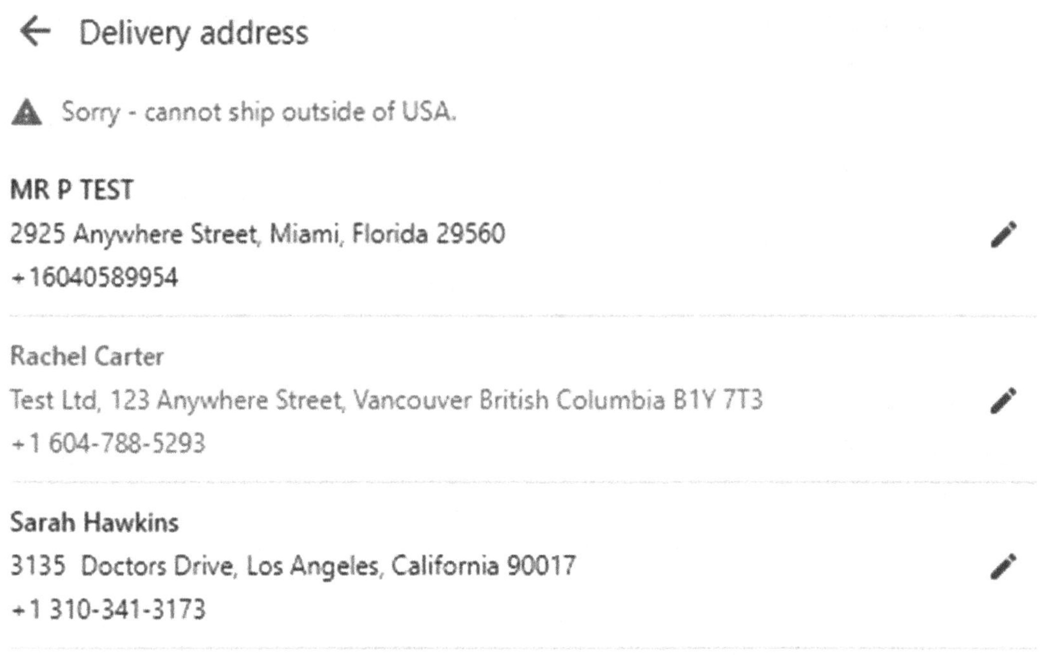

← Delivery address

⚠ Sorry - cannot ship outside of USA.

MR P TEST
2925 Anywhere Street, Miami, Florida 29560   ✎
+16040589954

Rachel Carter
Test Ltd, 123 Anywhere Street, Vancouver British Columbia B1Y 7T3   ✎
+1 604-788-5293

Sarah Hawkins
3135 Doctors Drive, Los Angeles, California 90017   ✎
+1 310-341-3173

Figure 13-8. *A warning to indicate an invalid address selection*

Notice how, this time, the delivery option is preselected for us and will only change depending on where the parcel is to be shipped – we cannot, for example, select free shipping if our address happens to be nowhere near the state of California!

11. If you choose the California address, it will close the selector and show the main screen again, with Free shipping in California as the selected option.

12. Try the same change again, but this time, select the non-Californian address – this should display the Standard shipping option, as indicated in Figure 13-9.

Delivery address	MR P TEST	
	2925 Anywhere Street, Miami, Florida 29560	▶
	+16040589954	
Delivery method	Standard shipping in US	▶
	$3.99	
Payment	Visa •••• 1111	**VISA** ▶
	MR P TEST	

Figure 13-9. *The updated delivery charge for non-Californian addresses*

Excellent, we've finished making our changes, and it's time to put this little demo into production! Okay, perhaps not full production as we have a long way to go before it is ready, but we can at least push it to somewhere that more closely resembles production.

Before we do so, I want to quickly run through the changes we've made in more detail – some are self-explanatory, but the address handler revamp exposes a few essential points that we should examine in closer detail.

Breaking Apart the Code

So what did we achieve? It was an extended exercise over two parts, but in summary, we've added some slight tweaks and upgraded the delivery options.

We started by adding some status messages – our original demo was rendering the sale results (or not, as the case may be) to the console log, which is a bit too rough and ready for customers! Instead, we added a simple #messages div and set the API to display suitable messaging based on the transaction outcome. At the same time, we added some rudimentary styling too – this is to help the messages look presentable on-screen.

Next up, we made a couple of small tweaks. The first one was to ensure that the sales tax displayed a figure to two decimal places; on occasions, I've seen it show three decimal places, which isn't necessary. Second, we also added a dollar symbol on the product page to make it more consistent with the API display.

The last change was somewhat larger – we swapped out the existing shippingoptionchange event handler for options based on the customer's location. The reason for doing this is that we want to keep delivery costs under control; shipping to destinations within a particular region will keep the costs manageable. We can still ship to destinations further away (unless we exclude them), but the costs involved need to reflect the greater distances involved in shipping.

From a technical perspective, we first amended the addresses stored in our browser – this had to include one address for California (where we would offer free shipping), one elsewhere in the United States (standard shipping), and one outside of the United States (the excluded area). We had to comment out/remove some existing functionality, as the current functions would no longer work.

We replaced them with a new `shippingaddresschange` event handler (and associated `updateDetails` function). This handler grabs the customer's country from their address and works out which shipping option we should apply based on their region code (in this case, US for United States, then CA for California). Depending on what was selected, it would display free shipping or standard shipping or tell the customer that the site cannot ship to their address.

Phew, that was indeed a prolonged exercise! We've almost come to the end of this chapter, but we should cover one more topic before we finish: what next? It's a good question – using the API opens up some exciting possibilities, so let's take a quick look at what we should consider the next steps when using this API.

Taking the Next Steps

Now that we've created the basis of a Gatsby-based site that can use the API, where can we go from here? It's a good question – we've touched on the basics of using the API throughout this chapter, but primarily in a development capacity. Now is an excellent opportunity to take a moment to consider our options in more detail:

- While the API does offer a very streamlined checkout process, it won't be for everyone – one of the deciding factors will be if your payment provider supports the API. Not all of them do – Stripe and Braintree are two examples of providers who do offer it in some format. I've created a cut-down version of Stripe's implementation of the Request Payment API demo at `https://codesandbox.io/s/test-react-stripe-and-payment-request-api-3dho4` – you can see a screenshot of it in action in Figure 13-10.

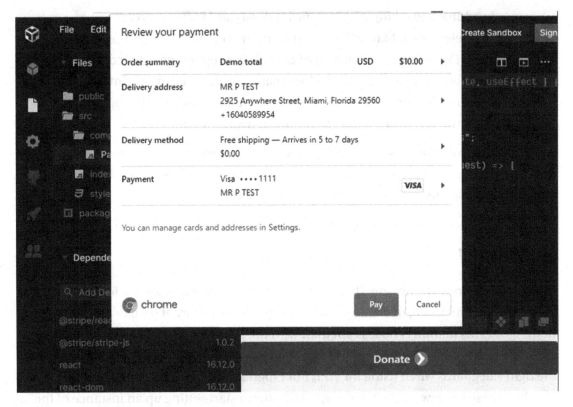

Figure 13-10.   *The API according to Stripe...*

You will need to register a free account with Stripe and add in your test Stripe key to see it work; otherwise, it will throw an error. Note: Stripe tracks usage of IDs and will block any that are used excessively!

- We should first run the `gatsby build` command – I know this might sound a little premature, but I've come across instances where something works perfectly in development but fails when building for production! It makes sense to do a dry run, if only for peace of mind!

- Of course, we can run the API in localhost, but in an ideal world, it needs to run in an HTTPS environment – why not push a copy out to a new site using Netlify? Netlify ties in beautifully to Gatsby, so we can quickly make and commit any changes. Bear in mind that Netlify does come with a limit on its free plan, so you may want to try that change first locally before committing to Netlify.

- In addition to taking a look at my book on the API (yes, sorry – shameless plug, I know!), I would recommend reading the Google Deep Dive article, available at `https://developers.google.com/web/fundamentals/payments/merchant-guide/deep-dive-into-payment-request`. It's a few years old, so not everything will apply, but it will give you a good grounding in using the API.

Hopefully, some of these ideas will give you a little inspiration – there is plenty more out there that we can do, so it's worth spending time researching the API in more detail if you decide to use this option for your future projects!

Summary

Anyone who knows me personally will know that I'm a great one for not following everyone else and trying new things – after all, how do we learn if we can't try anything new, right? This mantra is no less apt than with the Payment Request API – it might scare some die-hards off from using it, but I maintain it is very usable, as long as we implement the right safeguards when using the API. But I digress...

Over these last few pages, we've explored how to start setting up an instance of the API in a Gatsby-based environment – we've covered a lot of code and a few tips and tricks on the way. Let's take a moment to review what we have learned in this chapter.

We started with a brief introduction to the API and its origins, before working through a couple of housekeeping tasks; we then moved on to setting up the base site, ready for adding the API.

Next up came the all-important task of adding in that API; we took a look at the code required to get it working before exploring some of the points around the broader picture when using the API.

With the demo now in place, we then turned our attention to extending the functionality; we added events to manage changes of shipping methods and how we might update what we display for the customer. We then added a few finishing touches before updating the event handler to tie available delivery methods to customer addresses.

To round out the chapter, we then explored some of the things we could work on as the next steps – we saw how just a few could begin to take our demo to the next stage, although this was just touching the tip of the proverbial iceberg!

Unfortunately, we've reached the end of our journey through creating an e-commerce site using Gatsby – it's been something of a roller coaster, with some monster exercises along the way! I do hope, though, that you've enjoyed the material, as much as I've enjoyed writing this book, and that you create some great e-commerce sites using Gatsby at some point soon!

Index

A

Animation, 198
APIs
   client-side, 317
   functionality, 329, 331–333
   functions, 335, 336
   Gatsby-based site, 342, 343
   Netlify, 319, 320
   payment request, setting up
      configure, 323–326
      operator, 327
      wider picture, 328, 329
   setting up project, 321, 322
   shipping restrictions, 337–339, 341
   WooCommerce, 319
Autoprefixer, 61, 64

B

blog.js file, 161, 162, 180
Blog page
   adding content, 174, 175
   adding images, 175, 176
   complete images, 176, 178
   refining, 178, 179
   style, 171–173
blogPostTemplate, 171
Blog template, 166, 167, 171, 180
Bogus Gateway, 130–132

buildShoppingCart() function, 327, 334
buyItem() function, 327

C

Cart component, 113, 125, 127
Comment system, 187, 190
Contact mechanism, 193, 194
   code in detail, 195
   update the link, 196, 197
Continuous integration (CI) tool, 211, 249

D

DatoCMS system
   adding data, shop, 76, 77
   CMS, 68
   constructing data queries, 80, 81
   database fields, 73–76
   database/media, 70–72
   GraphiQL, 68
   housekeeping, 69
   implications, 79
   integrate, 77–79
   MySQL, 67
Deployment, production
   adding demo banner, 236, 237
   adding manifest file, 233–235
   CI tool, 249

Deployment, production (*cont.*)
    content, deploying, 247, 249
    custom domain, 250, 251, 253
    deployment process, 246
    final tidy-up, 238
    gatsby, 239
    preparing host, 239–242
    setting up offline support, 235
    uploading content, 242, 244–246
    working final steps, 231, 232
Disqus comment system, 190

E

.env.development file, 98, 99
expect() or assert(), 211

F

Fine-tuning, 132, 185, 310
Four-stage process, 121, 122

G

gatsby build command, 343
gatsby-node.js file, 105, 165, 166,
      168–171, 178, 271
Gatsby-remark-images, 159, 161
Gatsby-transformer-remark, 159–161
GitLab/GitHub, 91, 93, 239, 320
GraphiQL interface, 99
GraphQL queries, 97, 118, 168, 171,
      175, 264, 277

H

Header image, 22, 33, 145, 146, 306

I

Index function, 163, 165

J, K

JAMStack principles, 12
JAMStack tool, 68

L

Laying solid foundations
    altering site layout, 26–28
    gallery/blog pages, 35–37
    housekeeping, 19, 20
    implementing components,
      pages, 37–40
    main index page, 22, 23, 25
    navigation menu, 28–31
    site architecture, 20, 21
    site components/pages, 33–35
    updating header, 31–33
    updating header, 31
Lineitem code, 127, 129

M

Main blog page, 161, 162, 165
Mobile
    accessing layout, 285
    auditing site Lighthouse, 303
    basket, 300, 301
    design, 286, 287, 289, 291–294
    fixing issues, 307
    Lighthouse report, 310–312
    menu, 295–300
    performance issues, 308–310,
      312, 313

performance report, 304–306

problem, 284

PWA support, 313, 314

testing layout, 284, 285

N, O

Netlify/Heroku, 8–10, 12, 63, 67, 90

P

Payment Request API, 140–142, 281, 317, 319, 322, 323, 325, 327

Plugins
install, 159, 160
main page, 162, 163, 165

ProductGrid component, 96, 103

productImage property, 84

ProductPage template, 106, 109

Progressive Web Application (PWA), 3, 231, 313

PWA E-Commerce
benefits, 4
definition, 4
Gatsby, 5
planned architecture, 7, 8
setting scene, 7
setting up development
  environment, 9
  change, 15, 16
  DatoCMS, 10
  getting account set up, 10–12
  placeholder site, create, 13–15

Q, R

query() function, 107

S

Search Engine Optimization (SEO), 181
adding capabilities, 182–184
comments, blog, 187, 188, 190
exploring code, 185
metadata, 186, 187
sitemap, 191, 192

Shipping
adding taxes, 138, 140
applying discounts, 142–144
completed set, 137
initial shipping, 136
set up, 135
United Kingdom, 136

shippingaddresschange event handler, 342

Shopify, 98, 99
adding cart, 108
  gatsby-node.js, 110
  ProductForm component, 109
  ProductGrid template, 109
  ProductPage template, 109
adding products, 100
adjusting cart, 110
checkout page, 146
code changes, 113
code warnings, 114
GraphQL integration, 101, 102
  Gatsby-node component, 105
  ProductGrid component, 103, 105
  ProductPage template, 106, 107
  query used, 103
inventory level, 150, 152, 153
limiting delivery, 147, 149, 150
Netlify, 115–117
updating cart, 111, 112

SiteNavigation component, 27, 87

Sourcing data
    pages/components, 88–90
    setting up sites
        DatoCMS, 82
        navigation menu, adding
          entries, 85–87
        page layout, 87, 88
        updating index page, 82–85
    testing shop, Netlify downloading,
        91, 93, 94
Static site generator (SSG), 5, 94, 257
Styling shop
    adding custom fonts, 48–50
    breaking apart changes, 62, 63
    choosing color theme, 46, 47
    code change, 58, 59
    CSS preprocessors, convert, 54–57
    decisions, 45, 46
    Sass, 59–61
    SVG image, 50–53

T

Testing/optimization
    accessibility issues, 223–226
    fixing build issue, 202
    gatsby build, 202, 203
    GraphQL query, 205
    performance issues, fixing,
        217–219, 221, 222

    performing Lighthouse
        audit, 212–215
    responding issues, 215–217
    testing site
        Cypress, 205
        exploring demo, 210, 211
        setting up Cypress, 206, 207
        statements, 211
        writing test, 208, 210
    tools, 227, 228
    viewing results, 226, 227

U, V

updateDetails() function, 334, 338, 342
useStaticQuery function, 40, 86, 90,
    104, 109

W, X, Y, Z

WooCommerce (WC)
    creating new site, 260–263
    exploring options, 277, 278
    Gatsby, migrate, 257, 258
    GraphQL, 276
    migrating content, 274, 275
    New Arrivals component, 259
    product page template, 272, 273
    proposed solution, 263, 264
    sourcing data, 264–271

Printed in the United States
by Baker & Taylor Publisher Services

Printed in the United States
by Baker & Taylor Publisher Services